PLEASE DON'T SIT
ON MY BED
IN YOUR
OUTSIDE CLOTHES

MORE BY PHOEBE ROBINSON

*You Can't Touch My Hair:
And Other Things I Still Have to Explain*

Everything's Trash, But It's Okay

PLEASE DON'T SIT ON MY BED IN YOUR OUTSIDE CLOTHES

Essays

Phoebe Robinson

An imprint of Penguin Random House LLC
penguinrandomhouse.com

Copyright © 2021 by Phoebe Robinson
Penguin supports copyright. Copyright fuels creativity, encourages diverse voices, promotes free speech, and creates a vibrant culture. Thank you for buying an authorized edition of this book and for complying with copyright laws by not reproducing, scanning, or distributing any part of it in any form without permission. You are supporting writers and allowing Penguin to continue to publish books for every reader.

Tiny Reparations, Tiny Reparations Books, and Tiny Rep Books with colophons are trademarks of YQY, Inc.

LIBRARY OF CONGRESS CATALOGING-IN-PUBLICATION DATA
Names: Robinson, Phoebe, author.
Title: Please don't sit on my bed in your outside clothes : essays / Phoebe Robinson.
Other titles: Please do not sit on my bed in your outside clothes
Description: New York : Tiny Reparations Books, [2021] | Identifiers: LCCN 2021022661 (print) |
LCCN 2021022662 (ebook) | ISBN 9780593184905 (hardcover) | ISBN 9780593184912 (ebook)
Subjects: LCSH: American wit and humor. | LCGFT: Essays.
Classification: LCC PN6165 .R64 2021 (print) |
LCC PN6165 (ebook) | DDC 818/.602—dc23
LC record available at https://lccn.loc.gov/2021022661
LC ebook record available at https://lccn.loc.gov/2021022662

Printed in the United States of America
1st Printing

Interior art: Emojis © Cosmic_Design/Shutterstock.com

To my parents, who only vaguely understand what I do
for a living but are supportive nonetheless.
And also to Michael B. Jordan, because he is extremely hot.

Contents

Contents

PLEASE DON'T SIT
ON MY BED
IN YOUR
OUTSIDE CLOTHES

2020 Was Gonna Be My Year! (LOL)

A year after *Mad Men* ended, I started watching it, which is very in line with my brand of "refusing to participate in cultural phenomena so as to not do what everyone else is doing even though I'd probably enjoy the very thing I'm missing out on." Some of you might be thinking, *Being left out seems like a curious brand*, to which I respond, "Well, we can't all be goop." Anyway, once I started watching, I was hooked. The show is such a master class in fashion, screenwriting, and acting that I didn't mind that it was no longer the topic of watercooler conversation. In fact, everyone moving on to more current shows made me feel as though *Men* and its numerous iconic moments were just for me. And one scene, in particular, towers above the rest in my opinion: The Time Betty Draper J'd Off.

I know, I know. The show has won Emmys, Golden Globes, and a Peabody Award. Made stars of Jon Hamm, Elisabeth

Moss, and January Jones. Helped define the era of Prestige TV and here I am writing about a masturbation scene, but hear me out, y'all. In the 1960s, Betty (sad, lonely trash) is married to an unfaithful Don (hot, tortured trash). On top of the stress from a fractured marriage, Betty is run-down due to raising their two kids by herself, cooking all the meals, and ensuring her hair is always on point. Sure, she's a white woman with easy-to-manage straight hair, so the struggle shouldn't be real, right? Wrong. Hair is *hard* no matter the texture, and seeing as I can barely make a tuna melt without sweating out a professionally done hairstyle that's been sprayed and pinned into place, I feel Betty's pain of ensuring the pot roast *and* her curls are poppin'. Moving on.

By the end of the first season, Betty was becoming increasingly depressed and horny. In the eleventh episode, a fine-ass door-to-door salesman showed up, talking about measuring her upstairs windows. Betty knew better than to risk it all for casual sex, so she asked him to leave. Then she started fantasizing about the salesman and j'd off by rubbing up against her vibrating Whirlpool washer machine. I immediately had two thoughts:

1. Damn, the 1960s were *rooooooooough*. I mean, obviously, because of the Civil Rights Movement, Women's Lib, and all that jazz.[1] But we all forget that vibrator

---

1. Lmao, Gloria Steinem and the ghost of Coretta Scott King are like, "What?" at me using the phrase "and all that jazz" to describe the tumultuous sixties. It's ridiculous to summarize something major with a throwaway phrase. What if Maya Angelou wrote, "I know why the caged bird sings, yada, yada, yada"? People would be like, "Uhhhh, lady, you may know, but we still don't, so care to elaborate?"

technology back then was most likely terrible, since getting intimate with a giant home appliance was best-case scenar. Like, what else were women doing? A Bruce Lee standing split kick against a belt massager while watching *The Tonight Show Starring Johnny Carson*, just to feel *something*?

2. Is this what I have to look forward to if I'm ever in a long-term relationship again? I could feel that lonely and unsatisfied even if my partner is there when I wake up in the morning and go to sleep at night?

Suffice it to say, I was very single when I watched this *Mad Men* episode, and this sad housewife story line only reinforced my feelings of not wanting to be in a relationship. Cut to a year later. It was 2017. I met British Baekoff (my bf's code name because he's British and likes to bake), and everything I said prior—I'll never date someone younger than me, I'll never date someone in a creative field, I'll never be in a long-distance relationship—went out the window. Here was this super interesting, handsome, charming, quick-witted, funny, infinitely talented British guy who was four years younger than me, a former drummer turned tour manager who traveled around the world with bands three hundred days a year and called Portland, Oregon, home when not on the road. More important, like me, he knew exactly what he wanted to do with his life. The goal was to tour for twenty years (we met eleven years into his career) then settle down in life off the road.

All of which was fine and dandy with me because I wanted to be extremely single. I'm talking no relationship, no to even

the occasional date just to spend a couple of hours with someone new, and definitely no to a situationship.[2] When I entered
my prev long-term relaysh, I was twenty-seven, and when it
ended, I was thirty-one. I needed to get acquainted with the
thirties version of Phoebe and find out who I was without a
partner by my side.

Still, when there's a spark, one ought to investigate it, so I
did, cautiously. And lo and behold, a month after meeting BB,
we were in a long-distance relationship. Not ideal, but I knew
what to expect thanks to movies. Or at least I thought I did: a
combination of drama-filled fights, missed phone calls, and
romantic getaways. Of course, there was some of that with
Baekoff and me, but mostly? It was just a lot of . . . scheduling.
Just two people looking at their Gcals and trying to make love
work. As hard as long-distance dating was, we did it for a year,
then moved in together, hoping the pain of being apart would
lessen. And guess what?!

Ain't nothing changed! I mean, he was still gone eight to ten
weeks at a time, working eighteen-hour days. The majority of
our contact continued to be stolen moments via texts or me
staying up until three or four A.M. so we could FaceTime when

---

2. To my understanding, this is when you are hanging out. But there are no labels.
Yet there is physical activity. However, it's devoid of the respect and sensuality that
existed back in the day when adults took lovers. So you just live in this gray area
until one of you finds someone to actually date *or* one of you catches feels for the
other, which effectively "ruins everything." Right. This sounds dumb as hell. Thank
goodness I'm off the streets because based on what relationships and dating have
devolved into, if I'm ever single again, I'd rather close up shop and put an obit for my
heart and vajeen in *The New York Times* (*NYT* is like, "Obits are for folks who made
a contribution to society") than get my *National Treasure* on and decipher vague text
messages from a mediocre dude.

he was done working. And when we both toured, we were often in different time zones, which meant that we couldn't check in every day. Then there was the booking of flights to see each other, which was followed by the unbooking of those flights because one of our schedules changed. Missing each other's important work and family events. Us not being able to hug each other when we had exciting news to share or needed our spirits lifted—or simply because a little physical contact would have been the perfect way to put a button on a disagreement we resolved—was a bummer. Thankfully, so much of the time he was home was lovely and romantic, and deepened our bond. As a result, I cried harder every time one of us had to leave because the longer we dated, the harder being apart became.

So we tried to cope. Date nights via FaceTime. Sending songs that reminded us of each other. Compartmentalizing our brains and hearts—work is the perfect distraction—and yet the ache remained. We were best friends. So on those days when the absence of my best friend felt truly awful, I'd think back to Betty and empathize. No, I wasn't getting intimate with a home appliance, but I was lonely. And he was, too. That's why when he decided to come off the road at the end of 2019 in order to start a travel business, I was overjoyed. After twenty-five months of dating, we were finally going to be *together* together. 2020 was going to be *the* year we'd be the couple of my dreams and do all the exciting (fly his mom out to New York, as she had never been to America before) and mundane (grocery shopping) things as a duo. Simply put, Baekoff and I were like, "Pass me those sunnies," because our future looked bright AF and we weren't afraid to tell the world.

Remember that person who Crip-walked to "Auld Lang Syne" and said "2020 is going to be our year"? And the friend who texted inspirational quote memes in group chats with the message: "Speak it into existence, boo"? And that homie who, on January 5, did a Usain Bolt–esque victory lap while draped in a "New Year, New Me" flag, which, by the way, is just a picture of Oprah holding a bushel of the healthiest-looking kale and frisée lettuce? Well, I. Was. That. Chick. Bae was that chick. Heck, we were *all* that chick. And who could blame us? We believed the hype that 2020 was *ripe* with possibility, so we took turns sitting on the Universe's lap like it was an underpaid and overworked Santa Claus at Dillard's and we put in our requests and set our intentions.

Cut to the beginning of March 2020. It was still early days in our understanding of Covid and many of us had no idea just how much it was going to upend our lives. Then, by the end of the month, the world stopped and we were all nothing but a bunch of Paul Rudds during his viral appearance on the YouTube series *Hot Ones* when he said his now-infamous "Hey, look at us. Who would've thought? Not me." Truly, none of us had a damn clue.

I mean, let's stop for a second and remember March 2020. If you were lucky, you were going from having a rich life outside the home (work, shopping, running errands, visiting friends and family) to abiding by stay-at-home orders. Adjusting to 24/7 interaction probably made you wonder how many "faux" shits you could take before your significant other / roomies / family members figured out you just wanted to be alone because at that point, the bathroom was the equiv of an Airbnb oasis in Turks and Cai-Cais aka Turks and Caicos.

If you weren't so lucky, maybe you were sick or dealing with the loss of a loved one to Covid. Or perhaps you were one of the essential workers—nurses, doctors, and other medical professionals, who are disproportionately Black and brown— and on the front lines, risking daily exposure to save lives for a public that was . . . well, how can I put this?

On one hand, there were grateful, conscientious folk: people opened their windows and stood on balconies, cheering for those aforementioned nurses, doctors, and other medical professionals. Families did drive-by birthday celebrations for elder loved ones so as not to potentially infect another person who could end up in the hospital, or worse. And there were those who were in the position to follow the stay-at-home orders and did.

As for that other hand? I hate to write it, but that other hand included a small number of ignorant older white ladies complaining about hair salons being closed, which resulted in these women not being able to maintain their dye jobs. Some older white men didn't do much better: They protested the quarantine orders and wanted to carry on leaving their homes for any and all nonessential reasons, such as purchasing Miracle-Gro for their grass.

Really?! Huh. Remember the days when marching and being politically disruptive meant you were reacting to injustices such as oh, I don't know, *racism* (Civil Rights Movement; Black Lives Matter), corruption within the Communist Party

(1989 Tiananmen Square protests), homophobia (Stonewall Uprising), inmate rights (Attica prison riot), economic inequality (Occupy Wall Street), family detention centers and deportation (2018 pro-immigration rallies across America), gun violence (Million Mom March), oppressive regimes and low standards of living (Arab Spring), and violent crimes against women (Take Back the Night), just to name a few? And now, white dudes were out here protesting 'bout not being able to get mulch whenever they wanted? The gahtdamn temerity. White women were raging against the dying of the light . . . color fading from their hair? MUWHAHAHA. The. Irony. Black women have been judged and disparaged for allegedly caring too much about their hair, yet in none of the news packages on these trifling protests did I see a single cocoa Khaleesi. That's because Black women were up in the crib with bags of wigs, backup packs of hair, Tracee Ellis Ross's Pattern Beauty products, detanglers, edge control, castor oil, Pink Oil, wide-tooth combs, etc. We stayed ready, so we didn't have to get ready. In fact, I was so ready that Bae told me because I was constantly doing my hair throughout the apartment, he got used to finding hair in various corners, so he's now no longer afraid of spiders. That's right, a bitch cured his arachnophobia *and* rocked a glistening and healthy 'fro while quarantined. John Frieda salon could *never*.

Jokes aside, medical workers weren't the only ones who faced difficulties during Covid-19. Some folks were (and still are) homeless. Some were (and still are) living in a domestic environment that made quarantining dangerous. While people such as myself were able to work from home, many others were furloughed or lost their jobs and waited on the ill-equipped federal government to hand out insufficient stimulus packages. School closings forced parents to homeschool—that is, if they were fortunate enough to have a computer, internet access, and enough food for their children. Speaking of food, grocery stores and some restaurants couldn't close because how else were people going to eat? Amazon, UPS, FedEx, and USPS workers couldn't stay home because how else would we get the items we ordered? And what about people of color who simply needed to go to the pharmacy or buy groceries and did so sans a home-made mask? Not because they were cavalier, but because, as multiple news outlets reported, some Black and brown men, in particular, felt unsafe wearing a handkerchief or anything that didn't clearly and immediately read as a protective mask for fear of being thought of as a threat. I mean, when I FaceTimed with my dad, who was in Ohio with the rest of my family, and he showed me the homemade masks he'd hand sewn, the first thing I thought was not, *My dad rules; he's so thoughtful and re-sourceful,* but *Thank God they are sewn out of plain light gray material and not bandana fabric so some dumbass won't think my AARP-aged dad is in a gang or going to rob someone.* But what about those POC who didn't have access to non-bandana material and lived any-where in America, especially my home of NYC, the birthplace of stop and frisk? They either risked exposure to the virus by being outside without a mask or wore a bandana on their face and hoped they wouldn't be harassed or worse.

These situations were, of course, just the tip of the iceberg, but whatever your 2020 quarantine situation was, it's safe to say you didn't see this coming. Honestly, outside of a select few (e.g., Bill Gates, who, back in a 2015 TED Talk, stated that many governments were woefully underprepared if a virus pandemic seized the world), most of us were too consumed with our day-to-day responsibilities to ponder potential doomsday scenarios. But another part of the reason Covid so totally and utterly blindsided many of us is because it happened in 2020. This shit wasn't supposed to happen then! Covid-19 showing up and canceling 2020 *felt* much more significant than it would in any other year.

I mean, c'mon! Astrologists and numerologists practically alluded to everything being amazing in 2020! Dreams were supposed to come true! Resolutions were supposed to be upheld! Did I lose some of you with "astrologists and numerologists"? Yeah, I figured, but hear me out.

According to many numerologists, the number 20 suggests transformation and an improvement upon what came before. This tracks, as 2020 was an election year with many major elections held in the US and worldwide. And with the Intergovernmental Panel on Climate Change coming to the conclusion that we have ten years to halve carbon emissions in order to avoid an irreparable climate catastrophe, the 2020 elections were all the more important. Honestly, if we *didn't* buy into the 2020 of it all based on that alone, we would've been fools. But there's more. Numerologists believing that the number 20 leads to a happy development that could involve a spiritual awakening? Sign me up. Astrologers suggesting to cut out distractions and get more involved in the community? Cool, I'll do a better job of refolding sweaters after trying them on in Free People instead of leaving them in tiny piles for other customers to rummage through. Intuitive consultant[3] Mary Shannon breaking down the Universal Year number (4, because 2 + 0 + 2 + 0 = 4) in an interview with Refinery29 with the following: "4 Years tend to be relatively stable and have a comfy-cozy homey vibe to them. They are characterized as a time of reflection after the growth that generally occurs with a 3 Year (aka 2019)."[4] Well, you best believe I'm wearing sweatpants and a T-shirt with a zit patch on my face and a blanket around my manicured toes because I was going to be comfortable AF in 2020. Matter fact, 2020, what else did you have in store??? I was ready to handle it!!

But even if I hadn't been lulled into a false sense of security by numerology, based on everything we were told leading up to 2020, I still would've felt it was going to be a special year in all the right ways. Like I legit thought my 2020 was going to be me standing butt-ass naked in the streets of New York à la Alanis Morissette in her "Thank U" music video and expressing gratitude for all the goodness the year had brought me: "Thank you, Brooklyn / Thank you, Peloton / Thank you, thank you, sweeeeeeetgreeeeeen." I mean, I had the whole acceptance speech ready to deliver on December 31, 2020, to my boyfriend while our muted TV showed Ciara doing the "1, 2 Step"

---

3. Look, I'm not entirely clear on what this "job" is, but it sounds a lot like my parents going, "Told you so," anytime I screw up my life. They've been doing that for free for thirty-five years and counting. Dear reader, can y'all keep this white nonsense of an occupation between us? Otherwise, Phil and Octavia will be trying to garnish my wages for back pay for all their "intuitive consulting."

4. In numerology rules, 2019 breaks down as the following: 2 + 0 + 1 + 9 = 12, which is further broken down as 1 + 2 = 3.

on *Dick Clark's New Year's Rockin' Eve with Ryan Seacrest 2020*. Clearly, I was naïve.

It was kind of like in 2015 when Eyebrow Zaddy aka Michael Keaton won the Golden Globe for *Birdman* and was the presumptive front-runner to win the Oscar for best actor. Instead, Eddie Redmayne's name was called and the camera caught Keaton tucking his acceptance speech back inside his tuxedo jacket. The world was robbed of his words and I think about that often. Probably not more than Keaton does, but I'm sure a close second. Anyway, I know I didn't achieve any of the things I set out to in 2020—so many of us didn't—but I do have the whole speech written and tucked away somewhere for safekeeping, so it seems like a waste *not* to—oh, are you *sure* you don't mind hearing it? Only if it's not too much of an imposition. Oh, jeez, I'm so not prepared. *immediately pulls out folded-up piece of paper from slit in bra where a gel insert should be* Thank you so much, dear reader! Okay. Here goes.

Phoebe Robinson's "2020 Was My Year" Acceptance Speech

Wait! Let me set the scene first: *I'm stunned to hear my name. After looking around (there's no one else in the living room except my boyfriend, British Baekoff, but damn if I'm not going to milk this moment), I mouth "Oh my God," then kiss him. I stand up from my West Elm couch. I'm wearing an Ankara head wrap, PJs, and period-stained undies, because why stop doing the things that helped me get to this point? I make my way to the TV, air-kissing an imaginary Kerry Washington as she hands me an imaginary award. I look at it, inhaling deeply.*

I can't believe it. Oh my gosh. This is too . . . I mean, who could've imagined that a little Black girl from Cleveland, Ohio, would be standing in front of you. Wow. Okay. Of course, I'd like to thank my fellow nominees: Reset Passwords Because I Forgot the Old Ones, My Determination to Eat Cheese in Public Despite Being Lactose Intolerant, My Hairstyle That I Managed Not to Sweat Out After Bone Bones with Bae,[5] Meryl Streep (because when is she *not* nominated), and Imposter Syndrome. All your performances this year were impeccable. *cut to meme of Meryl Streep from 2015 Oscars clapping and pointing at stage from her seat**

My 2020 wouldn't have been what it was if it weren't for everyone who attended the final dates of my "Sorry, Harriet Tubman" stand-up tour, especially those who confused me for literally any other Black woman who works in Hollywood. *Maybe* Alfre Woodard does have a tight hour-long set on her boyfriend's uncircumcised penis and living in New York City, but do you think she drank an Ensure to get out of bed and perform for one hundred and fifty people *in Sacramento* who are noshing on chicken wings? Still, this was my first solo tour, so despite the occasional audience confusion about who I was, I will cherish that tour forever.

I'd also like to thank Duolingo, because without you, I wouldn't be able to butcher Spanish when calling Oaxaca

---

5. #WontHeDoIt

Taqueria to place a dinner order—"Meh gustaría TRES carNAY Aah Sah Dahs, *por favor*"—and then lie and say my name is Karen, as butchering another language is total Karen vibes. 😎

Mother Naych, I used to treat you like you weren't much more than what I experience when waiting outside for the Lyft ride I *definitely* should have called fifteen minutes earlier, but since I didn't, I will totes blame the driver for not *Tokyo Drift*'ing in a school zone so I could get to work on time. I was wrong and thank you for opening my eyes. This year, I went on five hikes aka waddled my melodramatic self over some autumnal leaves. And I did it all while wearing a fringe fanny pack, booty shorts, a Target tank top, and Sorel hiking boots aka "Silicone-Free Tomb Raider meets Shopbop Fashion Week."

Many thanks to Aldo Shoes' jewelry line because I was able to fool many a heaux into thinking I was iced out in diamonds when I was room-temp in cube zircones.

OMG! Can't believe I forgot! I ran a 5K! I'd like to thank the training apps I used to accomplish this feat. Alright, fine. It wasn't an *official* 5K that raised money or included other runners. I just ran three miles, in poor form, on a treadmill in my building's gym one time and realized halfway through the run that I forgot to wear my Apple Watch, which meant there was no record I could show of what I did. So I just ran . . . for my health? Hard pass.

To my parents, Phil and Octavia, you're now both in your sixties yet look just as good as, if not better than, me. Thanks for giving me hope that I will age as well as y'all despite the fact that you're vegan (I eat whatever), don't drink (I love me a Moscow mule), don't stay up late (two A.M. is a reasonable time for me to go to bed), don't suffer from adult acne (I haven't had clear skin since I was seven), and generally have calm demeanors (a game of Monopoly has me looking like a U.S. president leaving the White House after two terms).

To my boyfriend, British Baekoff, you put up with a lot, namely me forcing you to watch two-hour-long U2 concerts (comprised of fan videos of wide-ranging quality) on YouTube. There's no one else I could do this with. Thank you. I love you.

Finally, I'd like to thank my laser hair removal specialist. It's been a long journey, and without you, I'd still have a mustache like the one Shemar Moore rocked on CBS's *Criminal Minds*.

As I soak up the love from this nonexistent audience, my boyfriend asks, "Can you stop blocking the TV?" I make my way back to the couch and see that he ate the last of the Cheetos Puffs, which would normally be a bummer, except I have an emergency stash for these kinds of moments. "God bless Frito-Lay and 2020," I say to myself as I pop open a fresh bag of Cheetos.

The. End.

Not bad, eh, dear reader? In all seriousness, while not everyone had a speech prepared, many of us did anticipate that 2020 was going to kick off the decade in spectacular or at least better fashion, which helps explain why the coronavirus felt like such a deeply personal attack. These are 100 percent valid reactions to the new world we're navigating. We have the right to feel duped. To lose faith and question whether we should've had it in the first place. For many, those fun butterflies in our stomachs have been replaced by, well, sheer panic, and that overwhelming sense of losing control—be it of our jobs, our daily routines, our finances, our health, or simply how we can spend our time—was paralyzing. Not that we ever had that much control in the first place, but we told ourselves what we had to in order to function, as the alternative—nihilism— seemed too dark a path to walk. So we devised plans. Set goals. Did all the things one does when constructing a life, like loving, hoping, fighting, hustling, thinking about tomorrow, etc. We were vulnerable in the face of the unknowable, and that was hard enough in our pre-coronavirus normal.

Starting over and being vulnerable in a world that is nothing like what you had constructed for yourself was scary, frustrating, and heartbreaking. Beginning again can feel like yet another tiny death of who you are and what you knew. And the older I get, it seems that adulthood is nothing but those tiny little deaths. Just reminders that all the things and people and even our self-identities that we hold dear are fragile. And perhaps by us spending so much time trying to forget that fragility, we are also forgetting that it's what makes those very things, people, and ourselves special and worth living for.

So why am I here, on the page, with you, in this book you bought? The best I can offer at this moment is that I am a funny person, and if I can make you laugh and forget your problems for a moment then I did something. Although I'm not on the front lines, I'm still living in this, too, and it's probable that my way of looking at life could be of use to someone who just needs to laugh. I crave levity because I don't want the time inside to rewire my brain or convince me to lose all sense of optimism. Because in the face of it looking like we're all fucked, giving up would be letting down those in my family and friends who haven't. So I won't give up today. And I'll try not to tomorrow.

Instead, due to my tendency to think (and overthink) about things—both the profound and the inane—I'll put them down on paper as a time capsule, if you will, of who I was and maybe who some of us were at this moment in time.[6] That way, I can look back and remember that people put themselves on the line so I could be here. That my parents lovingly teased me over FaceTime so I'd laugh. That I played a bootleg version of "Lean on Me" for my boyfriend when he had a down day on a cheap keyboard I purchased. That despite the tiny and not-so-tiny deaths that the coronavirus brought, there were also all those little sparks of joy, those small, happy moments that helped make my life, *my life*. Same with those sad times.

So, dear reader, my hope is this: that when you look back on 2020, if you need to punch, yell, kick, scream for the dreams deferred and the lives lost, do it. If, when you're feeling low, you recall seeing yourself on the other side of this even though

---

6. California's Redwood National and State Parks is like, "Lol. Mofo, do not kill my fifth cousins twice removed aka the state of Indiana's entire forestry to talk about hot peen and your artsy neuroses." Point. Taken.

you had no idea how you were going to get here, live in that memory for as long as it takes for it to help propel you forward. If stripping away all the luxuries and circumstantial nonsense put you on the path to start appreciating what truly matters, stay on that path, too, because it will lead you to a more enriching and special life. Any and all of that which made this ordeal life-altering? Forget none of it. Hold on to it. Use all of it as fuel to help make this world and us better than we were before. Because given everything we've been through, it's highly unlikely that we'll ever feel that specific kind of pure joy and naiveté that comes with the "This is gonna be our year" energy that we possessed at the end of 2019. And while there's a part of me that mourns the loss of our last bit of innocence, I'm encouraged by what I've witnessed in the wake of Covid's destruction. Through all the heartbreak, setbacks, survivor's remorse, poor leadership, unexpected and welcomed surprises, renewed appreciation for the small and sometimes intangible moments, we said, "The hell with the idea that some date on the calendar signifies when it's gonna be our year; these are gonna be *our lives* and we can show up and fight for them and for the right to be happy whenever we choose."

Fuck the rules of waiting for the first day of the year or for the stars to align perfectly according to our horoscope or for the numbers to add up. Truthfully, there is no "right" year or moment. We know this now. Actually, we've been knowing this. All that we have, in many ways, is the knowledge that we don't know how much time we have left in our lives. So let's keep rolling up our sleeves and continue writing and revising and enacting new plans on how we can make *this* the best *life* of our lives.

Full disclosure: I will be approximately ten minutes late to all the meetings, and I understand that I just stated how time is a precious resource, but my mantra in life is "No matter the year: same me; same trash." Cool?

Yes, I Have Free Time Because
I Don't Have Kids

There are only a handful of toys I still remember from my childhood. The Skip-It, which I was convinced made me an athlete, my Pee-wee Herman pull-string talking doll, and my favorite one: a baby doll I creatively named Baby, which eventually got decapitated, but still, every night, the head and the rest of her body slept side by side with me in bed. Don't ask. Wait, actually, you should because what I just described was a low-key serial-killer-in-training thing to do. Okay, so. Long story short, one day, my brother and I, playing with our various toys, decided to put the doll in the washing machine, and her head got chopped off. I was devastated, but because I loved Baby so much I never wanted to replace her. Instead, I would sometimes walk around the house, carrying her head in my arms, and everyone in my family just acted like this was . . . normal. What the hell, Mom and Dad?! Y'all have never met a hotel doorknob that you didn't inspect thoroughly for several minutes and give a *Silkwood* shower to, yet not once were you like, "Let me investigate why our daughter is living her best low-budget Wednesday Addams life and mothering a decapitated doll head"?

Anyway, since I was having heart-to-hearts with a doll head and feeding it imaginary Similac, it was clear that I was super into the idea of being a mom. Then I got a little older and became what some would call a "tomboy" because I played pickup basketball with my older brother and his friends, didn't want to wear pink, and loved watching action movies. Still, you would find me baking with my dad, playing house with my dolls, and, of course, the game of MASH.

If you're too young to know what MASH is, don't worry, I got you. It's a pencil and paper game you play with friends. Lemme stop right there. Do some of you even know what that experience is? To play a game where the only components are number two pencils, lined pieces of paper, friendship, and imagination? I mean, that shit (and me) sound old as fuck! Generally speaking, I feel young until I start explaining something from my childhood such as MASH, then I second-guess and think to myself: *Damn, was I a part of the original expedition across the Oregon Trail with Lewis and Clark in 1804? Was I the secretary who got carpal tunns while taking minutes during the inaugural NAACP meeting in 1909 because W.E.B. Du Bois didn't know how to shut up? Was I the middle-aged Marriott hotel concierge service that Mathew Knowles called when LaTavia Roberson and LeToya Luckett were kicked out of Destiny's Child in 2000? Why do my knees hurt when it rains?* Moving on. MASH.

In summary, it's a game you play with friends that's

supposed to predict your future. Hence M = Mansion, A = Apartment, S = Shack, H = House. You can also determine what street you're going to live on, who you're going to marry, and how many kids you will have. And because I enjoyed having an older sibling, I always wanted to end up with two kids at the end of the game. Not because I had any deep-seated desire to be a mom. How could I? I was just a kid and simply assumed I'd emulate what my parents did: marriage, children, and owning a house. But again, I was just a kid. All those responsibilities seemed like faraway fantasies such as going to outer space, being a pop star, or cussing my parents out and living to tell the tale. I know I'm not the only one who, after getting in trouble and being sent to my room, would pace back and forth, whisper-cussing and saying things such as, "Oooh! Say something else to me! S-say something else to me! Y'all gonna push me to my damn limit and I'm going to move out. Oooh!" LOL. Move out and go where and do what? I was twelve with zero life skills, no funds to pay for the upkeep of my chemically straightened hair or rent (notice how hair came ahead of housing?), and no luggage or mover's starter kit from U-Haul. You ever try and pack up your life inside a JanSport book bag that your parents bought you during an OfficeMax back-to-school sale? Y'all, a copy of *To Kill a Mockingbird*, a six-pack of cherry Squeezits, some cheese cracker sandwiches, and jeans and a T-shirt from Sears legit take up about 63 percent of the book bag. Spoiler alert: You ain't getting very far; in fact, you'll last one afternoon, tops, before returning home with your tail between your legs.

But I digress. The point is I went through my childhood,

middle school, and high school years believing I was going to be a mother, a belief that not only stemmed from society selling the idea that motherhood is "natural" and the "final destination" for a woman, but because, for the most part, public figures and celebrities portrayed being a mom as a wholly instinctive, perfectly peaceful, and life-affirming paradise. Based off everything I'd been fed, my understanding of motherhood boiled down to the following:

- Morning sickness happens, so probably wise to have a bunch of extra trash cans around my house. (simplehuman company: "Lol, wut? But we will take your money.")
- Once my baby bump is pronounced, I'll schedule a nude photo shoot à la Demi Moore with famed photographer Annie Leibovitz. (My bank account: "Lol, wut?" Annie Leibovitz: "How did you get my number? But also, I'm going through some tax issues, so okay.")
- I'll obvs give birth real quick. (My vagina: "Bitch, iz you dumb?" Me: "I iz.")
- I won't sleep much yet my sunny disposition will remain unaffected. (Everyone who knows me: "You get a full seven hours of sleep nightly yet you're still a literal nightmare if anyone talks to you too early in the morning, so . . .")
- Breastfeeding will be a completely peaceful experience *every single time* in which I will sit on a cozy couch, surrounded by pillows, Tracy Chapman music will play in the background, and my baby will latch on to my boob

without any issues. And once I'm done with breast-feeding, my boobs will magically go back to being couture titties aka high, tight, and small. (Gravity: "Da fuq?")

- I'll lose the baby weight easily and quickly. This notion is, of course, based on the copious amount of magazine and TV profiles on celeb new moms who said all the weight melted off them (and somehow they also have toned, athletic bodies) merely from chasing toddlers around and lifting them up while wearing ballet flats. (My body: "Um, I think you kind of just have to exercise *in addition* to doing this as it's mostly, if not entirely, the working out that would create the weight loss and toned body." Me: "Hard pass!")

- Fast-forward past all the school stuff, especially helping my kids with their homework (not interested in relearning algebra) and PTA stuff (not interested in interacting with other parents because I'm a tad anti-sosh) and land squarely on prom night, where despite the fact that one of my kids is now seventeen and I didn't start having childrens until I was in my thirties, I have somehow remained eternally thirty-five. (Time: "Bruh, did you go to school? Read a book? Understand what aging is? Looked at a clock before?")

- Oh! Almost forgot. Even though I was a royal shit to my parents when I was a teenager, my adolescent kids and I will be the Black Lorelai and Rory of *Gilmore Girls*, just bff'ing it and talking out all of our feels. (Reality: 😑 😑 😑)

Yep, this is real ignorant, but can you blame me? Ever since I was a child, society painted motherhood as this effortless job that every woman automatically knows how to, wants to, and is always happy to do, because the patriarchal narrative is that every woman is the same, thinks the same, and wants the same things. Huh? Women can't even agree on whether man buns / ponytails are attractive or terrible on men[1] but we're supposedly all on the same page about something as life-altering as motherhood? Err, I don't know who keeps flapping their gums and telling this lie, but they need to stop. Actually, I *do* know who keeps this theory about women alive: basically EVERYBODY. Seriously, the notion that women are destined to be moms and if they don't fulfill that destiny, something is wrong with them is reinforced everywhere. I'm talking about the friends who warn women that they will regret not being a mother, family members who pressure women into carrying on the family legacy,[2] acquaintances, strangers, you name it. Practically everyone has a vested interest in women carrying out their supposed "duty," and the people who are typically the loudest about their interest are, you guessed it, men. Oh,

---

1. I'm #TeamAttractive because I'm not ignorant. Hair is hair, y'all, and some folks are talking about "it's not manly for a guy to have long hair" or "long hair never adds to the attractiveness of a man, but it can subtract from it" or "men with short hair look good, but it's really rare to find a hot guy with long hair." News flash: SO MANY MEN WHO HAVE SHORT HAIR ARE BUSTED. IN SOME CASES, THEIR SHORT HAIR HAS CONTRIBUTED TO THEIR BUSTEDNESS. JUST BECAUSE A DUDE LOOKS LIKE A BASIC-ASS iMESSAGE AVATAR DOES NOT MEAN HE'S AUTOMATICALLY CUTE. Get a grip. Kiss a man with whom you can buy Goody elastic ponytail holders in bulk and stop this gendered nonsense. Live a little.

2. I've been alive thirty-six years and I've yet to meet one family where I'm like, "We need sequels." Usually, I'm just like, "How about we call it? Time to wrap this up."

men just *love* having opinions about and creating the parameters women are supposed to live within that then get passed down from generation to generation, shaping communities and societies and ultimately resulting in a suffocating definition of what a woman can be and what her life can look like.

As I'm approaching my late thirties, I can't help but marvel at how the boundaries of modern womanhood are expanding, thus allowing more of us to architect our lives. That is certainly worth celebrating. However, though we've evolved significantly from how women were treated during the fictional events of the sixties (*Mad Men*), as well as the real-life events of the sixties (having trouble getting a credit card; Yale refusing to admit women until 1969; women being discouraged from entering the workplace), there is still much to do in terms of reconceptualizing what it means to be a woman and to be a mother. Being honest about how messy, complicated, and difficult child-rearing can be sometimes still puts mothers at risk of being viewed as failures (because motherhood is supposed to be a joyful breeze) or ungrateful complainers (because voicing any normal frustrations is proof of one being unappreciative about the miracle of life), when it should be viewed as someone acknowledging the complexities of being a mom. More and more women speaking their truths on issues such as postpartum depression, the uneven division of household labor in two-parent homes, how the love for your child is unlike any other kind of love in the world, and that there's no storybook, one-size-fits-all way to be a mother actually allows people who want to have kids to make a more informed decision rather than being duped by a fantasy they'll never be able to live up to. But it's not just about making sure soon-to-be mothers are making informed decisions. It's about guaranteeing that *no matter what a woman chooses*, everyone will refrain from judgment because choosing to be a mother and choosing to be childfree are *both* decisions worth celebrating because the celebration is in the fact that a woman chose the trajectory of her life.

That's right: Celebrate the childfree. Not the way we do with moms and Mother's Day. No one's asking for that. Women who don't have kids want more than merely being "accepted" or "tolerated." Celebrate them the fuck home as Kenny Loggins sang. I'M BLACK, I SWEAR! In all seriousness, society has a long way to go in its treatment of childfree women. Such as: People must learn to not treat them as an inconvenience that's been thrust upon them, or even concern themselves with why some women opt out of motherhood, and, most important, the public must put effort into resisting the almost Pavlovian impulse of relegating childfree women to the outskirts of society. And, finally, we must task ourselves to stop pitying or invalidating a woman's life simply because she doesn't want to be a parent. Because the path to becoming a voluntarily childfree person is not an easy one. While the process is uniquely different for each person, what I can say with absolute certainty is that, across the board, not being a mother is one of the most internally scrutinized choices of a woman's life, even if the woman has known since she was a child that she doesn't want children. Society will do its best to sow the seeds of doubt about that decision within her and it may take some time for her to uproot them. Well, if it's not clear by now, *je suis* one of the childfree, and I guess now would be a good time to resume our currently scheduled program that's already in progress: *Motherhood: How I Went from "I Wanna Be a Momma" to "That's Gonna Be a No from Me, Dawg."*

Being from the Midwest and attending a private Catholic prep school, even though I'm not religious, meant a lot of things—having a sense of humility, caring about the greater good, eating at Wahlburgers more often than I care to admit to—but perhaps the biggest aspect of being a Midwestern gal was the expectation that I would most likely follow the path of steady job → marriage → house → kids. Many of my former classmates were doing just that in Ohio. Securing well-paying jobs with retirement benefits. Falling in love. Buying the houses of their dreams with their spouses. Getting pregnant and having children. And preferably, all before the age of thirty. Meanwhile, my life in NYC looked nothing like that as I was entering my late twenties. I still had a day job because despite being a few years into my comedy career, it rarely paid in anything other than beer and chicken wings. I was saddled with debt, and paying rent on time was a rare occurrence. And to make matters worse, except for a few over-before-they-started relationships, my hopelessly romantic behind was very single. Just watching *27 Dresses* and identifying way too hard with Katherine Heigl's Jane, who is always the brides-maid (twenty-seven times, duh), yet never the bride: "See, she's totally me if I liked weddings. And enjoyed being a bridesmaid. And had that many friends." Anyway, one eve-ning after a long day of work, stand-up comedy, and feeling like I wasn't measuring up, I logged on to Facebook for a distraction.

LIES! Okay. Let me preface this by writing that I know I'm not the only person who does the following nonsense, so take your Judge Mathis glasses off and refrain from criticizing me. Truth is I logged on to Facebook because sometimes when I'm down in the dumps, I poke at the wound a little bit and wallow in the sadness because, in the moment, that's easier than pulling myself out of it. Anyway. I began scrolling and it was business as usual: people posting BuzzFeed articles, selfies, funny videos, etc. Then I saw one of my former high school classmates. She was standing in front of a ranch-style house with her husband and their child, holding a set of keys with a caption that read: "We did it! We're officially homeowners!" Instead of just letting out a single *Glory* tear and then moving on with my night, I wrapped myself in my comforter and began ugly crying and mumbling about how my life was a mess and that I was so behind. That feeling, which I had held inside for several years, was finally and messily spilling out of me. "So behind, so behind, so behind" became the refrain of the night, and since there was no one there to snap me out of it, I cried and cried and cried until my eyes puffed up and I choked on saliva. Then I cried some more and remained in a funk for weeks.

See?!?! This is what not minding your business gets you: wailing like you're in *The Handmaid's Tale*. All I had to do was keep my masochist-in-training behind off social media and deal with my thoughts of inferiority either by myself or with a friend / family member, and I wouldn't have tempted fate and gotten my feelings hurt. But truth be told, there was no reason for me to be throwing myself a pity party because I didn't even want kids! Or the ranch-style house, for that matter! Don't get me wrong; at the time, I would have *loved* to have been financially stable, have a decent apartment, and be dating someone amazing. However, in spite of all those perceived failings, my teenage dream was to live in New York City and build a career in entertainment. I was doing just that and still, I felt as though my life was nothing but a series of shortcomings, which is by societal design.

A woman can be achieving her goals, which people swear is one of the tenets of feminism, but if those goals are not in line with what the world at large has deemed as the ultimate objective—settling down and becoming a mother—she might conclude that she's completely missed the point of being an adult. Worse than that, she is made to feel that she *chose* to fail at being a woman, a failure that is not an individual one, but an attack on the greater good. The punishment for this crime can range from being isolated from friends and family, to mini existential crises, the seeds of which society planted in her long ago, which then bloom anytime anything good happens so as to undercut the joy she feels, to potentially no man wanting to spend the rest of his life with her if they know having kids is not an option. Hence the waterworks from me that night. So, there I was, twenty-seven years old, sobbing alone in my apartment, fearing that because I didn't want to have kids it meant that I also couldn't have a soul mate.

Now, nothing major happened that made me decide to not have kids. There was never a deep conversation with my parents or a best friend that set off alarms that motherhood might not be for me. I didn't have a pregnancy scare that rattled me to my core nor did I babysit one of my friends' kids for an afternoon and think, *No thanks*. It was most likely just a series of little moments throughout the years coupled with the fact that as I got older, when I envisioned my life, children were never in the picture.

Still, I couldn't shake the feeling that I *should* want them and that maybe all I was doing was tricking myself into believing I was living the life I wanted when, in actuality, I *did* want kids and I was merely putting off the inevitable and refusing to grow up. Or worse. Perhaps the fact that the choice to be childfree wasn't a torturous one meant that I'm intrinsically broken, which, for a hopeless romantic, feels devastating. *If I don't want to be a mom, I must be damaged, so why would anyone want me as their wife?* is something I'd ask myself routinely, because despite the messaging that all women are baby crazy while men have a "take it or leave it" attitude toward being a parent, it's simply not true. A 2013 Associated Press poll found that 80 percent of men wanted to be fathers in comparison to 70 percent of women. The AP noted that "dads were more likely than moms . . . to say they saw positive effects from fatherhood on their love life and career" (no surprise there), and 14 percent of men stated that the top reason for becoming a father someday is "to carry on traditions or family history."

The idea of "someday" haunted me and mutated in my brain to mean "someday, my biological clock will chime, alerting me that I should have a family," "someday, I'll find the One and realize that all along, I wanted to be a mother," and "someday, if I have children, then maybe, just maybe, I'll be what a woman should be." Every day, I wasted energy hoping that "someday" would turn into "today," and the anxiety I felt would disappear. Until it did, I stalled with any dating prospect, because while I continued not wanting kids, I *wanted* to want them so I could feel normal and hopefully the guy would choose me.

So I projected the idea that when it came to motherhood, I was keeping my options open. I went from "Maybe in my thirties," to "Once I'm in my thirties and I'm not where I want to be professionally, I'm definitely freezing my eggs," to "I mean, I can always do IVF in my forties like some of my friends have already done," to "Who knows? Maybe in my fifties, I'll be like Janet Jackson or Sandra Bullock and want to be a mom. I can always adopt," to "When I'm eighty-nine years old and about to Crip walk into Heaven as a Kirk Franklin song plays in the background, perhaps I'll be ready to raise a child." Clearly, the subtext in all this text was I'M STALLING TO THE POINT THAT I'D RATHER BE AT DEATH'S DOOR THAN SPEND FIVE MINUTES ENTERTAINING MY OFF-SPRING BY DOING A REMIX OF "HEAD, SHOULDERS, KNEES, AND TOES" WHILE MY HUSBAND BEATBOXES AN 808 BEAT. A subtext I'm sure that everyone in my life picked up on while my goofy behind was the last to know. Sort of like the time when I thought Jon Hamm wanted to date me because we emailed twice, so I started talking to some of my friends about how I'm down to be bicoastal since he lived in L.A., and while they were supportive as all good friends are, they were also like, "Uhhhhhh, y'all have only exchanged basic-ass Gmail addresses, so maybe stop doing Kegels while calling your

Alaska Airlines rep to cash in those miles?" Clearly, there have been many times in my life where I was de–Looney Tunes. And this whole song and dance about how I was going to be a mother one day was yet another example, but I couldn't help it.

The finality of rejecting motherhood seemed so . . . rigid and stubborn. Like not having children was due to my unwillingness to change my mind about motherhood one day rather than because I'm a rational person who knows what's best for my life. And we all know, according to society, there are few things worse than the *perception* that a woman is uncompromising, as if being a mother when you don't want to can even be considered a "compromise." So I kept pretending and relationships kept not working out, which I never realized was partially because I was not being my authentic self and the stress from that manifested in me being a workaholic or more neurotic than usual because distractions are always the easier option than facing the reality of who you actually are.

Then I met British Baekoff. Being in the presence of someone who has their own doubts and insecurities yet walks through life certain of who he is and what he wants was dope to witness. I mean, if he could so thoroughly like me for me and never once second-guess those feelings, then I ought to stop questioning myself and my feelings when it comes to parenthood, especially because he was giving me an out to reveal my true self by hinting at not wanting to be a father. Right?

Nope. At least that's how I felt in the early stages of our relationship, since he's younger than me. How many times have we watched a grown-ass man living the bachelor / serial monogamist life, professing that "kids aren't in the cards" for him, and then he turns fifty-one and a half and all of a sudden, he wants a son to play catch with; meanwhile, his geriatric sperm is going, "Uh, I was fully enjoying going to the cinema at three P.M., drinking room-temp Metamucil, and wearing the memory foam sneakers that retired NFL quarterback Joe Montana wore in a Skechers commercial"? All. The. Damn. Time. Now, does this man adopt a child and become a single dad like many a Hollywood starlet? No. Does he date and eventually marry an appropriately aged single mom and get an instant family? Hell no! He decides only the carrier of the youngest (of legal age, of course) and freshest womb is worthy of being his wife. Le sigh.

Whenever I see pictures of [insert famous/wealthy man], age sixty-six, and his new girlfriend [insert ridiculously attractive woman trying to turn a gap year into a gap life], age twenty-four, and the pics are accompanied by an article about all the things they have in common, such as them both knowing her checking account and routing numbers, I truly wonder if not working is worth it. Like, I get that obtaining money and nice things without actually having to work is tight, but . . . IF STARING DOWN THE BARREL OF A TENURED PEEN HAS YOU TAKING A DEEP BREATH LIKE JAPANESE COMPETITIVE EATER KOBAYASHI IN THE FINAL ROUND OF A HOT DOG EATING CONTEST, PUT THAT DONG DOWN AND UPDATE YOUR MOTHERFUCKIN' LINKEDIN PROFILE. LIKE, GET A REGULAR OL' JOB AND FILL OUT TIME SHEETS BIWEEKLY. IT WON'T KILL YOU.

Point is, I knew British Baekoff was the One early on in our relationship, but I was afraid that all his jokes about not wanting to be a dad would eventually stop once he turned thirty, or thirty-five, or forty, or older. So I either didn't say anything in response to those comments or I chuckled and assured him that he would be a great father. After all, I'd rather be right all along about my unfounded fear that he would eventually leave me to start a family with someone than be blindsided that I was not the One for him. Again, he repeatedly said he didn't want children, but that truth wasn't louder than the paranoia in my head. So we kept right on with our relationship without me being all the way honest about my concerns until we moved in together.

I'd just turned thirty-four. After sixteen years of hustling and saving, I finally owned an apartment. In Brooklyn. It was my first apartment without a mouse or cockroach problem and the first time I ever had a washer and dryer! That's right! Just down the hall from where I sleep I can do *laundry*. Aah, I made it. Anyway, one afternoon British Baekoff and I stood in our brand-new kitchen. I was content . . . and yet.

"Do you think you'd be happy if this is it?" I asked.

BB was sipping tea while scrolling on his phone, so he distractedly responded with "What?"

"I mean, if it's just you and me. No kids. Just us. For the rest of our lives. Would that be enough? Would your life feel full?"[3]

---

3. Why do so many couples do this? When discussing whether to merge their two LLCs aka move in together, they'll spend hours deciding between Verizon Fios or Spectrum as their future service provider and –28 minutes figuring out big-picture items such as if they want a family. Y'all, please have the hard talks *before* cohabitating; otherwise, you risk unnecessary heartbreak when you realize you two aren't on the same page. And, by the way, you *keep* having those talks throughout your relationship. People change and so does what they want.

He put his phone down. "You're more than enough to fill my life."

Aww! How sweet! Now, the prevailing thought is that when a straight man says this to a straight woman, she'll become so overwhelmed with love that she'll want to poke holes in all his condoms like they're a tray of choux pastry buns that a *Great British Baking Show* contestant has to fill with hazelnut buttercream before time's up. But in the case of my boyfriend and me, we just high-fived to not having children and carried on with our Saturday afternoon. In all seriousness, I was relieved. I finally believed him and stopped fearing that he would walk out the door one day and find someone much younger to have babies with. I was also touched that *I* could be enough. That *we* could be enough. Sure, I have a small circle of friends who are voluntarily childfree, which made me feel less alone, but when it's your soul mate, this like-mindedness feels like a cocoon that you didn't know you needed, but now you can't live without it. There is safety in numbers. There is safety in knowing that another person wants the same life as you. So I no longer needed to be afraid in my relationship; it was just the world that I had to contend with. And the world is a busybody with sciatica, a cute wardrobe, and a penchant for gossip, especially when it comes to women and whether or not they have kids.

Ever since I turned twenty-five, the top three conversations of my life have been: 1) career ups and downs, 2) figuring out who has Lactaid, and 3) when am I going to be a mother, which has probably moved into the top spot since my boyfriend and I started dating. Sigh. I understand parenthood is one of the biggest choices anyone will ever make, so it being a recurring theme is not unsurprising; however, it's one of my least favorite topics of discussion. Look, if it's with a good friend or loved one, I don't mind going deep, but with the average layperson, I just feel judgment emanating from them and end up feeling not that great about myself, unnecessarily stressed, and that I should've just kept my Black ass at home. Like, Howard Hughes, I know you became agoraphobic because of a near-fatal plane crash, but have you ever been at a house party and dealt with a nosy-ass heaux whose idea of small talk is interrogating you for not having kids and is practically on standby, speculum in hand, to look up your coochie and around your lady walls while you're just trying to get the last spanakopita? It ain't fun, Howie!! Aaaaaaaaand that's why I don't wanna go out no more where I have to interact with random or judgy people about anything real in my life. If it ain't about what I did over the weekend or who makes my wigs or what I've been watching on Hulu and Netflix, I ain't talking about shit with you! Okay, that's a tad extreme, but can you blame me? There is no winning for a woman if she is on the receiving end of this question.

If she's single, folks behave the way I do after I put concert tickets in my Ticketmaster cart and a countdown clock appears on my screen. I get flustered and yell, "It's impossible for me to enter my sixteen-digit credit card number in the allotted amount of time!" Seriously, the unjustified hysteria is real and it doesn't matter how young or old the woman is, if she's not already with child, she's made to feel as though all is almost lost. "You know what you should try," they say, which is followed by suggestions to get her eggs counted or to dive into the $10,000, three-week process of freezing her eggs. Listen, heifer, are you about to offer this woman zero-money-down financing like she's trying to lease a Tacoma during Toyota-thon? If not, don't come up in here with a "You know what you should try" as though proposing someone embark on a $10K procedure (that's not guaranteed to work, by the way) as casually as recommending trying out a new tapas restaurant or switching bodywashes.

Now, if the woman is in a relationship but not married, people want her to get engaged, then married, and quickly get down to the business of becoming pregnant. Ummmmmm, on *Shark Tank*, Mark Cuban is always cussing someone out for scaling their business too fast because they had six months of decent sales, but as soon as a couple is legally monogs and the woman has Gene Kelly's umbrella from *Singin' in the Rain* aka an IUD installed in her uterus, everyone wants her to instantly immediately scale up and start raising children, which is, of course, enriching but incredibly stressful. What is the rush?!?! Why is society so hell-bent on forcing people into life-changing scenarios as though there is some universal timetable we're supposed to be living by? All the outside pressure does is make the couple on the receiving end feel anxious and awkward in mixed company, and, worst of all, it can force them to jump to conclusions (e.g., if we're not married now, we'll never get married; if you don't want kids right now, you'll never want them) instead of taking their time. Oh, hell no.

I mean, I don't even want kids, and I'm taking my time

with Bae, making sure we're right for each other. I only want to get married once. Not because of some moral issue; getting divorced (and getting married again, tbh) seems as annoying as moving, and I am not living that celebrity life where jumping into marriage and dipping the fuck out when they're "over it" is the norm because money and supporting oneself is not an issue. However, if you're not rich and unbothered (and quite frankly, even if you are), it's wise to take a beat, or several, and think about which, if any, society-approved boxes of adulting you want to tick. It's even wiser for those outside of someone's relationship to not apply pressure to something as monumental as marriage. Everyone's timetable is different, and while many are on track to be partners at What's Mine Is Yours, many aren't and that's not everybody's business. You know what else is not everyone's LLC? When a woman is married or in a long-term committed relationship and childfree. Yeesh! The fog of judgment is thiiiiiiick, and not the good kind of thick like actor Milo Ventimiglia's thighs in booty shorts, but thick like gas that a comic book villain uses to attack a city, thus making it nearly impossible to breathe.

For real. If a lady is married without kids, people look at her like, "So y'all just fucking for pleaszh?" I'm not married, but I mean, yeah? Don't people do anything simply for the enjoyment of it anymore?! Just like not every hobby needs to be turned into an Etsy business, not every act of lovemaking needs to result in a child. Serious question: Why is the underlying theme of marriage that you're supposed to be boning your spouse for the express purpose of adding a dependent

on a W-4? That sounds sad as hell. Sex is one of the most exciting and incredible things humans can experience, and sometimes it happens in hopes of creating a person, but a lot of the
time, it's happening because it feels good. So making married
women feel like their relationship is somehow invalid because
they're not reproducing is not only terrible, it can put them on
the defensive or, in my case, the offensive. I'm not even married, but I'm used to being the aggressor in the "why I don't
have kids" conversation as a means to protect myself.

In the very recent past, whenever motherhood came up, I'd
generally come out the gate with, "I don't want kids because
I don't have the capacity to be nurturing." Not a "maybe I
don't," which could signal to the person I'm talking to that
I would like for them to reassure me otherwise. Instead, what
I offered up was a hard truth that I'm not only supposedly
deficient in a characteristic that society believes all women
should possess, but that it's impossible to fix that deficiency
within me. It just always felt easier to project the image of
whatever I suspected the average person must be thinking
about my childfree status (usually that I'm heartless) because
if I could beat them to the punch, then their words couldn't
hurt me. There was just one problem: What I said was bullshit.
I know how I am with my friends, employees, and family. I
am the resident hype woman, encouraging them to reach beyond the stars. I share books, quotes, and life lessons I've gathered along the way because I don't believe in hoarding
information. I celebrate their achievements and help them talk
through their doubts. And pre-Covid, I was doling out hugs

left and right. If anything, I love nurturing others; I just haven't given birth to or adopted any of these people. But I was taught that none of those traits mattered since I wasn't a mother. In fact, since I wasn't a mother, a part of me suspected that perhaps none of the aforementioned things that I do ever really happened. That's not where the self-flagellation stopped.

I would also claim that I was too lazy to be a mom even though I run multiple businesses, and while I know that's not akin to the 24/7 job of parenthood, most people who know me would not describe me as shiftless or one to shirk responsibility. And sometimes, I'd get straight to the point by stating that I would be a terrible mother who wouldn't pass on any of my good qualities, just the neurotic tendencies, to my hypothetical children, thus creating an army of Black Larry Davids. That I would be utterly hopeless and would never learn on the job, and no parental instincts would ever kick in for me. I have spent much of my adult life trying out different justifications to explain why I don't want to be a mother, not only for others but also for myself. I needed to diagnose my "shortcoming" as a woman. Let me tell you something: It's tiresome and painful to constantly poke and prod at yourself in the hopes of finding proof of your brokenness that you can offer up as penance to every person you see. As if self-hatred and shame are somehow a sufficient payment for one's childless time on Earth. As if self-hatred and shame should somehow be acceptable armor in order to get through a conversation.

Sadly, I'm not the only person who did or still does rely on the self-blaming technique. It continues to be used by us voluntarily childfree people because we have had these discussions a million different times and in a million different ways, so we can easily decipher who has good intentions and who doesn't. And more often than not, people are "concern trolling." Meaning, they aren't actually concerned or interested in understanding you or your life choices; rather, they want to condemn you under the guise of questioning. As if over the course of one or several conversations, they will discover the *real* cause that you were too dumb to realize or too ashamed (there's that word again) to admit. The reasons can include, but are not limited to:

Ambitious ~~Partner~~ Wife: LOL. Let's be real, we all know that an ambitious man is never considered the reason for the season of childlessness. A husband can opt to not have children and put his career first and be celebrated for his devotion to his craft and be labeled a genius (a word, by the way, that's rarely used to describe women) and told that it is a "worthy sacrifice" if it means society is on the receiving end of his professional contributions. But a woman? She will be blamed, chastised, and labeled "selfish" for investing in her career. And despite all the ways that she may be an incredible wife—her thoughtfulness, her giving nature, her love for her spouse, etc.—she will still be seen as a horrible person who's denying her husband the joys of fatherhood, all so she can climb the corporate ladder. Some folks might even predict that the husband will eventually leave her and find someone else who can give him kids. And if he doesn't leave, people will just assume that when she gets older, she will admit that not having children is the biggest regret of her life. That is how the story is supposed to end for an ambitious woman who never became a mother. She must be punished by all-consuming grief.

Silly Person Who Hates Children and Is Too Stubborn to Overlook That Hatred in Order to Sign Up for an Eighteen-Year Commitment: But also . . . isn't that a good thing? Like, have you ever had a bowl of tagliatelle Bolognese that was prepared by a chef who was in a stank-ass mood and didn't give a damn about you, your life, or your taste buds? That garbage will make you wanna power wash your tongue like you're a city employee cleaning a sidewalk. Point is, just like the best food, the best people are made with love. We absolutely do not need folks who *loathe* children begrudgingly making babies and creating a whole new generation of Mitch McConnells. I don't care if the hate you have in your heart has nothing to do with being anti-children and is just temporary because someone cut you off in traffic prior to you getting home; if you don't tell your wife/girlfriend/partner to greet you at the door with burning sage to wave over your peen while John Legend's "Ordinary People" plays in the background, you are not to have sex for fear of any negative energy that may still be in the dong. That's just science.

You Just Haven't Thought It Through: Since the beginning of time, women in particular have been programmed with messaging that they should be straight, a wife, and a mother. Whether it's playing house or being warned to not have certain traits that would make them undesirable to men (confidence, opinions, wits, joie de vivre), it seems all that girls have been trained to do is to be a mother *without* ever thinking about if that is something they want. Therefore, determining that motherhood is a no-go is something that has been thought about *a lot*. Let's stop underestimating women's ability to think critically about the choices they make for the betterment of their lives.

You're Trying to Get Your Peter Pan On Instead of Being a Grown-Ass Adult: I know the Peter Pan reference is meant to be taken as a slight, but Peter Pan is dope. He can fly, he encourages people to be adventurous, and his tights never have a run in them, unlike mine, which as soon as I step into stockings, thirty-two rips and tears appear and I look like a *Rocky Horror Picture Show* backup dancer. Anyway, Peter Pan is great, so I refuse to accept being called him as a form of shade. What I do reject, however, is the notion that because I don't have kids, I'm resisting being an adult. No. I'm 10,000 percent an adult. Peep the stats: 1) If I sleep at a seven-degree angle that's different from how I usually sleep, then for the next ten days, I have to turn my whole body in order to look at the person I'm talking to; 2) every day, I click "Later" on the "Updates Available" notification on my laptop; 3) my home is always at "sorry for this mess" (even when it's not) when I invite people over; 4) I'm utterly confused by any and all prices in the grocery store like it hasn't always been this way; 5) when I find out there won't be seating at an event, it's reason enough for me to stay home; 6) when I get home from work and realize I've forgotten to take the chicken out the freezer, I call my parents to commiserate because I finally understand why they always made a fuss about this mistake; 7) chores are seemingly and depressingly endless, but still I love to complete them then go to my to-do list, write the task down, and immediately cross it off, which, much like the Pizza Hut / Baskin-Robbins combination shop, is a fresh hell / a sweet treat. I could go on, but you get my point. I adult. All people, once they reach a certain age, adult whether they have children or not. Just because the things and responsibilities that make up one person's adulting look different from another's doesn't mean it's not happening. While we've evolved to where not being a parent (either by choice or circumstance) is more commonplace—one out of five women in their early forties have never had a child—it's clear that the heteronormative expectation is for straight couples to make babies. Evidence is everywhere for that, but none might be clearer than when a public figure finally "settles down."

George Clooney got married at fifty-three and became a father at fifty-six. Cameron Diaz had her first child at forty-seven. And it was almost as if society let out a sigh of relief as if to say, "Finally! They decided to grow up and get on with life the way it should be lived." What about those who never change their minds and are content with not having kids? They're pitied and viewed as irresponsible because, sadly, it seems that the *real* reason being voluntarily childfree bristles some people boils down to a perceived lack of morality. Bella DePaulo's *Psychology Today* article "The Cost of Choosing Not to Have Kids: Moral Outrage" examines this. More than any of the other reasons people may disapprove of the voluntarily childfree—presumed laziness, immaturity—the biggest grievance is that opting out of having children breaks the societal contract of "contributing" to the greater good. After reading a study psychology professor Leslie Ashburn-Nardo shared in a 2017 issue of the journal *Sex Roles*, DePaulo provided her analysis of the data:

> The people who decided not to have children were denigrated more than the people who wanted to have children. They were seen as less psychologically fulfilled and less well-adjusted.
>
> The analyses the author did seemed to suggest that the feelings of moral outrage were driving the skeptical views of the psychological health of the people who chose not to have kids. When participants learned that the person they were reading about had decided not to have kids, and stood by that decision years later, they were morally outraged. That outrage seemed to fuel their harsh judgments that the people who chose not to have kids were probably not all that fulfilled or well-adjusted.

Dr. Ashburn-Nardo believes that the married people who chose not to have children were viewed harshly because they were violating an expectation that is so strong, it is almost a cultural imperative: You must have children! Couples who violate that norm suffer backlash for doing so.

Ummm, how about we keep cultural imperatives to less invasive things, such as not walking around barefoot on flights and banning "free trials" that require us to enter our payment details? Like, if it is free, then why you tryna force people into a contractual agreement? That'd be like if I went to Sam's Club and as an employee is about to give me a free sample of

Honest Tea iced tea, she says, "Let me get that expy date, security code, and billing zip from you real quick so that we can charge you monthly for a case of tea that we both know you always say you're going to cancel but never do." If I heard that, I'd be like, "Lol. Wut? I'm fine being parched as fuck as I walk around this warehouse looking for premade mac and cheese, makeup wipes, and dried acai berries."

The point is that shared, universal beliefs make sense with lightweight issues, but something as personal and transformative as having a family ought to be a decision that each person must make for themselves. Especially if it's a decision that is tied up in the mythology that it's something we should all do because we're in this (and by "this," I mean "life") together. Look, I get it. On some level, I understand the desire to pretend we're in a utopian community. The fantasy that we're operating as our best selves for the benefit of the group makes us feel warm and fuzzy inside. But that's not reality! Time and time again, we behave in ways that best serve the self rather than everyone.

Littering has been proven to have disastrous effects, as researchers estimate that more than *40 percent* of the world's litter is simply burned in open air, which releases toxic emissions, yet every day in New York City, I see people toss paper, plastic, and cardboard on the ground as though they're about to have a romantic evening with Oscar the Grouch and the garbage is the equivalent of a rose petal trail that will lead to a heart-shaped hot tub. Many folks refuse to respect the humanity of the LGBTQIA+ community and to agree that they should have the same rights as cis, straight people. We overlook the harmful effects of the "gig" economy and instead promote the narrative that people having to work around the clock in order to make it demonstrates an "excellent work ethic." We allow abusers and sexual predators to go unpunished if what they provide culturally—music, art, athletic achievement, technological advancements—is deemed worthy. We don't care about our elderly, our veterans, or anyone who isn't able-bodied. Despite the tragedies of Sandy Hook Elementary, Marjory Stoneman Douglas High School, and a long list of other school shootings, we don't protect our students and restrict the kinds of guns that can be purchased because some people's allegiance is to the Second Amendment and not to the safety of our youth. Hell, look at the national response to Covid-19 in America. We can't even come together in the face of a global pandemic. After nine months of the federal government spreading disinformation, coupled with the nation's "me first" mentality, which resulted in many people refusing to wear a mask and socially distance, more than three thousand people were dying per day, meaning that each day we were surpassing the total deaths on 9/11. So the notion that not having children is this grand disrupter to an otherwise idyllic civilization doesn't hold water.

Also, while women of all races and socioeconomic classes are typically expected to be mothers, American history has shown that the mandate to have children for the social, political, economic, and, yes, racial benefit of this nation was a specific directive for white women. Better known as pronatalism, it was not a concept promoted to women of color. In fact, quite the opposite happened as the bodies of WOC were violated in order to maintain white dominance. For example, we oft hear about the post–World War II baby boom, which led to an estimated 78.3 million Americans birthed during this period. But looking deeper at this time period reveals a different story for non-white women. Desegregation was a threat to eugenics believers who felt the country would improve greatly if Anglo-Saxons and Nordics bred. Therefore, anyone who didn't fit in either of those categories—Blacks, Native Americans, and, yes, some poor whites—was sterilized in order to "control" those populations. University of Michigan professor Alexandra Minna Stern writes:

In North Carolina, which sterilized the third highest number of people in the United States—7,600 people from 1929 to 1973—women vastly outnumbered men and Black women were disproportionately sterilized. Preliminary analysis shows that from 1950 to 1966, Black women were sterilized at more than three times the rate of white women and more than 12 times the rate of white men. This pattern reflected the ideas that Black women were not capable of being good parents and poverty should be managed with reproductive constraint.

But as we're all aware, these actions haven't been left behind in the past. Unfortunately, they're still prevalent today. For instance, Dawn Wooten, a nurse at the Irwin County Detention Center, which is an ICE facility, became a whistle-blower in 2020 when she came forward with allegations of medical neglect at the center, including ICE failing to contain the spread of Covid-19 and coercing mass hysterectomies. More than just who is allowed or encouraged to have children, the topic of motherhood is a significant part of the culture wars. Senator Mike Lee (R-Utah), in response to the proposed Green New Deal, suggested the following: "The solution to climate change is not this unserious resolution, but the serious business of human flourishing—the solution to so many of our problems, at all times and in all places: fall in love, get married, and have some kids." This statement, of course, was backed by a photo of Luke Skywalker on a tauntaun. Yeah . . . women are supposed to follow the good word of a grown-ass man presenting us with a picture of a *fictional character* in the equivalent of a Canada Goose down coat, riding a *fake creature* in the heart of winter, as the prediction of what America and the world's future could be like if women don't hurry up and fall in love with *somebody, anybody!* and have kids. Y'all, I just know aliens are watching us and quoting reality TV star NeNe Leakes, one of the great scholars of our time, when she visited her frenemy Kenya Moore's new home in what NeNe considered a less-than-desirable neighborhood: "Whew, chile. The ghetto! The ghetto, the ghetto." Seriously, aliens probably don't even feel like it's worth killing us to inhabit a place that has been drenched in foolery and buffoonery by our so called leaders. A buffoonery that is, of course, never aimed at men.

While I've spent the majority of my adult life trying to figure out why there wasn't a dull ache in my heart because I didn't want to have children, my boyfriend has not. When he's asked if he wants to be a father, he simply replies, "No, I've always known I didn't want to be a father." No one has follow-up questions, no one reassures him that he will change his mind one day, and no one is upset over this choice, as though he is not "contributing to the greater good." They tend to accept his feelings at face value and move on, because fatherhood is never thought to be a fulfillment of man's purpose and evidence of his selflessness. Similarly, his not wanting to be a father is not considered selfish. He is just seen as a person who analyzed his life, weighed the pros and cons of parenthood, and came to the conclusion that's best for him.

Obviously, this reaction to BB's choice is not groundbreaking. We're all aware of the double standard women face when it comes to parenthood; however, it's important to note that the perception is that women who are childfree are *losing* something. And perhaps that might be true for those who want to have kids and for a multitude of reasons cannot. But, for Baekoff and me and, I imagine, for countless other people, I believe I have *gained* by not having kids. To not have kids in the face of a world that chastises those who make that decision is to know oneself deeply. To trust my decision-making skills in a society that has trained me to doubt any choice I make that is not in service to the patriarchy is profound. Not that you can't feel that way if you decide to have kids, but it is clearly much more widely accepted and celebrated and a choice that is more prevalent, so it's easy to identify with. The decision not to isn't.

And that's what a lot of the topic of motherhood boils down to in a lot of ways, right? Identity. More often than not, our identities are defined by either what others do or don't have, what qualities they do or don't possess. I'm good because this person is not. I'm happy in comparison to my friend who is struggling. I should strive for more because I saw one picture from a classmate I haven't talked to since high school graduation who has a different life from mine, so maybe they are doing it right and I'm not. And when we sense our identities don't align with others, instead of accepting that, we look for fault and attempt to get rid of whatever we deem to be wrong.

Well, there's nothing wrong with me. There is nothing wrong with the life choices I've made. I'm happy in ways that people with children aren't and vice versa. I think people forget that. It's not that voluntarily childfree people are just crowd-surfing through life (although that may be the case for some) or that parents feel that raising kids is their calling and they wouldn't trade that for the world (although that may be the case for some). No one is 100 percent content in their choices all the time and doesn't wonder what their lives would be if they chose differently. We're all in that boat together. What we all, women especially, have in common is the what-if. That no matter what we choose, we're going to have moments of imagining a drastically different version of our lives. That's fine. Hell, I encourage it. Fantasizing doesn't mean you're unhappy. It means you're human. So making peace with our ability to dream of a different life for ourselves without it meaning the life we did choose is tinged with regret is something that ought to be one of the most natural things to do in the world.

Because if I'm being honest, writing this essay has naturally stirred up feelings in me. There are moments when I look at British Baekoff and imagine how good of a father he would be. The way he is with my niece and nephew is touching, and once in a while, I feel a slight twinge of sadness that he's not going to mold a human being. I've also occasionally thought about baby names. The thought of how much our parents would dote on our fictional kids (we really did hit the jackpot with loving and giving parents) makes me feel warm inside.

But seeing how good he is with kids isn't enough for me to want to be a mom, and me being a nurturing boss at work isn't enough to make him yearn for fatherhood, and we're both fine with that. And I think that is sometimes what people who have kids misunderstand about us childfree folk. The misconception that not having kids means that we live at the extremes of either deep, painful regret or that our lives are perfect and every day is just cartwheeling and doing light rhythmic gymnastics like the heauxes in the IUD commercials. Actually voluntarily childfree people such as myself, while very content, can feel the totality of all the emotions yet land on the side of "out of all the choices in the world, not being a mother is a decision that will help increase my chances of reaching peak happiness and peace." And without children, I will have the freedom I've dreamed of, the free time I've always enjoyed. I will be the woman I'm destined to be. And that's what I want for everyone, especially every woman reading this.

I haven't written this essay to brag about how brave I am or how great my life is because I don't have kids, although I do feel both of those things. But that's not the point. I write this because like most things I do in my career and/or my life, I don't want anyone to feel even a second of the doldrums, the misery, or the anxiety that I've felt when it comes to motherhood. It's important to me that people who don't want children for any other reason than it's not for them to feel that choice is legitimate and not a cop-out. I write this in the hopes that these words will embolden you, so you don't succumb to pressure from your families, friends, and partners as if your life is not your own. I write this so you don't have to feel alone or cry yourself to sleep because you've been conditioned to feel like not being a mother means you are a failure, incapable of love, incapable of making the world better than it was before you entered it. I write this so women can free themselves from the pain and anguish of feeling like they don't know how to be a person. You are a person. You are worthy. You are whole. You are healing *while* you are whole. You are recovering from every comment, snide remark, and hurtful attack on your womanhood. I see the scars and they are healing. And after the healing is over you can go on living, or start living for the first time, the life you have dreamed for yourself.

Guide to Being a Boss
from Someone Who Has Been Building
a Mini Empire for the Past Two Years
and Counting

Almost a year into the pandemic, *The New York Times* published an article entitled "Arizona Man Is Accused of Faking Own Kidnapping to Evade Work," in which they detailed how nineteen-year-old Brandon Soules faked his own kidnapping, stuffed a bandana in his mouth, bound his wrists behind his back, and planted himself by some dusty-ass train tracks (talk about commitment!) all because he wanted time off from his job at the Tire Factory. When I read this story, I reacted the way a dog does when looking at itself in the mirror: I am you, Brandon! And you are me!

Growing up, I watched many Black actresses in interviews say they didn't feel seen until Diahann Carroll's historic turn in the titular role on *Julia*, the first American TV show starring a Black woman in a non-stereotypical role. Well, I didn't feel seen until this white man wasted taxpayer money and police resources all because he wanted a time-out from slangin' tires.

I repeat: Slangin'. Tires. By the way, I'm not implying that being a tire salesman is small potatoes. Responsibility is responsibility, whether you're an entry-level employee or the CEO of a Fortune 500 company. And when you've had enough, you're through, and, clearly, Soules was so fed up with being in charge of tires that the only conceivable way for him to take a breather was to call the po-po with a fake-ass request to get Liam Neeson to come find him. Let that sink in for a sec. Soules wasn't aiming to finagle ransom money. Or blackmail anybody in hopes of ruining their reputation and life. Or trying to fulfill his desperate need for attention by making up this kidnapping. Brandon Eugene[1] Soules was just WEARY! Do you know how tired you have to be in order to write, produce, wardrobe-style, and star in your own independent movie called *When You're Born with a Dollop of White Privilege But Still Find a Way to Fuck Your Life All the Way Up*? The answer is extremely, and I feel that tiredness deep down in my Adele-fresh-off-a-breakup, Paul-Robeson-"Swing-Low-Sweet-Chariot," drama-calling-Mary-J.-Blige-from-a-burner-phone soul.

Truth be told, I'm low-key impressed with Soules. He did something I've dreamt about but never had the audacity to do. Well, not the faking-a-kidnapping part, but the blowing-up-my-life-spectacularly-so-I-can-get-out-of-work-for-a-few-days

---

1. Okay. I Googled but could not find out what Soules's middle name is, so I took a guess based on my opinion that so many white dudes' middle names are often the first name of their great-grandpappy who built a house with his hands. That's why it's always some goofy shit that doesn't quite flow perfectly like David Prescott Bartholomew Young, Eric Woodrow Baker, or Joe Aloysius Miller. So Eugene it is for White Nonsense Hall of Fame inductee Brandon Soules.

bit. What Soules attempted to pull off requires gumption, un-wavering self-belief, and tenacity, which are key qualities I look for in an employee, so normally, I'd offer him a job, but we all know he wouldn't show up, then I'd get a call days later about how he was kidnapped by a Mexican cartel and I'd have to be like, "Isn't that a season four plotline in *Ozark*?" #FoolMe-OnceBitch. In all seriousness, what Soules did was irresponsible, reckless, selfish, self-destructive, and ridiculous, and yet . . . I understand it! Because the stakes only get higher the further one gets from an entry-level gig like selling Michelins, which is something I know about.

I've worked my way from being a receptionist at New Line Cinema in 2006 to being the founder of my own production company—Tiny Reparations—and literary imprint—Tiny Reparations Books—on top of maintaining my stand-up, pod-casting, and hosting gigs. Often, and especially when I'm in the thick of it, I take stock of my career. The businesses, the never-ending to-do lists, the decision-making, the copious amounts of reading and writing I do on a weekly basis, the countless meetings / phone calls / Zooms, delivering bad news, receiving bad news, the victories and nice surprises, the stress and anxiety, the learning on the fly, taking ownership of mistakes, managing personalities and expectations, the pangs of guilt that someone or something is being neglected because I have to tend to another project, the delicate dance of being fully present yet also thinking one, two, and even five years in advance, keeping myself motivated when I'm dog-tired, because as the boss, I definitely cannot be the one who throws in the towel and gives up.

As I look at the list of all the aspects of my professional career I have to juggle, I can't help but be impressed. Proud. Curious if I'm capable of putting more on my plate. And the fact that I continue to build and want to expand into other arenas is proof that, on some level, I welcome and enjoy the pressures that come along with being a leader. I'd even go as far as to admit I love being a boss.

Still. Almost every day I'm wondering, HOW. CAN. I. GET. OUT. OF. THIS? WHO MADE MY WORLD LIKE THIS? CAN I SPEAK TO THE MANAGER BECAUSE I WOULD LIKE A REFUND FOR THIS LIFE OR, AT THE VERY LEAST, SOME STORE CREDIT FOR WHEN I SEE A DIFFERENT LIFE THAT TICKLES MY FANCY AND MIGHT BE INCLINED TO TRY THAT ONE OUT? I know it sounds like I'm joking, but I'm serious. Take this book, for example. Every single week of the nine months it took me to write it, I thought to myself, *What if I don't turn the manuscript in to my publisher? What they gon do? Ask for the advance money back? Well, I'm not gonna give it back. So then what? They'll sue me? Well, SUE ME then, bitch.* WUT?! I sweat when a TSA agent asks me to reconfirm my birthdate because I'm convinced that even though I've done nothing wrong, I'm about to be shipped off to Guantans aka Guantánamo Bay, but I'm out here pretending I'm big and bad enough to welcome litigious energy into my life.

See, this is what happens when you're new money, but acting like old money. Like, just because I've set my bills to autopay, signed up for Seamless+, and have a plethora of S'well water bottles to choose from with which I can obnoxiously make a production out of hydrating myself by unscrewing, sipping, and rescrewing the stainless steel top back on during Zoom meetings, I'm acting as though I'm financially stable enough for Penguin Random House to serve me papers. Y'all, I cannot afford more than a fortnight of billable hours from a lawyer, and even within those fourteen days, I'm praying the lawyer takes half days and that their Verizon Fios Wi-Fi, cell phone, and landline are jank, so they'll stop working for hours at a time. Obviously, I do not have the money or emotional *strenf* to deal with a lawsuit, but in moments of weakness and exhaustion when I have to choose between ruining my career and honoring my commitments, blowing my life up doesn't seem like that bad of an idea, which is why I understand how so many people in the public eye and/or in the C-suite self-sabotage their lives. The stress is too damn much!

When we witness CEO after CEO and corporation after corporation indulging their worst capitalistic and law-breaking impulses and not settling for stealing a little (which is still absolutely reprehensible behavior, by the way), but embezzling funds to such a comical degree that it's impossible to ignore, the idea that they operated as though "they were too big to fail" gets thrown around. Hmm, maybe. No doubt that some of these folks' reckless behavior was the direct result of unchecked arrogance, but I suspect that a good number of them subconsciously wanted to fail *precisely* because the crimes had gotten so unmanageably big. Because they couldn't envision a way to get off the hamster wheel of corruption, being found guilty either in the court of law and/or the court of public opinion could, in its own bizarre way, be a salve when carrying the secret of misdeeds proved too mentally and emotionally taxing. When Tiger Woods was outed for spending years being the Jehovah's Witness of thottery by spreading the good Word aka his peen, everyone was confused. I wasn't! He'd been playing golf since before he was *one year old*, was expected to be the faultless face of brands, be the example of a morally perfect person, rarely acknowledge his race in any meaningful way (which means he also couldn't address the micro- and macroaggressions he endured either), win every tournament big and small, and help line the pockets of agents, managers, lawyers, etc. Not that any of those circumstances excuse him for repeatedly cheating on his wife, but when one lives in a gilded cage of pressure, they're liable to destroy their life in dramatic fashion like . . .

Charlie Sheen! When he was fresh out of rehab in 2011, he bad-mouthed Chuck Lorre, his boss and the creator of their hit TV show *Two and a Half Men*, and stated he would return to the series only if he was given a 50 PERCENT RAISE. He was promptly fired and many folks were dumbfounded at how things could have ended that way. I wasn't! Carlos Irwin Estévez being so unreasonable at the *start* of negotiations is shit a person does when they have no intention of staying at that job. Seriously, the average person might suggest a 10, 12, maybe even 15 percent raise (if they're bold), all the while knowing they'll settle for something in the 5 to 8 percent range. But opening with 50 percent? Dude dropped that number because he had probably already started the termination process before publicly disrespecting his boss. I bet like six hours prior to TMZ reporting on this nonsense, heauxes were already getting email bounce backs because Charlie hit up the IT department to have them cancel his Charlie.Sheen@CBS.com email address.

Now, I could keep going with examples of people ctrl + alt + deleting their lives, but you get the point: It's not all that uncommon that when one is burdened with too much responsibility, whether real or imagined, they might feel trapped and seek ways to free themselves, and often those ways are categorically destructive. And as you know now, somewhere deep down, I, at times, have this same impulse, but lack the courage to do something so inconsiderate. Still, more often than not, I'm the one turning to the Universe and saying, "Gimme the ball, coach; I'll bring home the victory."

If I'm being honest, these conflicting parts of myself have existed for as long as I remember. After all, I spent all of my teenage years coasting because I was too afraid to put in the effort only to end up failing; too knowledgeable about the fact that anything I wanted to do would require immense amounts of energy; too lazy to do the work because living in my head is easy and safe; too terrified that all my work would pay off, I'd finally get what I wanted, and then I'd have to deal with newfound responsibilities. Well, as I've learned time and time again, when I did get what I dreamt of, I simply rose to the occasion, then took everything I learned and welcomed the next challenge. Each challenge, no matter the outcome, filled me with more confidence and the conviction that I could handle *more*, not less, hence how I ended up thirteen years into my Hollywood career with a mini empire in the making. Clearly, despite fantasies about dismantling everything I painstakingly built, every day I continue to make the choice to do the opposite. In fact, doing the opposite doesn't fully encapsulate what I'm doing. I'm aggressively doubling down whenever I can, assuming more and more responsibility, which will only prepare me for whatever new and exciting opportunities are bound to come down the pike.

So how did I end up in a leadership position where the stakes are constantly raised and I have to stifle the #JokesNot-Jokes urge to burn my life to the ground? Glad you asked.

You know the saying: "Yes, hardworking Beyoncé can have an even harder-working and sassier alter ego of Sasha Fierce, but what's actually cooler is that Phoebe Robinson's hardworking self has an alter ego of Black Garfield: just lounging in bed, eating lasagna, and avoiding wash day." Oh, you're not familiar with that old adage? Then you should probably read less James Baldwin and more of my diary. And yes, this is the first time in Black history that someone has suggested reading *less* James Baldwin, which is why I will never be a professor, because I'd be like, "Class, did y'all read what happened on the Shade Room last night?" and then give everyone A's regardless of their answers. Moving on.

The point is that while some folks possess two modes—work hard and work harder—I, on the other hand, am made up of opposing philosophies—alpha leader and lazy piece of garbage—that are constantly duking it out, and what typically ends up being the deciding factor that overrules my listless tendencies is that I'm a visionary. Not in the sense of folks like

Frida Kahlo or John Rockefeller, who changed the world and left their marks on history, but in the sense that I love the process of creating. More than sleeping in, enveloping myself in a wool blanket on a couch, or binging my favorite TV show, I get the biggest high when a bolt of inspiration strikes and a fully realized image pops into my head as I become almost obsessive with making what I envision a reality, or when I have a germ of an idea and collaborating with others elevates it to a level I never would have reached alone, or simply when I or the Universe asks the question of "What if?" A query innocent enough that's usually born out of "I mean, yeah, maybe this seems outrageous at first glance, but is it really? What if this is actually pretty reasonable and the only outrageous thing is that it hasn't happened *yet*?" That curiosity is how I ended up going from freelancing to launching a production company and publishing imprint within a year of each other and overseeing a handful of employees.

After the second batch of *2 Dope Queens* HBO specials premiered in 2019, I was secretly happy to put that project to bed (Jessica Williams and I started it as a live show back in 2014) so I could focus on my dream of having my own scripted half-hour comedy series on TV. Except the Universe was Dikembe Mutombo'ing this hope every chance it got. It was either not the right idea, or the right idea and not quite the right collaborators, or the network / streaming platform enjoyed the idea, but not enough to put their energy and money behind it. Whatever the case was, it yielded the same result: rejection. Enter ABC. They were casting a show that received a pilot order[2] and sent me an offer to be one of the leads without having to go through the nerve-racking audition process. Pause. If you don't know, that is a big deal. Usually, you schlep your wares (aka self-esteem and acting talent) all over town in the hopes of booking a job, only to have Hollywood mostly turn their noses up at you as if you just opened a Tupperware container of grilled salmon and asparagus,[3] so when an opportunity presents itself to bypass all that desperate "choose me" energy, the word "yes" should just tumble out of your mouth, especially because starring in a network sitcom can be life changing.

But I was reticent. Locking myself into someone else's vision that I had no hand in shaping felt, well . . . not like prison, which is what people usually say. You know what I'm talking about. Sometimes, famous actors will occasionally complain by saying, "Working on such and such show was like being in prison," and I'm like, "Have they been to pris? Do they know anyone who has been to pris?" Clearly, I haven't and I don't

---

2. Basically, a pilot order means the network / streaming platform likes the script and the TV series idea, but they wanna shoot the pilot script first to see if they like it enough to order an entire season. It's kinda like when you start dating someone and then introduce that person to your friends who, like you, also have boo-boo taste sometimes, before locking Bae down. None of y'all know what the hell you're doing, but somehow it all works out. *Frasier* was on the air for thirteen years and everyone knows someone who has been married for thirty years.

3. Fun fact (for who, I don't know): I am that person. And it's even worse because I'm the boss, so my employees are forced to settle for mentally cussing me out over this ignorance, which is fair. Salmon *and* asparagus? That's a fragrant as fuck combination. If the Diptyque candle company ever had a product with a scent that strong, they'd have been out of business two hours after their website went live.

because I'm giving it a cutesy nickname like "pris"! But what I do know is an acne-free person getting paid obscene amounts of money to kiss other acne-free people and becoming famous and, in exchange, having to prioritize that TV show over other things they want to do from time to time is not prison. That's a champagne problem. Like when a bottle of Veuve Clicquot (how do you pronounce that brand because every time I make a go for it, I sound like Elizabeth Berkley saying "Versayce" in *Showgirls*) has lost a bit of its fizz, but it will still get you tipsy. So no, I refuse to compare ABC's sitcom offer to pris; it simply just didn't fit right with my spirit because I still wanted to bet on myself and create a TV show.

A few weeks passed and I was in the middle of the slow-churning process of developing a pilot for my own scripted series (which was serendipitously falling apart) when ABC Signature (a studio under the Disney/Fox umbrella that creates shows for ABC, Hulu, Freeform, FX, and other platforms) hit me with: "Ever thought about running your own production company?" Call me naïve, but I didn't know you could tell a big entity no and they would come back with something juicier that's impossible to refuse. But more important? Y'all, I accidentally played hard to get and . . . it worked? WHAT?! I always thought "getting what you want by playing hard to get" was a myth, like shaving your arm hair makes it grow back thicker, but I'm now filing "turning down one offer can potentially lead to being presented with a completely different and better one" under shit that's actually true alongside the neck test (aka wrapping a pair of jeans around your neck and if the waistline comfortably meets at the back of your neck, the jeans will fit) and that Black people always have a case of unrefrigerated bottles of water around their houses.

In all seriousness, this offer from ABC Signature made me realize I should've been keeping it coy my whole life! Instead, my thirsty and eager-to-please Midwestern self has been walking around like, "MAY I HAVE YOUR ATTENTION, PLEASE? I AM AVAILABLE AS FUCK! For employment, friendship, romantic relationships, to give my uninformed opinions on everything, to give business advice, read other people's writing, help pick out presents for loved ones, talk shit, convince friends to buy a Peloton bike, etc." Not to say that my tech-avail energy hasn't benefited me thus far, but as this business proposition taught me: Playing it cool sometimes just *feels* more badass than being an emotionally exposed Earnest Ernestine. Moving on.

The point is I always assumed I would start a production company in my forties, but ABC Signature wanting to take me off these dodgy freelancer streets and put a ring on it trumped any arbitrary timetable I had set for myself. If they believed I could handle all the responsibilities that came with running a production company in my thirties, then why shouldn't I? After all, it seems as though many people are good at their jobs because they developed many of the skills *on* the job, and I'm a quick-ish study, so this shouldn't be too difficult of an endeavor, right?

Call this a classic case of "you don't know what you don't know." Because I'd been freelancing for several years, I assumed that starting a production company would be like any of my other hustles. Anyone who has freelanced before can understand that assumption. You start out hopeful and rosy and then immediately you are bedraggled as fuck. Every single day of freelance life was comprised of endless mini heavy lifts: drumming up work, booking stand-up gigs, auditioning, doing paid and unpaid writing gigs, tracking down payment for work I did weeks and weeks ago, strategizing which bills I could be late on so that I had enough money to pay my rent, and sometimes taking jobs that underpaid but overextended me because some money was better than no money, etc. Therefore, as exciting as the offer of running my own company was, part of me was too locked into a grizzled vet mindset and believed it would be taxing the way my work had always been, so I didn't fully comprehend just how my career and life were going to change. No longer was it going to be just Mai (you'll learn all about my second-in-command in my "Black Girl, Will Travel" essay) and me against the world. Contracts were signed. Expectations from everyone, especially myself, were born. I was *founding* a company. I was going to be a boss . . . with THREE whole employees—😦 😦—and counting, as I would soon find out. We'll get to that in a second, but first, more about Tiny Reparations.

The production company was put together while I was in the middle of my stand-up tour. So when we weren't on the road, Mai and I looked at office spaces, interviewed people to fill the head of development and personal assistant positions, wrote an employee handbook, and had countless discussions about everything from the fundamentals (monthly overhead costs, health insurance plans, defining the office cultch aka culture) to the minutiae (where do we want to hang the artwork, how many team-building lunches do we want, is it a bit much to get matching U2 T-shirts for everyone? The answer is yes, but I still did it and then ended up keeping all four shirts for myself because, thankfully, I realized how ignorant I was being). Then there was the matter of the production company, ya know, producing something. The studio wanted me to come up with a TV show for me to star in, so I was meeting showrunners and began brainstorming and before I knew it, months later, Tiny Reparations officially launched while I was in Scotland for the Edinburgh Festival Fringe. Word to the wise: If you have to start a business venture remotely, make sure it's not in a place like Edinburgh that's just unseasoned food and personalities.

Once I returned home, Tiny Rep demanded my undivided attention (I started production on a limited-run talk show for Comedy Central while developing an idea for a scripted series with showrunner and all-around wonderful human being Jonathan Groff), and then I did the only sensible thing: I put my dream of running a literary imprint on the back burner. Yeah . . . I'm aware how this sounds. I spent so much time at the beginning of this essay lamenting how much I secretly want to get out of all my responsibilities, yet the more I write, it's obvious that I was on the path to building an empire.

What can I say? I contain multitudes, y'all! And I'm not the only one. All of us do, which is what keeps life interesting or tiring, depending on who you ask. So, this is why despite my countless protests about working too much, I would still dream about launching an imprint. Speaking of which, the idea for that came about over a rainy afternoon lunch with my then soon-to-be lit agent, Robert, way back in 2014.

He and I quickly bonded over our shared love of pop culture, corny jokes, attractive men, and a penchant for planning for the future. Sensing that I'm not a one-book-and-done kind of author, he asked me what my endgame was. I knew that, for a time, Toni Morrison was a book editor while she wrote her own, and though I'm forever impressed by her ability to juggle, I also felt that was—*youguessedit!*—waaaaaaaay too much work, so I told Robert, "Editing is too time-consuming, so I'll just have my own imprint instead." I still chuckle at this. The word "just" is so hilarious and lovably innocent. Just. "I'll *just* have an imprint" was said with the same casual energy I have when, after a waiter presents all the dessert options, I say, "I'll just have the check. Thanks!" I swear I wasn't trying to play it cool; I honestly had no idea really what all went into running an imprint. I just loved reading books and believed that having my own imprint would allow me to be surrounded by books all the time . . . which is actually correct. My apartment with Baekoff currently looks like an indie bookstore called "One Day I'll Read All These Books, but Honestly I'll Just Keep Buying More and Trip Over Them." This store is not very successful, guys. Anyway, ever since that lunch, Robert and I would briefly talk about an imprint and I'd claim it wasn't the right time because my plate was full, and late 2019 / early 2020 was no exception. And yet . . . I decided to do an exploratory call with Plume, the publisher of my two previous books.

Ooooooookay, we can all agree this is getting ridiculous, right? I was behaving the way politicians do when they create exploratory committees to see if they want to run for president. These politicians make announcements about how they're *not* running for office; they're merely thinking about it. Mm-hmm. They're full of it and so was I. Telling myself and everyone around me that this call with Plume was not going to set things in motion was nothing more than a sweet little lie that I justified with the following stream-of-consciousness thinking:

This is just to loosely talk about maybe, somewhere down the line when I'm older, what running an imprint would look like, even though I'm not *really* entertaining the thought because, again, now is NOT the right time, but if we can have an hour-long conversation and then someone can send me a follow-up email with a PDF deck of what the company structure would look like *if* I *were* to run my own imprint, which I am not gonna do because *Iamverybusy,* so busy that I haven't given it much thought except that I would call it Tiny Reparations Books, I've already written a mission statement, I've decided that I want to publish literary fiction, nonfiction, and essay collections, and I would like to be heavily involved and read submissions / meet with authors and agents, which, now that I think about it, let's THOROUGHLY walk through my bullet-point list of questions and the three-page document I created about how Tiny Rep Books fits in the marketplace, but, again, and I don't know why no one understands this, I will not launch an imprint at this time, but also, I will 100 percent launch it and be overwhelmed even though working this hard is the high I chase. END SCENE. Yep, I tire myself, too. But this was the story I was sticking to even after the call and through the early parts of Covid.

I was reading for hours every day not solely for pleasure, but also to distract myself from the fact that the coronavirus upended every single project I was working on. The additional free time meant that besides reading, I also had time to think, which is how the idea for this book came to be and why the literary imprint seemed more realistic than ever before. Diving into a new business venture could be *just* (there goes that word again) the thing that would lift me out of my depression. When I reconnected with #TeamPlume and my publisher, Christine Ball, after our initial conversation, it happened to be shortly before #PublishingPaidMe went viral, which only further proved the timeliness of my mission to have a highly inclusive imprint, not just on the author side, but behind the scenes. On one hand, it's frustrating that it takes a collective uproar on social media for there to be transparency about how authors of color earn significantly smaller advances than their white counterparts, but on the other hand, you bet your sweet ass I took this industry dustup as a sign to get my piece of the pie so I can spread it around, because I remember what being a newbie author was like.

When I was shopping around my first book in 2015, *every single* imprint (except for Plume, obvs) flat-out rejected it for the following reasons: "Black female authors don't sell," are "not relatable," and "readers aren't interested in funny stories from Black women." Mm-hmm. Only a year prior, in 2014,

Pew Research revealed that the person most likely to read a book is a college-educated Black woman, so what were these publishing execs talking about? Did they think Black women in 2015 *all decided to decide not* to read Black female authors? Like we're hitting each other up in Slack, "Girl, we gotta talk about Ernie Hems"? This was not to say that Black women *only* read books written by Black women. That's equally as limiting a narrative as the notion we don't read at all. Matter of fact, we'll throw some white authors in the mix, like one puts parsley on garlic bread, while at the same time we *love* reading Black female authors. We are hungry to have them promoted and marketed to us, so we can discover their works. This assumption that the dominant demographic would want to read everything EXCEPT works from folks who look like them and have shared experiences is simply nothing but racism.

I knew that I didn't want Tiny Reparations Books to be yet another place that made debut as well as established POC/LGBTQIA+ authors feel like they didn't matter. That their stories and voices weren't worthy. So, much like with my production company, Plume and I quickly got to work building the imprint of my dreams, which included having a Black woman as the editor and letting my publicists, also people of color, have a hand in shaping the PR and marketing for all the titles under Tiny Rep Books. And as I was jumping between reading book proposals, writing my own book, and developing and pitching TV shows while Hollywood slowly started to return to form, as well as leading team meetings and checking in on how my employees were doing mentally in the wake of quarantining indefinitely and the mental anguish that summer 2020 brought, it dawned on me: I'm a boss. I mean, yes, I knew I was the one in charge, who did the hiring and firing and set the tone for the company, blah, blah, blah. But all the nuances as well as the micro and macro facets of what being a boss entails: being a leader, having to manage people and their expectations, observing dynamics between coworkers, being an example of how to execute conflict resolution, understanding that weekly, I would be making hundreds of decisions regarding the big and little things, maintaining my own mental health, etc., and everything else in between? Oof, all things I didn't truly understand how much they factored into the totality of my newfound position.

There was so much I didn't know and even more I didn't know I was *supposed* to know, but that wasn't because I wasn't trying. I listened to business podcasts hosted by entrepreneurs such as Gary Vaynerchuk, read books including Kim Scott's *Radical Candor: Be a Kick-Ass Boss Without Losing Your Humanity.* And I peeped profiles on executives in magazines such as *Fast Company* and watched interviews by successful businesspeople. Real talk: Most of these interviews and resources are garbage. For every good one—Simon Sinek's *Leaders Eat Last*—there's usually a litany of old, crusty white dudes who are eleventy years old and worth two billion dollars, delivering the same tired advice that sounds great on a magnet or looks pretty written in calligraphy on social media—"Invest in yourself," "Build a reliable network," "Don't be afraid to make mistakes." It's perfectly serviceable yet absolutely surface-level information that's devoid of specificity and insight into what it takes to run your own business or build an empire. What I needed and wanted was for these business luminaries to be frank about the nitty-gritty of what it's like when you're no longer working for "The Man," but *are* "The Man."

Just once, I wish someone said, "Heaux, why are you suggesting bowling night for team building? They do not want to hang out with you outside of work hours." Or, "Please understand that if you email your employees at 5:53 P.M., asking them to do last-minute work, the only reason they're not putting in their two weeks' notice is cuz you got them that 'good good' [health insurance]." A blunt "Aww, it's so cute that you hoped to save money by stocking the office with low-budget snacks. People did not join your *widdle* start-up so that when they're stressed out, they could comfort themselves with whack-ass reduced-fat Utz chips" would've been nice. An honest "Hey, boo. Here's the deal: The office printer you bought will almost always NEVER be used for professional purposes. And when the print box appears on your employees' computer screens, they will absolutely bypass the option to print in black and white. Yep, that's right. They're going to use up all that cyan and magenta ink printing out their StubHub tickets for *Dear Evan Hansen*. And you better not say shit about it" ought to be mandatory information given to all new bosses and business owners.

And finally, I would've appreciated advice specifically about being a Black female boss. There's not a whole lot of information or books on that topic, and what does exist, you really have to dig to find. Like, where's *Lean In* for us? Now, it doesn't matter whether you agreed with everything in Sheryl Sandberg's book, there's no denying that it broke through the zeitgeist as a solid resource women can refer to; however, the same isn't true about BW leadership. The ones that tend to break out are books such as *Year of Yes* by Shonda Rhimes, which is great, but is more about her personal journey transforming her life over the course of a year and less concerned with getting down to brass tacks when it comes to business in the way I had hoped. Thankfully, it appears the tide is turning, and no longer is there a complete dearth of business books written by Black women as there used to be. Folks such as Minda Harts (author of *The Memo: What Women of Color Need to Know to Secure a Seat at the Table*) and executives Elaine Meryl Brown, Marsha Haygood, and Rhonda Joy McLean (coauthors of *The Little Black Book of Success*) are a part of the latest generation of business books written by BW. Thankfully, the conversation about Black women in business is becoming louder and harder to ignore. So it seems as though there's no better time than now for me to join the conversation about being a Black lady boss. If I may have a word . . .

Being a Black woman and a boss is the shit! I know, I. Know. Despite all evidence displaying the multitude of the Black female experience, society is, more or less, intent on boiling us down to an outdated and monolithic narrative that BW in charge is nothing more than just breaking down one civil rights barrier after another, delivering rousing speeches at the ready, and Negro spiritual humming when the going gets rough. The common perception is that being a Black woman in a leadership role equals overcoming obstacles only to encounter more trials and tribulations, and while I didn't believe that, I still was a bit anxious about what it would be like for me since I didn't have personal examples to use as reference points. I've never had a Black female high school teacher or college professor. Same goes for having a Black woman as a boss. Sadly, this is the norm, especially in entertainment.

During my stints at film and internet companies as well as freelancing at various corporate offices, a Black woman was never in a managerial or C-suite position. Not only is the lack of Black women in leadership roles due to racial bias, it's also a missed opportunity for businesses to tap into a more than qualified talent pool. According to the NCES, the National Center for Education Statistics, Black women are the most educated demographic in America when it comes to associate and bachelor's degrees. Damn. Just think of all the Black women whose maximum potential is not utilized and how their different perspectives could positively impact margins. After all, Black buying power is $1.4 trillion, is projected to grow to $1.8 trillion by 2024, according to the Selig Center for Economic Growth, and is outgrowing white buying power. OH, REALLY?! Okay. Listen up, white people, you have been put on notice: If you wanna keep up with us, y'all need to start shopping more at Madewell and buying TRESemmé and Vidal Sassoon (clearly, I don't know what kind of shampoo y'all use) in bulk because we are leading the charge and will eventually become the de facto market that's catered to. Meaning elevator music at the dentist's office will be Al Jarreau (HOW FUCKING OLD AM I?), tiny bottles of cocoa butter lotion will replace mints on pillows at hotels, and the nash anth, on good days, will be "September" by Earth, Wind & Fire, and on days when we're feeling petty: "Hope She Cheats on You (With a Basketball Player)" by Marsha

Ambrosius because that is specific and bitter as fuck and some days that's how we're all feeling.

Anyway, what I'm getting at is Black women have so much to offer as bosses, but because of the constant negative media depiction of us, we are underpaid, disrespected, and discriminated against when we're clearly qualified, and, as a result, we are not considered for leadership positions. And outside of Shonda Rhimes, there weren't a whole host of examples to call on that I could use as guidance in building the kind of career I imagined for myself, which not only saddened me, but fueled me to be the Black lady boss I didn't have in my life.

So, for all my employees, I'm passionate, funny, thoughtful, incisive, decisive, compassionate, artsy, intense, and collaborative. I have weaknesses that I take ownership of, weaknesses that are slowly becoming strengths, and I believe that all of us at Tiny Reparations and Tiny Reparations Books can create incredible TV shows and books that are not only funny but have something thoughtful to say. There's tons of joy in it. Still, I don't want to paint too rosy of a picture. My Blackness and gender can trip up the ignorant. For instance, are there people who underestimate my business acumen because I'm a Black woman? You betcha. Have I been underpaid because of the way I look? Absolutely. Have there been scenarios where someone around me underdelivered or was sloppy because they think Black women will accept subpar quality? Hell, yes. And am I hyper-aware sometimes that I will be unfairly judged as harsh or mean or demanding if I'm not treating people with kid gloves? To say anything other than "yes" would be a lie. Although there is no true way of "preparing" for the uniqueness that is being a

Black woman who is also a boss, some insider information and personal experience working for a BW would have been greatly appreciated. So, this is where this essay and I come in.

I'm sharing what I've learned in the hopes that you will be a little less in the dark than I was years ago. Is some of what I'm about to tell you going to be ignorant or ignorantly presented? I think we all know the answer to that question. So thanks for signing up for this DeVry University version of Harvard Business School. Please note there are no refunds, I'm the only faculty member, my office hours are the minutes I spend waiting for my Lyft XL, and the only required reading on the class syllabus are my two previous books and *Rich Dad Poor Dad* by Robert Kiyosaki, who filed for bankruptcy in 2012. Aww, Rob. Like Ferris Bueller famously said, "Life moves pretty fast!" Anyway, here's what I've learned from running businesses and building a mini empire for two-plus years:

What Warren Buffett Should've Told Ya #1: For Some of Your Employees, This Is Just a J.O.B.

This rule is not what any business owner wants to hear, but the sooner this reality is accepted, the more effective and successful you and your company will be. The truth is that no one on payroll, no matter how loyal, will ever, ever, *ever* care as much about your company as you do. Which means that yes, for some of your employees, it is JUST. A. JOB. That's right: They're there for the 5G Wi-Fi, cheap snacks, and because, like all of us, they have rent due on the first of the month. Similarly, there will be times when they don't want to be there, so they'll occasionally call out sick, kill time surfing the internet or texting friends, and, yes, leave work early to go to a dentist appointment. Call me cynical, but I don't believe anyone goes to the dentist. Fine. Maybe Lupita Nyong'o does because her teeth *are* blindingly white. But for the rest of us? Uh-uh. No way. Like everyone is going to the dentist, yet we're ALL walking around with our teef looking like Sherwin-Williams off-white paint swatches at Home Depot? I'm talking Ecru, Cappuccino White, Chantilly Lace. Suuuuuuure. Anyway, knowing that some of your employees are not emotionally invested in the success of your company can bruise the ego, but I beg you to remember: This Is Not Personal. Most employees are not going to give 1,000 percent or maybe even 90 percent or 75 percent of themselves to a company, and why should they? The company does not have their DNA swirling up in its helixes, so there isn't that unbreakable bond reminding them that, at the lowest points, it'll be worth it. Sounds like common sense, but it's easy to forget when you're deep into the day-to-day.

You have to remember that your company is not *your employees'* dreams. Some are in a financial pinch and need steady income to tide them over until they can either get back on their feet or find something better. For others, you and your company are the fallback option for the dream gig they didn't land. And finally, there are those who legit heard everything you said the job did and didn't entail, agreed to the terms, and then when they started doing the job, made it clear that they don't want to do said job and made it appear as though you pulled a rope-a-dope on them. This leads me to . . .

What Warren Buffett Should've Told Ya #2:
Every Single Person Lies During a Job Interview,
So Don't Believe Everything They Say;
Instead, Listen to Your Gut

Much like dating, in which you don't really know the person you're with until three months in, when the honeymoon period is over and everyone stops acting on their best behavior, you don't *really* know who you hired until they've been working for you for a while. Take me, for example: According to all my employers when they hired me, I had the typing skills of a court stenographer, could put together PowerPoint presentations like a modern-day Don Draper, and my biggest flaw was that I worked too hard. Cut to me having that job: I typed with a maximum of four fingers (and still do!), copying and pasting an image from the internet to a document stressed me the fuck out, and every day was senioritis as I generally went on autopilot shortly after lunch. But I said what I had to say in order to get the job, so why wouldn't the candidates do the same to you?

I firmly believe most people aren't lying to you out of malice. They have bills and responsibilities and, like you, they're also adulting and, unless they are a trust fund baby, they need money to live. So it only makes sense that they'll present the most idealized version of themselves even if it's for a job they don't really want. I write this not so you'll turn into a distrustful person, rather, I want you to hone your gut instincts so that you'll listen to your Spidey senses when a job candidate says or does something that doesn't sit right with your spirit. I learned this unfortunate truth when I had to fire my previous personal assistant.

Look, much like death, taxes, and leaving your house wearing foundation that doesn't match your neck,[4] firing people is an unavoidable and unpleasant part of life. Sometimes it's not working, and to delay the inevitable is a drain on resources, team morale, and the sanity of both you and your employee, who is probably aware of how they are dropping the ball. And as someone who is an empath, I tend to give people fifty chances when two or three are all that's needed. Now on with the story of how "B" and I ended up parting ways.

When I interviewed her, she mentioned that one day, she'd like to be a writers' room assistant on a future Tiny Rep show and work her way up to eventually showrunning her own TV series. This path of PA → writers' room assistant → staff writer and beyond is a well-worn path in Hollywood, and I was excited that she envisioned being at my production company long enough to work her way up the ladder. Turns out my optimism was misplaced.

Apparently, what she meant by "one day" was "right fucking now." Like, she hinted that she was ready for a promotion after one month on the job (lol, get a grip), made careless and sometimes costly mistakes, such as ignoring passport and

---

4. This is why it's imperative to have summer and winter foundations, because everyone's skin lightens and darkens depending on the season. If you try to have one foundaysh that you use year-round, you'll end up looking like Boo Boo the Fool. #HowManyWhitePeopleAreGoingToGoogleThatTerm #ALot

visa deadlines related to business travel, and shortly after I gave her one last chance instead of firing her, she FaceTimed me because she conveniently got offered her dream gig and wanted to weigh the pros and cons of staying with me or taking the new job. Ooof, if there was ever a moment to learn that some people will misrepresent their motives to get a job, that was it. It became clear to me that B had no interest in being my assistant—it was almost immediately about the next thing. And at first, I felt that was my fault. That if being a personal assistant was somehow cooler, she would have liked it all more. No. Just no. For all you current and soon-to-be bosses, let me save you a lot of strife and headache: Providing solid employment in exchange for a salary, perks, and health insurance is not a hoodwink. It is not your responsibility to make work feel like summer camp. If someone agrees to a job offer yet is unwilling to hold up their end of the bargain because it's not glamorous or fun every second of the workday, they're wasting your time because you're here for business and they clearly . . . aren't.

I'm aware social media convinces everyone that people in the public eye are living one endless loop of sipping margs, getting free shit that they can afford, hanging with celebs, and receiving cunniling-ling to a soundtrack of Sade and Anita Baker, but you want to know what I'm doing right now? Instead of hanging out with my boyfriend on this lovely spring day and having a picnic on the roof or brunching with a famous friend, I'm writing this very essay with my dirty hair thrown into a messy bun, slight BO wafting up my nostrils, and rocking three-year-old underwear, which I just learned is allegedly disgusting because we're supposed to replace our undies every six months.[5] To be honest, that's what the majority of my days look like, with the addition of showers, of course. However, I believe she expected working for me to be like a curated Instagram story, and because I wasn't going to promote her on *her* timetable and she wasn't meeting famous people day in and day out, I must have duped her. I didn't, and obviously she duped me, even though early on, deep down in my stomach, I knew she wasn't the correct fit. See?! This is what I was referring to when I mentioned listening to your Spidey senses. I hadn't, because that would've meant letting go of the fantasy I created of mentoring her. She, in little and not-so-little ways, revealed that she didn't want that kind of relationship with me, no matter how much she made it seem she would be interested in that during the job interview.

There will be many times when the circumstances are

---

5. Who the hell made this rule?! Listen, I get that the longer we evolve as a society, the more hygienic we're supposed to be, but I'm sanitary enough. Okay, fine, "I'm sanitary enough" sounds like something a trifling person would say, but I promise I'm clean! Like, I wash my hands, don't believe in the five-second rule, and, duh, I don't let bitches sit on my bed in their outside clothes. But buying a brand-new underwear collection EVERY SIX MONTHS?! Who's got all these spare panty pesos? These full-cut brief francs? These thong Turkish liras? Yeah, that one was a mess, but you feel me. I thought the agreed-upon life cycle of underwear was as follows: new → then over time, natch discharge moves them to the period panties category → then they go back into everyday panty-wearing rotaysh because they're cute AF on the outside → until wear and tear eventually makes them holey and causes the waistband to lose its elasticity → then your significant other comments on the Swiss cheesiness of your Underoos, so you playfully tell them to kiss your Black ass and continue to wear the underwear for another *full* year → until you see that Calvin Klein has a clearance sale, so you buy some new ones and hold a funeral for your raggedy drawers by going to the nearest lake, putting them on a barge, and shooting a flamed arrow at the barge like you're the Blackfish sending off Lord Hoster Tully in *Game of Thrones*.

even more cut-and-dried as far as your candidates are concerned. So recognize it, take the dreams and fantasies out of the equation, and trust your gut. You and your business deserve more than someone half-assing it because they show up on day one with one foot out the door.

What Warren Buffett Should've Told Ya #3: Have Some Damn Fun

As much as I joke around, I'm a pretty tightly wound person. Not in a way that I take myself seriously, but as my astrologist so accurately put it: I don't believe that success can come without pain and suffering. So bring on the sleep deprivation, anxiety driving my creativity, and not taking care of my mental and physical well-being. If the outcome means I accomplish what I set out to do, then it was all worth it, right? Ehh . . . maybe not? I'm sure this sounds rich coming from me considering I have quite a few things to show for my laborious efforts, but trust me. I've spent most, if not all, of my career consumed with crossing off and then quickly adding to my to-do list out of fear that work will dry up and because I was so hyper focused on achieving my dreams that practically everything else—friends, family, moments of peace—took a back seat. While I'm not filled with regret when I look back on the first thirteen years of my career, there are twinges of "Hmm, I should have enjoyed that more" and "I wish I took time to celebrate this with a friend *in person* as opposed to firing off a quick 'thx, queen' in response to their celebratory message." Not absorbing the fact I was making my dreams come true also meant I wasn't absorbing the lessons I'd learned on the path to those victories or appreciating the people who were at my side, cheering me on and/or playing an integral part in my success.

You can be happy *and* enjoy your work. You can goof around *and* still be the boss everyone will answer to and respect. You can take a break, go on vacation, have a relaxing dinner with a friend, or a long and leisurely phone call with your parents, and you're not going to fall behind. I know the stakes are high when your livelihood and reputation are on the line, but don't let everything else that makes life worth living fall by the wayside. You owe it to yourself and your business to have fun and relish the good times because running a company is simply just too hard of an endeavor if you don't stop and savor any of the delicious moments that come along.

What Warren Buffett Should've Told Ya #4: Get Yourself a Lawyer

I know we all think we can lawyer because we've watched legal dramas on a lazy Saturday afternoon, but a) we don't know shit, and b) what we will most likely need a lawyer for isn't to help us fight a murder charge, but so we don't sign a boo-boo contract in which we're getting paid peanuts. After all, the show was called *How to Get Away with Murder*, not *But What Do Those Royalties Look Like Tho*, which, if that show had a hot dude in it, I would watch. #HabeasMyCorpus! What I'm getting at is rarely, if ever, are we privy to discussions about what the possession of a trademark logo entails or why we should care about limitation of liability / indemnification. I mean, if *Behind the Music* taught us anything, it's to read a contract before signing it, but if we don't know what any of the words or legal phrases mean, then what's the point?

Legit, before I got a lawyer (but also even now that I have one), sometimes when I had to sign a contract in front of someone, it may have seemed like I was really absorbing what I was looking at, but in actuality, I was just thinking to myself, *I am reading. This is what reading looks like. Squinting and hmm'ing so I appear smart. More reading and nodding and nodding and reading. Pause for a moment and hold the pen up to my bottom lip to show that I'm thinking. Is this how people look when they're thinking? Will Google that when I get home. And now I'm signing. Fingers crossed I didn't agree to fuck my life up.* This is trash, but I know I'm not the only one who does this. The law is hard, and I'm not sure about you, but for me, legalese does one of two things: hurt my brain or become my NyQuil.

Honestly, once I see the words "in accordance" and "heretofore," my Black ass is sound asleep. I know parents struggle with newborns not sleeping through the night and I wanna be like, "Have you tried reading your baby a merch agreement between a client and a merchandising and branding company? That shit is like chloroform to the nostrils in a Hitchcock movie." Like most people, I can't get through reading a legal document, and guess what? All of this is perfectly fine and normal. No one expects you to know all the ins and outs of the law, which is a bad thing because there are always going to be snakes looking for easy prey, but it's also a good thing because you can dedicate your energy to what you do best and hire a lawyer to protect you.

In my opinion, a lawyer is one of if not the most important hires you will make. When you lawyer up, negotiations suddenly get taken more seriously by the opposing side, you prevent yourself from being taken advantage of, and, finally, a lawyer is probably one of the most objective people you can have on your professional team. Even if you have a good, friendly relationship with your lawyer, their job is to remove emotion from the situation. I don't care what anyone says or how controlled a leader is, when you are the big kahuna, you're always at risk of clouding a situation with your own feelings and biases because, despite the cliché that business isn't personal, it. 1,000 percent. is.

While a business isn't who you are, it was birthed from you, and every day, you're making professional decisions that have a direct effect on your future. Business becomes personal, on some level, once you have skin in the game. So you need an objective professional who will help you make the best decisions for your future. Honestly, one of my fav parts of a phone call with my lawyer, Josh, is when he's walking me through something and I'm silent for a whole five minutes. Sometimes, the pause will be so long that it might seem like the call has been dropped. But he immediately knows I don't understand what's going on and then he ultra–breaks down the legal word salad into plain old English and then we'll talk about our favorite parts of *Hamilton* that make us cry. I'm pretty sure he's not billing me for that last part, but if he was, I wouldn't complain too much. Josh has, over the years, improved my bottom line and prevented me from being screwed over. He's worth every penny. Btdubs, I'm aware that lawyers aren't cheap, so if all you can afford is one on a case-by-case basis, do it. I beg of you.

What Warren Buffett Should've Told Ya #5: You Didn't Get into This to Dracarys a Bitch

Or maybe you did. I don't know your life, but what I do know is acting a damn fool anytime anyone dares to breathe in a way you don't approve of or behaving like a dictator will create not only a high turnover rate, but an environment where your employees talk shit about you. For real, if your employees' impersonation of you is so good that Lorne Michaels is booking them a window seat in economy plus so they can join the *SNL* cast, then you done fucked up and need to reexamine your draconian behavior. But let's put a pin in a potentially bruised ego due to office trash talk because, frankly, that self-absorbed reason shouldn't be the motivation behind the way you carry yourself at work. What should motivate you is making the decision about whether you want to be a boss or a leader and figuring out how best to execute that.

What I've observed from me and my friends' experiences is that the typical boss stops at making demands, caring only about the bottom line, and treating people as though they're disposable. And I get it! Ruling with an iron fist and intimidation can get the desired results. Just look at dictatorships, politicians, and Jamaican hair braiders. If avoiding being cussed out is the overarching goal, of course employees are going to toe the line, but, frankly, that sounds miserable for everyone involved. I mean, it's demoralizing to be on the receiving end of vitriol, and to be the one doling out that awful wrath does nothing but mess up your skin. Seriously, being a tyrant will have you going from Dorian Gray to Steve Bannon in a New York minute. #ShallowButTrue. But leaders, especially the successful ones (note: Success is not limited to amassing wealth; I'm talking interpersonal skills, encouraging their employees to exceed their potential, etc.), are a different breed. Leaders are inspiring, make their employees feel like they're in the fight with them, and show they care about more than the bottom line, all of which can cause their employees to exude the most coveted yet illusive quality: loyalty. I mean, who is loyal to a boss? No one? Maybe a few, but truthfully, those few are loyal to what the boss *represents* and *provides*: money, power, and access.

Some people have been in jobs where someone has tried to poach them yet the person declines the offer. Basically, money is nice, but just like you can't buy love, you can't buy long-term dedication from your employees unless you give them other reasons to stay. Those reasons include but aren't limited to being mentally present, prioritizing work-life balance, providing opportunities to be promoted from within, equipping employees with sufficient onboarding and training, giving them the freedom to be creative in ways that aren't directly related to their positions but can lead to innovation down the line, and, lastly, ensuring that management and leadership are not a dumpster fire. That's right. Terrible managers and leaders are surefire ways to make employees leave.

In fact, Steve Miranda, the managing director of the Center for Advanced Human Resource Studies at the Cornell University ILR School,[6] concluded that about 80 PERCENT of turnover is because the environment created for the employee is so bad that Al Gore is like, "One sec. Let me get my Samsung so I can film this and release it as the sequel to *An Inconvenient Truth*." Get it? Cuz the orig *Inconveen Troof*—that was ignorant—was about global warming and how we're ruining the environment? Guys? Guys? ANYWAY! The point is don't be a nightmare and perhaps you'll earn the devotion that every single leader craves. After all, as Simon Sinek, bestselling author of *Start with Why* and *Leaders Eat Last*, so aptly stated on Twitter, "A boss has a title, a leader has the people." Trust me, you want the people.

What Warren Buffett Should've Told Ya #6: Ooooh, Child, Surround Yourself with People Who Will Keep It Real

This is pretty self-explanatory. Not every idea you're going to come up with is going to be that next great idea that will elevate your company. In fact, some of your ideas will be shit. Straight-up clangers that make contact with every square inch

---

6. That . . . is a mouthful. Go 'head, Steve, keep giving the world that *Game of Thrones* "say my whole damn name and house" energy. We will bow down, boo.

of the toilet bowl on their way down the drain. And you need to have cultivated an environment and hired the person (or people) who knows that doing their job includes letting *you* know when you're taking things down the wrong path. Obviously, this should be done with tact. No one's asking for *Real Housewives of New York City*'s Bethenny Frankel energy where you're going to be roasted for jokes. But you do need to have someone who can interrogate your thoughts and opinions because they have a different perspective than yours, which is probably part of the reason you hired them in the first place. Does your employee pointing out how a potential decision of yours could be disastrous feel great in the moment? Of course not. You might get defensive or be embarrassed when presented with evidence that what you want to do is actually *not* in the best interest of your company, but get over it. Take a beat to process and understand that what your employee is doing is solely to help you. It's because they care. It's because they want themselves, you, and the business to thrive.

Now, yes-people, on the other hand? Sure, they'll stick with you when the going is great and make you feel good with empty praise because everyone loves being around a winner. However, when you're about to #StruggleBus it for a while, as all businesses are wont to do, these suck-ups are nowhere to be found. They're either gone and on to their next meal ticket or standing silently when speaking up could turn things around. Now, it's up to you as to who you want in the trenches with you, but for me, I'd gladly take someone who's bold enough to tell me what I don't want to hear if that information is in the best interest of my business, over a heaux paying me lip service and guiding me toward disaster because all they care about are the checks clearing (aka getting paid) and that they feel like they're my "favorite."

What Warren Buffett Should've Told Ya #7: Ask for Feedback

It's not enough to have your employees' input on the direction of the company; they also need to have input on *you*. Oh, you thought you were only going to *give* and never *receive* feedback? Like you were just gonna hand out your Amazon.com customer reviews on what your employees need to tweak and improve and you were going to get nothing in return because . . . what? You're infallible? Ya ain't Black Jesus, walking on water or turning water into wine. At best, you're turning water into Crystal Light, which no one asked for, so yeah, there are areas that *you* need to improve on. That's why you better learn how to take critiques that, by the way, aren't even going to be that harsh because your employees are nervous to say the wrong thing that, at best, will cause you to treat them negatively or, at worst, get them fired. Trust me, it's way more difficult for them to give you feedback than for you to receive it. Still, it's tough to hear constructive criticism.

In the beginning, every time my employees gave me criticism, I wanted to vomit. My skin got hot. My mind raced as I felt like I was the worst boss and that my employees had already uploaded their résumés to Monster.com because they were ready to leave. But that was my own shit. That was me being emotion-minded and not understanding that feelings aren't facts. Can you tell I go to therapy? Anyway. With time, my adverse reaction to hearing how my not-so-great tendencies affect those around me has lessened as I've learned to accept this truth: Not all feedback is negative or ill-intentioned. Now, if you've employed some messy folks who have ulterior motives and are whispering in your ear to manipulate you, then at least you found out you've been carrying a Iago on your payroll, but that's not what's happening in most cases. Your employees, when given the opportunity, want to help you get to the next level because it means they're going with ya. That's why I tend to end most meetings with, "Is there anything that I can do that will make your job easier?"

This phrasing is intentional. I want them to be as effective as they can be, and that can only happen if *I'm* operating in a manner that doesn't intentionally or unintentionally get in their way. So if they can suggest changes and tweaks on how you could make their lives easier, which in turn will help your business reach its ultimate potential, you'd be a fool not to hear them out. And before you know it, you'll be taking it on the chin like Muhammad Ali.

What Warren Buffett Should've Told Ya #8: Stay On or Under Budget

Y'all, as much as I wanna claim that the math don't be mathin', it turns out the math indeed do be mathin'! I say this because as a Libra, I have expensive tastes. But also, maybe it's just how I was raised. I'll give you an example. I talked to my dad recently and he said, apropos of nothing, "The only mustard Trey [that's my three-year-old nephew] wants to eat now is Grey Poupon." Uh-huh . . . right.

"Dad, pray tell, how did he end up explicitly requesting Grey Poupon?"

"Well," Phil began, "I gave it to him to see if he would like it. Just wanted to expose him to different kinds of foods and condiments."

WUT?! Usually, when you want to expose toddlers to different kinds of foods and condies, it's pineapples or bite-sized pieces of cooked chicken or mashed avocado on toast, not bougie-ass condiments! Give him French's yellow mustard, which is $1.79 at Target. We don't need to waste fancy mustard on garbage toddler taste buds. I love my nephew, but he still smiles after licking the living room floor. His palate is not elevated, but now he wants the finest things in life because my dad is out here doing the most, which was a common and sweet occurrence for my brother and me growing up. After all, I've been eating Grey Poupon since I was a kid as well because my parents instilled in us that enjoying nice things (even if they are minor like Grey P) is not just for rich people.

So thanks to Ma and Pa Robinson, my astrological sign, and experiencing a snippet of what the world has to offer, I am now a bougie bitch.

Meaning I start each day with a Pressed Juicery green juice, *Architectural Digest* was the design bible I referenced when coming up with ideas for how I wanted my office to look, and I have a monthly subscription for goop Balls in the Air multivitamins that are for "people who function at an intense pace." Yep, I eye-roll at this, too, but also, I double down on my bloop aka Black goop ways. And while my bougie tastes led me to living beyond my means (along with student loans, of course), which kept me in financial trouble for the entirety of my twenties and early thirties, I'm now older and wiser. Still, I was tempted when I was launching my production company.

My last corporate job had unlimited snacks and breakfast items, a FreshDirect vending machine, endless office supplies, state-of-the-art printers, and more. The head honcho would throw pricey holiday parties. The temperature in the building was always perfect. There were cozy lounge spaces where people could chat when they got sick of sitting at their cubicles. A wellness room for when we needed to take a nap or use a breast pump, or simply have some peace and quiet. I could go on and on, but you get the gist. My last office job was an enjoyable place to work, so enjoyable that it was easy to believe this was the standard. To assume that a fully stocked array of cereal brands to go along with any and every kind of milk was not only normal, but the bare minimum. More than those unrealistic expectations, I convinced myself that all these bonuses were signs of what a "real" office does, what a "real" boss provides, and that if I'm ever in charge, this is what I must do or my employees will stage a mutiny. Cut to opening the Tiny Reparations office, where it was my turn to foot the bill.

I was like, "Hol' up, hol' up, hol' up. What we charging on my business Amex?" Like, yes, I do, too, prefer almond milk in my bowl of Cheerios, so I don't have bubble guts during an eleven A.M. meeting, but also? This ain't Meals on motherfucking Wheels. These are grown-ass twenty- and thirtysomething adults. I don't need to provide them with EIGHT different cereals and myriad milk options. They can purchase that mess with the salary I pay them. And I didn't stop there. You better believe on CB2's drop-down menu, I clicked "Sort by Price: Low to High" when I was searching for decorative items for the office. And I walked around asking my employees, "Do all these lights need to be on?" Lol. Okay, I didn't go that far. However, what did happen was that all the things I thought were must-haves quickly fell under the category of "fringe benefits." It was in my best interest financially to be frugal and decide what were, by no means, requirements, but would add to the work environment; what were the things that were nice and we could, hopefully, implement down the line; and, ultimately, what was an absolute waste of money. Because, as we all know, ♪ It's a whole new world ♪ when you're the one footing the bill.

By the way, this isn't about being cheap. It's about being realistic. That company I worked for had five-hundred-plus employees, East Coast and West Coast offices, and had been around for over twenty years. Tiny Reparations was just getting off the ground, hadn't started making money yet, and had only four people, including myself, working there. Splurging on perks when we didn't have revenue coming in would set us up for failure. This meant my "bad and bougie" tastes got downgraded to "reasonable and paid in full at the end of the billing cycle." Has a nice ring to it, don't it? I wish I could say I got this reality check all on my own. I didn't. Mai looks over all the expenses with a fine-tooth comb as though she's performing an audit. If there's a pricey item I like, she'll present me with the Wayfair option because blowing money on a bunch of cute shit from Restoration Hardware so the office can look fly for the 'gram is irresponsible and *not* what a boss does.

But it's more than just office space. You need to have an emergency fund to tide you over during your low-grossing periods and must be able to afford your overhead, of which a big chunk will be employee salaries. I've already covered the importance of having a lawyer, but your other must-have will most likely be an assistant because, trust me, you're not as efficient as you think you are. Unsure about the right time to hire an assistant? When feeling like pulling an Usher in an R&B music video aka being so emo that you start dancing in the rain, not caring if your jeans are soggy, becomes a regular occurrence, ya need some help. And the only way you can afford this help is if you're living within your means not only personally, but also professionally.

So remember, the numbers don't lie, be clear about what is a need vs. a want, and understand that your profits increasing isn't a license to ball out of control, but to build your future and maintain your financial independence. However, if you do want to splurge on Grey Poupon for the office (and also your life!), go for it. That mustard is good as hell.

What Warren Buffett Should've Told Ya #9: Understand What You're Not Good At / What You Don't Like Doing and Have Other People Do That Shit

Orgasms are great, but have you ever tried paying someone to do things you don't wanna do and gained hours of your life back? I don't know about y'all but, to me, delegating feels like a rebirth. Like I just hatched from the egg that Lady Gaga stepped out of during her performance of "Born This Way" at the 2011 Grammys. My face has the collagen bounce of a pre-pubescent Korean gymnast. My energy is that of an early-aughts college student hopped up on Four Loko the night before their senior thesis is due. There's nothing more coun-terproductive than bringing an "I ain't really trying to fuck with this right now" vibe to tasks I loathe (expense reports, scheduling meetings across various time zones) or that aren't my strong suit (super schmooze-y calls because I hate kissing butt to get what I want), because I'll make careless mistakes, take twice as long to get things done because I'm dragging my feet, or my negative energy will be a buzzkill for everyone around me. Believe me: Once you get to a place where you *don't* have to do everything yourself, you shouldn't, and instead, you should trust others to help take care of the smaller details so you can focus on the big picture, which is you being as successful as you've always dreamed. And to have free time making curated U2 playlists for your friends even though they didn't ask for them. Just me?

What Warren Buffett Should've Told Ya #10: Your Employees Don't Have to Like All Your Decisions, but They Gotta Respect Them

When I was a kid, I desperately wanted L.A. Gear sneakers. I don't know why, but I had my heart set on owning a pair of shoes with soles that lit up like a Times Square billboard every time I took a step. So I asked my parents and they politely said, "Hell no," and told me my Keds Champion[7] leather shoes would suffice. True, but I was ten! I didn't want sensible-ass sneakers! I wanted something that looked dope and oozed suburban wealth. None of that fazed my parents and they held steadfast that their money would be better spent on food, mortgage, and other practical bills. Sure, I was annoyed for maybe a week or two, tops, but I didn't act a fool. I simply got over my disappointment, put on those Keds, and played with my classmates. And if my parents weren't wholly confident in shooting me down (they probably were since they're not label people, so, if anything, L.A. Gear's popularity only made them more inclined

---

7. Bitch, Champion where? Y'all, do a quick Googs of "Keds Champion leather sneaker," look at that shoe, and tell me what championship that shoe represents? Keds is messy as hell to name this shoe that when it should be called "participation ribbon for doing the bare minimum of showing the fuck up."

to decline what I was asking for), they didn't show it because they knew that buying me whatever I wanted whenever I wanted it could turn me into a shallow person.

This is what you have to understand when you're the boss: You're going to call some shots or do things your employees won't like. They have to get over it, and you have to get over the fact that you're going to disappoint some people, because guess what? Sometimes, what's in the best interest of your business will be at odds with what your employees want, and that's okay.

Your company cannot be run by committee, so you've got to make the executive decisions. And if you want to (and more often than not, I think you should) explain your reasoning behind the choices you make so your staff understands your thought process, gets a sense of when you're open to taking risks and when you're not, and can have a better grasp on how they can come up with ideas that align with your vision, do it. Still, there'll be times when you'll want to go a different way. Your employees have two options: They can lick their wounds and get on board with Keds, or be rude, dismissive, and demand L.A. Gear, which you can address in hopes of finding a solution, or agree to part ways if they're incapable of respecting your authority. Either way, what matters most is you set the tone and they follow it. Basically, you're Kirk Franklin, they're the choir, and y'all about to perform the fuck out of "Melodies from Heaven." Good luck!

What Warren Buffett Should've Told Ya #11: This Could've Been an Email

Working from home can be lonesome. So sometimes folks are jonesing for human connection via Zoom. I empathize with all that. Still . . . I. Do. Not. Need. To. See. Your. Face. You do not need to see mine. We don't need to *Hollywood Squares* this situation when a short and simple email would have sufficed. Is an email a little impersonal sometimes? Sure. But also, isn't writing each other how couples survived the Civil War? Like, didn't soldiers send letters home to their wives and that was enough for the wives to get through the loneliness and another week of making the same tired corn bread? If letter writing could keep a marriage alive during the entirety of the Civil War, then I'm sure my working relationship with Heather can thrive via the emails I send her while taking a dump. If this stance paints me as antisocial, then so be it. I just believe that working from home during a global pandemic is taxing enough—after all, we're expected to maintain the same level of productivity we had pre-Covid—so having to carry on as though we're not experiencing collective trauma, all the while putting on our professional bests or code-switching for the Zoom cameras is . . . well, frankly, none of us are getting paid enough to do that.

But worse than the people who want to use Zoom as the default means of communication are the tricks, who, at the last minute, decide a scheduled conference call should now be a VIDEOCONFERENCE CALL. Wait a damn minute. Why are people calling audibles last minute as if we aren't all dressed like it's day two of our periods? Even if you can't have a period or never had a period, you're dressing like your uterine lining has just finished a ropes course aka you look a fucking mess. The audacity, to assume folks have washed their faces that day. Taken a shower. Brushed their teeth. Put on an outfit. I ain't wasting my cute clothes just so I can sit at my makeshift desk (aka the dining table) and work. This is an athleisure and sweatpants household until further notice. So stop it with the Zoom surprise meetings. You can't do that to people, especially Black women like me. Because now I'm pulling a muscle diving for a wig so I can put it on my head before I click "Join with video" and have to spend the rest of the day IcyHot'ing my back. So, in the future, when you want to set a Zoom, ask yourself, *Could this be an email?* And if the answer is "yes," then bitch, clickety-clack, click-click on your keyboard like a Delta Airlines employee trying to rebook you on a flight and keep it moving.

Well, I hope this provided some guidance on how you can operate your own business. I know there's a lot to figure out, and it will always be a lot because there is always more to learn, tweak, experience. The magic is not in doing it how Warren Buffett or Shonda Rhimes or I have done, but in customizing the rules to fit your wants and needs.

Some leaders have zero interest in conquering the world; they just want to monetize a passion or skill set and make a nice living and be a part of their small business community.

Others have grand designs on changing the industry they're in or leaving a mark on history or pushing the conversation forward. Whatever the case may be, just do your work and create a legacy you'll be proud of, and if grit, determination, creativity, and the occasional fantasy about destroying your life in spectacular fashion are what's needed to get the job done, you're my kind of CEO. Let's chat.

But not on Zoom, please. If I get a Zoom invite from you, I will definitely fake my own kidnapping.

#Quaranbae

I'm not saying you should shit yourself in front of your significant other (IS THIS THE MOMENT WHERE I RUIN
ANY CHANCE OF BEING AN OPRAH BOOK CLUB SELEC-
TION? I. FUCKING. THINK. SO.), but I believe that unless you
do mortifying things, accidentally or not, that make your partner pull a Walter White and get a burner phone so they can
create a Raya dating profile to search for fresh peen or vajeen,
then, frankly, you aren't in a relationship. Y'all are just com-
rades who are sexin' and passing time like prisoners in Litch-
field hoping to get released early on good behavior. But a
relationship? That, my friends, is, among other things, a com-
pilation of inside jokes and annoyances, romantic moments
and unforeseen problems, and, most important, the sobering
reality that no one else in the world would put up with your
specific brand of nonsense quite the way your partner does.

This is especially true for soul mates. British Baekoff's mine,
and not because he said I was his a few years ago while

nursing me back to health from a nasty flu as we watched *Hidden Figures*. He's the One for many reasons. Nobody makes me laugh, nurtures and challenges me, loves and likes me in spite of my flaws, believes in me completely, and makes me feel secure and at ease the way he does. And I'm not talking "a tank top and well-worn sweatpants on a lazy Saturday afternoon" type of comfortable. I mean a comfort so freeing that my breathing calms and my heart beats at a steady rhythm that stays right in the pocket like a thumping bass line in a funk song. With him, I'm at my safest. With him, I'm at home. Matter of fact, he is home. And you know what I do when I'm at home? I shit. Regular old deuces as well as those close calls where I give my toilet seat a thumbs-up and go [insert Denzel Washington laugh], "My man!" The point is the second I'm with Bae, all my body's defenses power down, which results in the occasional burp or fart, followed by an "Oops, babe!" or "Sorry, boo!" However, three months into the 'tine aka quarantine, my body had betrayed me in front of Baekoff like never before, and that haunts me to this day. Like, I'll be going about my business and my brain will troll me by queuing up this memory, which stops me in my tracks. Then I stare off into a random corner of the room I'm in like I'm Angelica Schuyler in *Hamilton* and start singing "Satisfied":

I remember that night, I just might (Rewind)

I just might have definitely, accidentally sharted in front of my boyfriend, who was shocked and also had a look of *Oh, this is what Maya Angelou meant when she wrote, "When someone shows you who they are, believe them the first time"* on his face. But c'mon. He had to have seen this coming, right? I had become lax in the whole "not passing gas in front of each other" department and coped with living through a pandemic by eating food in weird combinations (e.g., an amuse-bouche of dessert, then dinner, which was followed by more dessert). It was only a matter of time before my stomach went *no más.*

This is probably why my boyfriend stifled a laugh and asked, "Did you just shit yourself?" This. Messy. Ass. Heaux. He knew damn well I did, but wanted me to admit it, so that "Remember that time when you shit yourself in front of me?" could be the "That's what she said" of our relationship. Well, my parents didn't raise me to go out like that. So, with my heart full of pride, I clinched my butt cheeks and said with the utmost casualness, "W-what? Oh! Nah, I mean, I get why you'd think that because my butthole emitted a deep, Johnny Cash baritone sound; however, let me assure you, good sir, that was merely a stage-one fart with a touch of bass because of the seaweed in this store-bought pho I just ate."

I quickly waddled to the bathroom to poop out the pho and two giant slices of three-layer red velvet Betty Crocker cake I had eaten and took a shame shower. Obvs, we didn't have sex that night. He and I straight-up 11'ed, aka each of us lay down on our respective sides of the bed, watching nineties sitcom reruns on Hulu as he periodically chuckled, not at the TV but at what had gone down in the living room mere hours ago. So how did we get here? I'm glad you asked. Welcome to my town hall, take a seat, and I'll explain the journey to how my booty-hole doubled as a 16 Handles fro-yo shop for a night.

Unlike some people—no judgment—my boyfriend and I were early adopters of quarantining. Although, if I knew then what I know now, my last outing in the Before Times (aka pre-coronavirus) might've been different or, at the very least, I might have pressed my luck and not stayed indoors until mid-March. Ah, coulda, woulda, shoulda.

Anyway, I remember the transition of me walking past piles of garbage bags while pretending that kind of moment is what JAY-Z and Alicia Keys were talking about in "Empire State of Mind" to keeping my Black ass at home because people can barely be bothered to be sanitary before the threat of an impending pandemic.[1]

So, there I was with a couple of girlfriends, wrapping up

---

1. One time, I went to use a public restroom with this woman I knew somewhat well. I washed my hands; she did not and, instead, walked her trifling behind to the door and reached for the handle. I swallowed the small bit of vomit that materialized in my mouth at this unsanitary display and asked her if she forgot to wash her hands. Lol, I know that no one forgets to wash their hands but I was trying to give her an out that she clearly didn't take because she hit me with this cavalier response: "Oh, I only peed, so no need. Now, if I went number two, then, of course, I'd wash my hands." She proceeded to walk out of the bathroom with the carefree vibes of women in emergency contraception commercials who can enjoy lemon poppy-seed muffins because they know they are childfree. Meanwhile, I stood frozen, replaying in my mind what she said "Only peed, so no need?!?!" Bitch, wut?! Don't Dr. Seuss this! The average toilet paper has the thickness of a dissolvable Listerine Cool Mint breath strip, yet she's acting like her pee-pee droplets would not penetrate the toilet paper and make contact with her fingertips as she wiped her vajeen? Jesus, take the wheel and my motherfuckin' memory of all the times I touched something this heifer had. Point is, humans have been up to speed on how unhygienic it is to urinate and not wash their hands, yet they do it anyway, but I'm supposed to have faith that as soon as the Covid-19 threat was real, the world was gonna be nothing but a bunch of Howie Mandels, just sleeping in a vat of Purell hand sanitizer and washing their hands anytime they weren't clean? Uh-huh . . . sure . . .

February aka Black History Month by going to see Céline Dion perform at the Barclays Center. IS THIS SOMETHING MALCOLM X WOULD HAVE DONE DURING BHM? Of course not, but also? Dion's "All By Myself" and her cover of "River Deep, Mountain High" are certifiable bops. I believe that if he had heard them, he would have put a pin in talking about Plymouth Rock landing on us in order to sway along, cup of white wine in hand, as she belts out notes. Cut to the end of the first week of March.

I canceled all my stand-up shows, told my employees that we'd work from home, bought three cases of canned tomatoes (Bae was convinced we were going to make and eat home-made chili exclusively) and decided that I wasn't going to leave my apartment or see anyone I knew unless it was an absolute emergency.

Despite my fear of the 'rona, as evidenced by my boyfriend and me being early adopters of quarantine—we started on March 6, 2020—we believed it would be only a temporary inconvenience. But as the days went on, the death toll increased, and the place I've called home for over half my life, New York City, became a coronavirus hot zone, I was no longer distracted by the hilarity of the now-disgraced Governor of New York Andrew Cuomo's no-nonsense daily press conferences and I quickly sobered up to reality. Bae and I were going to quarantine in an apartment, possibly for months, with no end date in sight. Just the two of us. No change of locaysh. Just inside. With recycled air. No trees.

With that realization I was sad, although I couldn't even name a brand of New York trees. Are trees called "brands"?

"Strains"? "Makes and models"? Kidding! I'm not that dumb. But for real, I knew nothing about trees except to say "tree" like Jodie Foster in *Nell* when I see one—#DeepCutReference— yet I instantly mourned the end of ignoring trees on my way home from Target after capitalizing on a two-for-six-dollars face scrub deal. Of course, that's a trivial thing to miss, but I believe that when soul-shaking, life-changing, world-breaking things like a global pandemic happen, your brain turns to anything that can help you self-soothe. For some, that might've been making a box cake and eating half of it in one sitting. For others, maybe it was buying three twelve-pack rolls of toilet paper. By the way, who were all these overly confident people who knew their shit schedule for the next six weeks? Y'all, I had a fruit salad and a fifteen-ounce green juice today and I'm still tossing up a prayer to the Virgin Mary that I'll drop my first deuce before the sun sets. But that's the point, isn't it? No one knew what their life was going to be, so they acted out. Ate their emotions. Hoarded instead of shared. Fixated on the nonexistent, e.g., my "relationship" with trees.

Because I didn't care about the trees. Wait, I did. I mean, I do. Like, I believe climate change is real. Viva planet Earth or whatever. But what I'm getting at is that I mainly cared about what those trees represented: my old life. Not being able to interact with those trees, no matter how superficial that inter- action may have been, was symbolic of everything I was leav- ing behind in order to shelter in place. No more strolling across the Brooklyn Bridge, reading a good book on my com- mute to work, or going to my favorite bodega and complain- ing about the price of Dr. Bronner's soap that the shop owner and I know I'm going to buy anyway. It was the end of sitting on rooftops with friends and eating sloppy breakfast burritos, flying home to Cleveland for a summer visit with my parents, or dancing my heart out with twenty thousand others at a concert. And work? Ha! In many ways, my work routine imploded. I wasn't going to spend thirty weekends on the road like I did in 2019. Traveling internationally for stand-up as well as for pleasure was instantly a thing of the past. So were my day trips to the West Coast for quick-paying gigs. Simply put, having my lifestyle upended because of the lockdown was unsettling. It was also scary, but for a different reason.

Like I wrote in the introduction of this book, pre-quar-quar, my boyfriend and I had never been together for more than two weeks at a time. And even when we were in the same place, he was working remotely / catching up on sleep and I was continuing to overstuff my schedule. Whether we liked it or not (oh, who are we kidding? We are tried-and-true workaholics, so we liked it), we were always, in some way, distracted. Our minds occasionally wandered during conversations. I stayed up until four A.M. writing while he was in bed and asleep by midnight. Being a tour manager for a rock band meant that he was never not on call. Not even when he was home on his time off. In short, there was always something stealing our attention. But quarantine would change that. Work was going to slow down. There weren't going to be outside activities to break up the monotony of coupledom. It was just going to be me and Baekoff. All the time.

Now, I'm not trying to sound ungrateful, because I know the alternative—quarantining solo—is rife with its own set of challenges, including boredom, isolation-induced dark thoughts, not having anyone to share newfound financial burdens due to unemployment or being furloughed with, and the absence of human contact. Touch deprivation became a topic of national discussion and legitimate concern during Covid-19 because of social distancing. And as time went on, some were starting to feel its effects. In Megan McCluskey's article "The Coronavirus Outbreak Keeps Humans from Touching. Here's Why That's So Stressful" on Time.com, she investigated this new normal and referenced a 2014 study conducted by psychologist Sheldon Cohen and other researchers at Carnegie Mellon University. The study concluded that hugging as a form of touch improves the immune system. McCluskey writes:

> The researchers had 404 healthy adults fill out questionnaires and respond to telephone interviews to assess their perceived daily social support and frequency of interpersonal conflicts and receiving hugs, for 14 consecutive evenings. Then, the researchers intentionally exposed each participant to the cold virus. Broadly speaking, the participants who had reported having more social support were less likely to get sick—and those who got more hugs were far more likely to report feeling socially supported.

A stronger immune system is not the only benefit of touch. McCluskey continues: "According to Dacher Keltner, a professor of psychology at the University of California, Berkeley . . . 'Touch is the fundamental language of connection. . . . A lot of the ways in which we connect and trust and collaborate are founded in touch.'" Think about it. That form of communication is everywhere we look. Whether it's parents skin-to-skin bonding with newborns, friends high-fiving, or a playful squeeze between romantic partners, touch plays a key factor in not only human interaction, but in helping us maintain our sanity. So, if I had to choose between quarantining solo or with my soul mate? I'm choosing "soul mate" every time. And because of that fact, some single folk assume that my boyfriend and I quarantining together was nothing but a bed of roses.

Throughout the quar, single friends (without roommates) would say things such as "Being inside 24/7 stinks, but at least you have each other!" and "I wish I had someone I could talk to anytime I wanted," and "You two used to travel constantly for work, so it must be nice to make up for lost time," and the classic "Don't get knocked up from all the sex you're having, lolz, lolz, lolz!" Lemme tell you something: Most couples weren't having as much sex as everyone thinks. Seriously, some of my single friends thought #QuaranbaeLife was just FuckFest2020 with the Red Hot Chili Peppers headlining and Flea slapping the bass for eighty hours straight. That wasn't happening. Why?

Relationships, romantic or platonic, aren't designed for the people in them to be around each other constantly. Not even for those couples we consider #Goals. I bet there were moments during the quarantine where my Forever First Lady Michelle Obama said to Barack, "Bruh, if you don't go put on some stonewashed dad jeans and play hoops in the backyard for two hours so I can have some peace and quiet," you're fooling yourself! Trust me when I write that no one is ever turned on by being around the person they love all the damn time.

You know why affairs are so hot and sex-filled? Because the people involved don't see each other all day, every day! Do you think on *Scandal*, Olivia Pope and President Fitz would have been banging in the Oval Office if the previous night Fitz overheard her in the bathroom trying to time her poop plops to the sound effects from an episode of *Star Trek: Picard* that he was watching? No! Do you think Romeo and Juliet would've been so into each other if their families weren't haters and hadn't kept them apart? Hell, no; they were fourteen, and Juliet would've dumped Romeo because she was sick of Mercutio's non-funny behind hanging around. You know why Diane Lane's character in *Unfaithful* smashed the first dude (a French guy named Paul) who helped her after she tripped and fell in the street while running errands one afternoon? It's because her husband, played by Richard Gere, was walking around the house every day, rocking the same waffle-knit sweater and not appreciating the *Barefoot Contessa* meals Diane was making for dinner. Meanwhile, Frenchie was all *oui oui* and *ooh là là* fromage'ing Diane Lane outta her Maidenform undies once a week. What I'm getting at is this: Space and absence are the foundations of sexcapades, not deep familiarity and seeing people at their most raggedy for months on end. So thanks to Covid-19, Baekoff and I were constantly invading each other's space because how couldn't we, given the circumstances?

And if I'm being honest, not invading each other's space was an issue in our small two-bedroom apartment pre-Covid, too. To give you perspective, walking the length of Oprah's estate takes, I imagine, probably the entire running time of *The Departed*. Our place? Literally a handful of opening notes from the Rolling Stones' "Gimme Shelter" that plays at the beginning of *The Departed*, which isn't bad when you're free to come and go, because that's the point of living in New York City.

Now this isn't some theory I made up, such as "because of Phoebe Waller-Bridge's astronomical success in Hollywood, when I finally make it, I'm only going to be known as 'Black Phoebe.'" The truth is people *do* move to NYC for the adventure. And that adventure typically exists outside the home. So when people say they live "in the city," that's because the city is where life happens—the transportation, the parties, the workplace, the gym, the theater, the bars, the museums, the parks, the backstreet shortcuts that get you where you want to go faster, the brunches, etc.—so home becomes just a place to shower, snack, smash, sleep, repeat. This explains why when I bought this apartment, we didn't mind how small it was because our personal and professional lives kept us away from home.

Cut to the 2020 quarantine. He was in the living room, editing an episode of my *Black Frasier* advice podcast while freeballing it in a Bed Bath & Beyond robe; meanwhile, I was writing this book in my "office" aka the kitchen table next to the couch he was sitting on while rocking a pus-filled acne patch on my face. Despite our unkempt appearances, we felt like a power couple and were happy to be our most comfortable selves around each other. Those were the good days. The not-so-good ones? Well, we were riddled with cabin fever and felt as though we'd never have privacy again. So, in short, quarantining in an apartment only heightened our emotions as well as amplified the ups and downs of sharing a life with another person.

For instance, reading. Escaping into a book keeps me sane. Since sound travels throughout the apartment, I wore headphones to drown out noise. So sometimes, when Bae tried to get my attention to ask if, for the seventeenth day in a row, I wanted some jank Barilla pasta in Prego sauce, I took an AirPod out of my ear like I was on the A train and a gaggle of youths just entered my car hollering about "Showtime" and started freestyle dancing to Chance the Rapper's "All Night." I. Was. Pissed. Like, duh, Bae! What else we gon eat?! Quit playin' like we got options. Plus, we both knew that query was just an excuse to chat for the next twenty minutes. Just be like that John Mayer song and "Say what you need to say."

Speaking of the kitchen, Bae never found a cabinet door he didn't want to leave open. Even if he went to get a granola bar and an apple, when he left the kitchen, all the cabinets were open as if he was trying to create an *American Ninja Warrior* obstacle course out of eco-friendly wood and chrome handles. I told some of my male friends about this and the consensus was "Of course you never close the cabinet doors because you gotta be ready for anything." I relayed this to Baekoff and he cosigned it with a "You never know what could go down." Huh? What do we have to be "ready" for? What is going to "go down"?! Our neighborhood was and continues to be boring AF. Our building was and continues to be quiet AF. We didn't have guests over. Every night, we chloroformed ourselves to sleep goop style aka spritzed our pillowcases with lavender because in your thirties, you don't simply just fall asleep. You've lived too long and seen too much, so you have to anesthetize yourself like some old-timey villain. Jokes aside, nothing of note happens here, much to our low-key disappointment. But even if something did, how would open cabinets help?! Like if a burglar broke in and was about to kill us, best-case scenar is British Bae going, "Oh, bollocks! This is how me life ends, innit? Jolly good that I left the cabinet doors open, which'll help shave a few seconds off the time it takes to look for a packet of chamomile tea, pop on the kettle, and have a quick cuppa before I die. Cheers, mate!"

Thankfully, no breaking and entering happened during the quar, so we never found out how Bae would've reacted. In fact, he and I were quite strict and no one was allowed at our apartment the entire time we hunkered down. This meant Baekoff and I were each other's go-to for conversation and connection. So we talked to each other. A lot. And we didn't always know how to get a break without coming off like an asshole. So you know what I did? I started meditating in the living room because I was like, "A bitch can't talk to me with my eyes closed." But you know what a bitch can do with my eyes closed? Go into the kitchen, which is mere inches from the living room, and turn on the Vitamix to make a protein shake.

When we weren't talking to each other or trying to steal a couple of private moments, we FaceTimed our parents. Of course, all the clichéd technological foibles occurred: Our parents' foreheads were the only visible image on-screen, they forgot the password to unlock the iPad and missed our calls, they could never prop up the iPad well enough, so it toppled over mid-convo, etc. Obviously, there was no middle ground when it came to the length of conversation. Either our parents would want to have a three-hour-long caucus with us about everything ranging from what went down at the supermarket to the trash Netflix movies they watched or they would go entirely MIA for days, as in the case of my mom that one time when she claimed she was unavailable to talk for an ENTIRE weekend because she had to spread mulch. LOL. Wut? Did she suddenly get forty acres and a mule overnight? Because I've been to her house *alls* my life and there ain't that much land. Spreading mulch probably took her five hours, but she hit me with an out-of-office autoreply like I was Carol in accounts payable.

Anyway! When the FaceTimes did go down, Bae and I made sure the other looked their best before these calls. Scratch that! Well, *I* held up my end of the bargain. Like when my boyfriend and I FaceTimed with my parental units, I did what they call in Hollywood "last looks," meaning I would make sure his clothes were neat and his hair and beard were on point and framed him up nicely in the camera. Y'all, I was giving him SAG-AFTRA union glam and Directors Guild of America–type professionalism on this nonunion set aka our couch. Meanwhile, Baekoff gave me no heads-up, and would FaceTime his mom at random hours of the day and just flip the camera on me when I hadn't smoothed down my edges and was sporting a Hanes Her Way T-shirt with years-old pit stains. Once the FaceTimes ended, I'd go, "Da fuq?" to which he'd respond, "It's fine. Who cares? She's seen you at your best." *Yeah* and I ain't trying to have her see me looking six degrees from a Katt Williams mug shot. Suffice it to say that Baekoff's allyship rating definitely took a hit after these trifling FaceTimes with his mom.

But guess what, boos?! As much as my boyfriend did things during the lockdown that could really burn my toast, it turned out that I, too . . . am annoying . . . to live with . . . sometimes? Most of you reading this are probably thinking, *Duh, mofo; everyone is annoying periodically*, but this was low-key startling for me. See, thanks to a healthy diet of watching nineties / early aughts sitcoms in which put-upon wives dealt with their ding-dong husbands, I assumed this quarantine was just gonna be Baekoff and I doing a deep dive on him and all the things he needed to work on and then when it came to me, I would be treated as though I just nailed a voguing competition: "Yaaaaas, bitch. Flawless. Stunt on these heauxes. Make them eat it. Legendary!" Cut to week two of the quar and my bf was starting to look like J. Jonah Jameson, the editor in chief of the *Daily Bugle*, because all my ignorance caused gray streaks on the sides of his head.

In all seriousness, despite the love of my life having the patience of a saint, there were still moments and days when he was absolutely sick of my mess. Sick. Of. It. I mean, I interrupted his video game playing with his friends overseas so he could do a quality control check on my two-strand twists. He listened to me on business calls uttering phrases such as "Let's circle back next week," "Would love some clarity," and "It's really important for our company synergy" ad nauseam. I have a twenty-dollar karaoke microphone and I walked around our home singing only the "aww baby," "ooh baby" parts of Ashanti's "Rock Wit U" because breath control I do not have. Sometimes I wore my plain-ass sleep bonnet until seven P.M., took it off, didn't style my hair, then put the bonnet back on at 9:30 P.M. because it was bedtime. I chewed and smacked my lips loudly while eating. Fear not, I wasn't born this way. Rather, because, prior to Baekoff, I lived by myself for several years, there wasn't anyone to check me with a "Hey, boo, every bite you chew sounds like the cast of *Stomp* clip-clopping around on linoleum tiles and tang-a-langin' on trash can lids. Close your mouth." Naturally, my "style" of eating worsened, and during the quarantine, British Baekoff knew that having a meal together meant subjecting his ears to a Live Nation ASMR concert he didn't ask to attend. So, yep, there's no way around it: I can be irritating. Case in point: Baekoff's not allowed to watch any TV series by himself, old or new, if there's even a hint of suggestion that I may *one day* be interested in it. Please enjoy:

Phoebe Being on Her Bullshit: A Play

Baekoff sits on the couch, enjoying his quiet British life without my loud American voice blaring in his ear as he watches TV. I see him

happy for five minutes and think to myself,
"Well, he had a good run."

Me:

You're watching the newest season of
Ozark? Interesting.

Baekoff:

Huh? Oh. Uh, yeah. The show
premiered before we started dating,
so . . . yeah, I've been
watching it.

Me:

I guess that tracks

10 DAYS LATER. Baekoff has headphones in,
watching TV. LOLOLOL. Like why is he wearing
headphones in this apartment? He trying to block
me out? I had a Ricola today because I was
bored. My vocal pipes are ready.

Me:

Babe. Babe. Babe. Babe!

He removes his headphones.

Me:

Is that the new season of *The*
Walking Dead?! There are 2.8 hot
dudes in it; why didn't you tell me
that so I could start watching the

show from the beginning[2] and catch
up before the new season started?

*Baekoff plays clip of a zombie getting shanked
in the head and I dry heave over his cup
of tea.*

*ANOTHER WEEK PASSES. We're in bed, scrolling
Netflix, trying to find something to watch.*

Baekoff:

What about *The Witcher*?

Me:

Ehh, that's just white people in wigs
doing goofy ish.

Baekoff:

That's literally what *Mrs. Doubtfire*
is and you love that movie.

FIN.

Does this play get a Tony? An Obie? No? Well, I tried. Moving on!

I'm sure there are folks reading this and thinking, *It's not*

---

2. Da hell was I talking about? I've never seen one singular frame of this show, but I was trying to convince him I was gonna watch *ten* seasons of a series I don't know much about. I mean, I know there are zombies . . . and it's set in Louisiana? Tennessee? Look, I know it's set somewhere in the South where people read strangers with the condescending phrase "Bless your heart." Is that the full title of the show? *The Walking Dead: Bless Your Heart*? That sounds fun and catty. I'd definitely watch.

that big of a deal. I pooped a little when I gave birth to our kids and my partner saw it. Nope. Does. Not. Count. Conducting the miracle of life overshadows all the ways your body may betray you during childbirth. But for me, there was no baby. No miracle. No breathy "ah-hahs" à la Maxwell in "This Woman's Work." Just a grown-ass woman standing in front of a grown-ass man, asking him to love her over the sound of her crapping herself. It was beyond embarrassing because losing control over my body like that meant I also lost control over how he saw me. Okay, fine. I wasn't exactly Miss Manners before this incident. Yet, I wanted him to see me in a certain light: as the cool, funny chick. Silly as that may be, we're all guilty of wanting our personas to remain shatterproof in our relationships at all costs. Like, some folks want to always appear unflappable in front of their partners. Others might strive to forever be the life of the party. Or the go-to problem solver. Or the compassionate shoulder to lean on. Whatever the case is and no matter how "real" people are when dating, everyone has an ego, which means a part of us is always stage-parenting ourselves to ensure we "book the gig" aka stay in the relationship for another day, week, month, year, or for eternity. And, in case anyone was curious, until me, I'm sure pooping oneself would not secure the gig with my boyfriend and would get nothing more than a "Don't call us; we'll call you."

Still, embarrassment was the least of my concerns. I was also irritated at myself because quarantine stress be damned, I was too old to be coping by eating my way straight to a number two. That's amateur hour. But mostly, I was annoyed. Why, at one of my lowest moments, did my boyfriend have pitch-perfect hearing? Do you know the number of times in our relationship when BB's eyes have glazed over while I'm talking to him and he cannot repeat back to me what I just said? Countless. But all of a sudden while he's watching an episode of *Peaky* fucking *Blinders*,[3] he has the hearing of a Labrador retriever vibing out to an instrumental track of Mariah Carey's dog whistles? Oh, hell no! So out of spite, I denied what he heard and suspected, cleaned myself up, and—oh, you know how the evening ended.

Fast-forward to three weeks later. Save for a couple of well-timed jokes from British Baekoff, Poopgate was behind us. We were too busy getting the hang of our newfound rhythm after overcoming the growing pains of coronavirus-induced, 24/7 immersion therapy aka quarantining. So at the end of a particularly good day, we chilled in bed. He scrolled his phone while I rested my head on his chest and enjoyed the rise and fall of his upper body as he breathed. It was one of those blissfully peaceful moments that I wanted to file away in my mind for later. Then I started cackling, which made Bae ask me what was so funny. Every time I tried to explain, no words got out, only more giggling.

Eventually, I managed to get out, "So you remember that night when you asked if I had shit myself?"

---

3. Honestly, the show should be retitled *Peaky Fuckin' Blinders* because every time I'd walk in on my boyfriend watching it, Cillian Murphy would be hitting someone over the head then saying, "We're the Peaky fuckin' Blinders!" And I'd be like, "In seas three you still have to announce yourself? Isn't the ONE rival gang up to speed on who would be beating their ass right now?" Even Jason Derulo stopped singing, *"Jason Derulo!"* after his second hit. We *all* get it, Cills!

I felt him put his phone down on the bed. "Yeah . . ."

"Well, you were right, but I didn't want to admit it. And I've been walking around these past three weeks dying to tell you because we tell each other everything. So, yep, I crapped my pants. There. I said it." Then I did that thing that Black people do when they are amazed by street magic: I ran away while laughing.

Baekoff gleefully yelled, "I knew it! I knew it! I knew you shit yourself!"

I came back in the bedroom and the two of us tried and failed to talk through our cackling. Hands down, this is one of my favorite memories from the Quarantimes, which is surprising for the obvious reason (deucing oneself is universally considered a lowlight) and not-so-obvious reason (owning up to said deucing brought my boyfriend and me closer). Actually, I'll take it a step further: Pandemic and devastating social and racial uprisings aside, quarantining was one of the best things that happened to our relationship.

Pre-Covid, Bae and I proclaimed that we were best friends. While I believe that we believed that, the truth is we weren't around each other enough to earn the title of "best friends." If anything, life with him mostly resembled the top six contestants' experience on an episode of *The Bachelor*. Meaning we spent minimal IRL time together due to our hectic schedules, so we'd have to meet in various cities around the world in order to see each other, like in 2017, when he surprised me by showing up in Croatia for the end of my movie shoot and then took me to London for my birthday. Uhhhh, yeah, I'm pretty sure I could be besties with anyone who took me on an international trip where we ate amazing food, went to a couple of museums so I could tell my friends that I experienced some cultch aka culture, endured my saying "Fanks" instead of "Thanks" to every sales clerk I encountered because I heard Adele say it that one time at the Grammys, and put us up in a nice hotel so that this $3.49-a-bottle Dial antibacterial soap loyalist could bone near overpriced bottles of Aēsop hand wash. I mean, if you did this for me, I'd be your best friend, your bridesmaid, would fashion you a Coachella flower crown out of the dusty-ass CB2 faux succulents from my apartment, be a character witness at your tax evasion hearing, and whatever else you need. If I'm being completely honest, the majority of my relationship with BB was about almost anything except having to deal with the day in, day out of dating someone. We weren't spending loads of quality time together, so we minded our p's and q's because we didn't see each other often. We weren't showing our worst flaws because we wanted every moment to be romantic and magical. So we were lovers. We were FaceTime partners. We were texting buddies. We were travel companions. We were girlfriend and boyfriend who missed each other more than we saw each other. We were friends. But legit best friends? Nah. Quarantine changed all that.

Voluntary confinement with a significant other comes with a choice: take on the Sisyphean task of trying to maintain appearances so a *version* of you can be loved, even if that love feels unearned, thus perpetuating the cycle of self-doubt you're so clearly stuck in, even if working to get the kind of rose-colored-glasses Hollywood kind of love you think you want is counterproductive to getting the specific, messy, nu-anced, unwavering love you actually need, and shrouding yourself in smoke and mirrors prohibits you from loving your partner completely and truthfully because you're unable to love yourself completely and truthfully. OR you tell your ego to take a back seat so you can lay yourself bare (in spite of all internal signs pointing toward self-preservation), all for the possibility of a love you've never known before.

Now, I'm not implying there is a wrong and right option here. Everyone's life and capacity to love and be loved, as well as the type of love they desire, varies and is impacted by lived experiences. However, I do believe that if you want a once-in-a-lifetime love, a love that not only withstands the worst parts of what each person brings to the partnership but can only exist if both people bring their best, truest, and sometimes hidden parts of themselves to the relationship, then ya better put it all—the good, bad, and ridiculous—on the table. And as much as I loved being the cool, funny chick he fell for when we met years ago, I knew letting go of that was the only way I could be what I am to him now: his best friend.

Now, some folks don't want to be best friends with their partner. They'd rather keep a little mystery in the relationship. Wut? You know why there are no Nancy Drew books when she's a grown-ass woman? Because *Nance is tired*. She ain't looking for clues no mo'. She's probably got a twenty-year fixed mortgage from City National Bank, acid reflux, and rogue hairs growing out the side of her titties (just me?). She's not about that solving-mysteries life. And neither am I! Life is confusing as it is; the hell you need to be piecing things together about your partner on a corkboard down in a basement? Like you on the grid, got Wi-Fi, some government employee named Darryl (and all of Russia) knows everything about you because of your sosh meeds, but you out here tryna hide from the one heaux, your bae, who will call National Grid on y'all's behalf because their meter reading led them to upcharging you seven dollars in April. News flash, the significant other who does that is your ride or die! That's why I don't understand all these couples out here waltzing around their relationship with a "you can't know xyz about me." You're a team! You think Tom Cruise woulda solved all those impossible missions if Ving Rhames left a bitch on "Read" for a solid two hours because he didn't want to seem too eager? I. Don't. Think. So. End the mystery, y'all! *Je ne sais quoi?* More like *Je ne sais* nah. Can you tell I barely tried with that one? ANYWAY! Moral of the story: You can be mysterious with anyone. That isn't special. But showing the authentic you? That's reserved for the person who's earned your trust and is interested not in the you up on that pedestal, but in the you that's down on the ground and in front of their face.

At least that's what I believe when it comes to Baekoff. Instead of prompting us to leave, showing our true selves made us double down and understand that some of our flaws could be fixed in months or a year, while others are just lifelong issues and quirks that we'll have to keep in check. It deepened our bond—a best friend bond that is unconcerned about appearances, shame, and embarrassment. In fact, all those things you wouldn't dare tell another soul are, sometimes, the only things you wanna talk about.

So often, over the weeks after #Poopgate, my boyfriend and I'd be hanging out, cooking, or sleepily asking each other about our roses and thorns of the day even though we knew the answers because we witnessed it all. And no matter how much quarantining tested us and our patience, we always returned to the fact that still, we wanted to share everything. Best friends share everything. So I fessed up and told my bestie about the time I shit myself because I knew how much it would make him laugh. I knew how much the two of us laughing until we choke is absolutely one of my favorite things in the world. I knew how much telling him was the last thing to free me from my ego of who I *thought* I wanted to and should be around British Baekoff. I knew telling him was going to allow me to fully be with him at home, in our home. He is my home.

Black Girl, Will Travel

⁓

In order for me to tell you about the time I tandem swung off a bridge in Victoria Falls in Zimbabwe, I must first tell you about the person I jumped with: Mai Huynh. Remember the episode of *White Living Single* aka *Friends* when Ross buys a new couch? Instead of having it delivered to his crib, which is nearby, he enlists the help of Rachel and Chandler to carry it up the stairs of his NYC walk-up apartment, then yells "Pivot!" with increasing urgency as Rach barely helps? Sometimes, that's what it's like to talk to my friend / director of operations of all my businesses / life coach / part-time therapist / #1 BTS fan, Mai. She'll stare blankly (At you? Through you? Past you to the immediate future where there's complete and utter quiet again? Who knows?) as you desperately grasp at anything to talk about: "You like reading books? I *love* reading books." Silence. "Eating out at restaurants is tight. Apps and then wet naps. Ya know, to wipe your hands."

I don't know about other folks, but her lack of response makes my mind go into a tailspin—*Why the fuck did you say that? Bitch, I don't know! I'm panicking here*—until I muster up the courage to break the silence. "Going on walks is . . . something? Um, there are parks. LoOKIng aT LeAVEs is nIce. hAVe you eVeR dOne tHAt?" Sure, it's funny now, but in the moment, you can feel as though you're failing the most difficult stress test known to humankind. Like, okay, NASA's Mark Kelly, you were pushed to your limits during your astronaut aptitude and physical exams, but call me after you've done a one-hour car ride to Newark airport with a petite Vietnamese-Belgian woman whose withering glances can cut through your soul like it's a preteen's earlobe at a Claire's ear-piercing station.

To be fair, Mai's not reserved because she's playing mind games; she's quiet because that's just who she is. She's like if comedian Tig Notaro and *Game of Thrones'* Jaqen H'ghar—minus the killing, of course—had a baby, which is the complete opposite of me. Yet like all seemingly mismatched buddies, our differences make our bond unique. I live to be effusive and loud and can revel in attention. As for Mai? Homegirl is always at a two, has a dry sense of humor, and is unimpressed with most things and people, including my thirsty ass. Deep down, I know Mai has a soft spot for me; but, honestly, she really only gets hyped for K-pop boy bands, snacks, and Hanson. *Hanson?* YES! That. Hanson. The white boys and their long, flowing flaxen-colored hair that you'd typically find on an Iowan cornfield thot? Yes, *that* Hanson.

The point is Mai is a chill person who can thrive in solitude, so naturally, she got through quarantine with relative ease and was rewarded greatly by the Universe for her resolve. Her skin became so radiant that the moon has written her name down in its burn book. Her spirit was renewed like the Tidal free-trial subscription I forgot to cancel. Her chesticles said, "Gravity, I rebuke thee," and lifted five inches. #SorryIsaacNewtNewt. I mean, she was legit in her studio apartment, working hard, wearing cozy PJs, and eating in peace without my nosy ass hovering over her shoulder and asking, "Ooh, what are you eating? Yeah? That sounds good. What's in it? How do you make that?" and her having to fight every urge to respond with: "BITCH, DO YOU SHOP FOR INGREDIENTS IN KOREATOWN? DO YOU OWN A SPATULA? HAVE YOU EVER READ A RECIPE IN ITS ENTIRETY? THEN STOP ASKING ME ABOUT SHIT YOU WILL NEVER INCORPORATE INTO YOUR LIFE!" Clearly, she has the patience of a saint, which I'm so grateful for.

However—and this is a big, juicy, oversized "however"—on that fateful day in March 2019 when Mai and I, with one arm around each other, stood on the edge of the bridge and stared down at a 230-foot drop over a gorge, I would have liked her to be less "Om" and more "I don't want to die either!" Turns out, as I learned later, part of the reason she was so unbothered is because without glasses on, her vision is, as the average optometrist would conclude, "mostly trash"; therefore, me, the bridge, the sky, the gorge, and the river were an amalgamation of shapes and colors. So while I was thinking about every single bone in my body breaking, she was experiencing the Disney+ version of tripping balls: none of the hallucinations, but all of the color palette that Bob Ross used to paint sunsets. Great.

Anyway, there we stood, displaying two ends of the emotional spectrum before attempting a death-defying stunt. The two men in charge of this activity gently kept their hands on our backs because surely they'd been down the familiar road of people chickening out at the very last second. I imagine folks who do that tend to fall into one of two camps: relief that they didn't follow through on doing something so risky OR regret that they didn't push past their fear for a once-in-a-lifetime experience. To me, it seemed these guys believed I would end up in the latter camp if I didn't do this, *plus* I kept delaying the proceedings with cries of "Waitwaitwait! I just need one more second." Realizing a steady hand wasn't working, they switched to tough love by reminding me that I was making this situation more difficult than necessary when all I had to do was look not down but straight ahead, then count to three so Mai and I could walk forward off the bridge and enjoy the fall.

Oh, really? That's *all* I have to do? Walk off a damn bridge with some ropes tied to me and hope I will survive? This is why white people get eaten by lions or end up on the side of a mountain looking like Jack Nicholson at the end of *The Shining* aka frozen to death because some fool boiled down the dangerous to a simplistic and casual "All you have to do is . . ." and the white people are like, "Great! Let's pack up the Patagonia and some Clif bars and I'll meet you there!"

But also . . . as much as I hate to admit it, these men were kind of right. Focusing on all the possible things that could go wrong only raised my anxiety and kept me firmly planted on the bridge. Tough love wasn't going to alleviate my fears, especially when all I wanted was for my irrational fear to be validated. A simple "You're right. This is hard. This is scary. But I believe in you. You can do this very hard, scary thing." Alright, so basically I hoped these guys that I just met twenty minutes ago would be my stand-in boyfriend while they just wanted to low-key shove me off this bridge so they could move on to the next customer. #MenAreFromMarsWomen-AreFromVenus. And Mai? Well, she was quiet as a church mouse except for whispering the occasional "It's going to be okay" to me. This little bit of gentle encouragement was all I needed, apparently, because I eventually gathered myself together. The men started the countdown and on three, I closed my eyes, Mai and I stepped out, and *whoosh!* down we went. Fast! The drop simultaneously happened in milliseconds and felt as though it lasted minutes. As we screamed, I thought, *You idiot! You're missing the best part. You're missing everything! Open. Your. Eyes.* So I did, and wow! Everything around us was beautiful. We were laughing, whooping. We felt alive and completely out of control. It was exhilarating and a reminder that these once-in-a-lifetime moments can happen only if you travel. So how did Mai and I get here? Glad you asked.

For the past few years, I've had the pleasure and opportunity to do philanthropic work with (RED), a nonprofit organization that teams up with various consumer brands to create products and experiences that people can buy. Proceeds from those sales help fund the fight to end AIDS, in part by helping reduce the price of HIV and AIDS medicine so that the people who need it the most can actually afford it. As the powers that be at (RED) know, it's one thing to study up on information and be a talking head or host events to encourage others to get involved / raise money, but it's quite another to get out on the ground and see the real-life results of everyone's hard work. So they invited me to join several donors on a trip to Zambia. I immediately said yes and asked Mai if she would like to join me.

See, I've always wanted to go to Africa, even long before I got my passport in 2015. The poverty porn that the world was determined to sell about various African countries, as well as the continent as a whole, never sat well with me. The voyeuristic, invasive, and zoo-esque energy always felt like propaganda, as if to say "Look at how uncultured, sad, and unfortunate Africans are. We shall either pity them or 'marvel' at their exoticness. We will absorb them as content, but not view or respect them as people. We will 'save' them, but only if they can still be dependent on us and never desire to have their own agency." Despite not having much evidence of the contrary when I was growing up—this was the nineties, after all, long before the internet and social media made it easy for anyone to show what I knew all along to be lies—I was certain that much of what I was told about Africa was far from true. I knew that, like everywhere else in the world, Africa is a complex place that's rich and overflowing with culture, traditions, stories, communities, and countries that cannot and should not be condensed to a tragic byline in a Eurocentric and falsely superior narrative. And even though I was in Africa for only four days and got to see a very small percentage of the continent, it was enough to change me forever.

Before I continue, I should note that while I reject the prevailing story line of Africa, I also don't want to pretend that it's a utopia. Both of the aforementioned narratives— overwhelmingly negative so everything is tragic and sad or overwhelmingly positive therefore everything is a Wakandan fantasy, which is a standard that no place can live up to—are damaging and deny the people in them their humanity. Now with that out of the way . . . y'all, their skin though! Have you seen it?!?! My. God. I know I just said to not generalize, but the Zambians? Their skin is rich and decadent like the center of a chocolate molten lava cake. Their hair is thick, kinky, and coily, exuding sovereignty that makes you feel like you, too, can possess their innate regal confidence, even if, deep down, you know you can't. And their teeth! Their freaking teeth. I am never smiling again, at least not when Zambians are just walking around with eighty-seven perfectly straight and white teeth. For the rest of my days (I'm talking my wedding photos, DMV license renewal, LinkedIn profile pic, etc.), I will be tight-lipped like the woman in the *American Gothic* painting because no one needs to see the insides of my garbage mouth.

Jokes aside, being surrounded by all the, for lack of a better word, "Blackness" felt a bit like getting pummeled by a series of tidal waves. For example, a group of children playing during recess would make my heart swell and my ovaries throb to the point that I could barely handle it, and just as I was gathering my bearings, boom! I was slammed by yet another wave of glorious beauty that felt absolutely foreign to me and also felt like the missing piece of myself that was finally being returned to me. Yes, African Americans and Africans are distinctly different from one another, and yet. Being surrounded by brown and Black skin, looking at billboards that featured nothing but people who looked like me or were as dark as or even darker than my mom, and being in an environment where Africans people are not the Other, but the standard, nearly rewired my brain. I'm not African and Zambia wasn't home, but it felt like the next best thing. I will be forever indebted to (RED) for giving me this powerful present.

Some of the people I got to meet now have access to and can afford the medicine they need to live. They've gained back years that can be spent with family and friends, working, laughing, breathing. And since, statistically, women of childbearing age are the most at risk of contracting HIV, it was powerful to see women planning for a future that before was in jeopardy. As for the countless other women and girls I met? I was envious of and inspired by them. Like when I met up with an after-school program that helps teenage girls start their own businesses, making and selling food, clothing/bags, jewelry, etc. Not only that, quite a few of the business owners came together to create a community pot to which a percentage of their earnings was dedicated to support their collective business endeavors. Oh, how I wish I could have experienced something like this when I was younger. Then there was the PEPFAR DREAMS site where a group of mostly teenage girls wrote, acted, and directed their own plays that had absolutely nothing to do with dating or liking a boy. Talk about passing the Bechdel test with flying colors! Considering how secretly boy crazy I was as a teen, I was bowled over by how these young women wove narratives that centered on themselves, their wants, and their needs instead of some guy's. So many grown-ass women spend a lifetime trying and failing to have the mentality these teens already possessed.

These are just a handful of moments that Mai and I still cherish from our four-day trip to Zambia. Many others would be shared and discussed over meals with the rest of #Team(RED), like on day three during a group lunch when Mai half-jokingly suggested that we bungee jump off a bridge at Victoria Falls during the few hours of free time that we'd have during an afternoon trip to Zimbabwe. Without thinking, I responded with, "Sure, why not?" I still don't know what compelled me to do so. I mean, outside of exercising, I'm not physically adventurous, and I live in a constant and irrational state of fear of breaking a bone all because I saw the *trailer*, not the movie, but the trailer for M. Night Shyamalan's *Unbreakable*. If you've seen neither, the basic premise is this: Samuel L. Jackson's character has type I osteogenesis imperfecta, a rare disease that makes a person's bones extremely fragile and prone to fracturing, and in one scene from the trailer, he falls down some subway stairs and breaks hundreds of bones. I do not have this disease, but needlessly worrying is my cardio, so here we are.

The best I can surmise is that leaping off a bridge is something Brooklyn Phoebe would never do. Being halfway around the world gave me license to be not myself. I was Africa Phoebe. And Africa Phoebe doesn't back down from a challenge.

The next day over breakfast, Mai let me know there'd be no hard feelings if I wanted to back out. I assured her that I was all in, so we headed to Shearwater Victoria Falls. Once there, we were told that they didn't offer tandem bungee jumping, but that we could tandem swing together aka walk off a bridge if we wanted. Hmm. Between Mai giving me the chance to bail and now this slight change in bridge-jumping options, I wondered if the Universe was trying to send me hints to not do this. But then I replayed the circumstances in my mind: *I'm in Zimbabwe. These jorts aka jean shorts got my booty looking high and tight like a floating bookshelf. And lastly, I already put on sunscreen and bug spray.* Yep, that was a major factor in me moving forward. Putting on both those items is a lot of effort, which is why I don't enjoy going camping. Like, I have to heat up my own can of baked beans AND slather on sunscreen and bug spray to protect me from the sun and prevent mosquitos from drinking from my skin like I'm a seven-dollar bottomless mimosa special? No thanks! Side note: Why is my camping cuisine the same as Heath Ledger's in *Brokeback Mountain*? S'mores exist. Hot dogs taste good. Treat yourself, Pheebs! ANYWAY. I thought about all the aforementioned factors and looked at Mai, who is one of the most badass people I know. And on that day, so was Africa Phoebe. We signed up to tandem swing. Then we were weighed separately and our respective numbers were written on our forearms, in big-ass handwriting, and with a RED SHARPIE. That way, they would use the appropriate cords and ropes that would hold our cumulative kgs. LMAOOOOOOO. Writing a human being's weight on their forearm for all to see is an attempted coup on their personhood and self-esteem. Now, I'm not one of those people who believes that a woman's weight must never be mentioned, but also can't there be some middle ground between information that's shrouded in secrecy and *Scarlet Letter*'ing my ass? But being branded with my weight was the least of my worries because I was now riddled with anxiety that mid-fall, the cords would give out and we'd drop to our death.

Obviously, since you are reading this book, that didn't happen because I lived to tell the tale. What did happen was I took a risk and it made me proud of myself in a way I never quite felt before. And it wouldn't have been possible if I didn't say yes. Yes to walking off the bridge, yes to traveling to Africa, yes to getting my passport, yes to listening to that tiny voice inside me, the one that often got drowned out by all the others saying that traveling isn't a possibility. That small voice remained steady and constant, believing nonetheless, and, it seems, so did I. Although I'm not sure how.

Simply put: My parents are not travelers. For instance, if I ever said to my dad, "How about the whole family pools their money together and Airbnbs a cute house somewhere warm for Christmas? Maybe even a place that has a pool for my niece and nephew to swim around in?" he'd probably respond with, "I'm good. I've seen pictures of rectangular-shaped things that have liquids in them."

For real though, he and my mom are homebodies, don't really have close friends, and don't desire to travel anywhere. They have lived long, intense, beautiful, demanding, unique lives and they're way the hell over it all: having responsibilities, opening mail, dealing with anyone who doesn't share their DNA, owning tote bags, answering the question "How are you doing?," their bodies aging, maintaining a pantry, witnessing how little society has changed when it comes to major sociopolitical issues, even though they're eating vegan, which is extending their life expectancy on this hellscape of a planet, etc. They have raised two children, have two grandchildren, and have managed to be together for over forty years. I feel like what's bubbling below the surface of their Midwestern niceness is a hearty "Did we win yet? Surely we must have at this point! Can we tap out now?!?!" Life has been one *looooooong* game of Monopoly in which Ma and Pa Robinson have been dealing with Baltic Avenue's bullshit and they don't wanna play anymore. Okay, I'm exaggerating. No, my parents aren't looking forward to dying. What they're looking forward to, I imagine, is ensuring that their streak of #NoNewFriends-OrAcquantancesOrWorldlyExperiences remains undefeated.

Ever since I can remember, my parents have never had any friends or hung out with anyone besides each other, which was in stark contrast to the movies and TV series that showed parents routinely leaving their kids with a babysitter for the evening or going on vacation with other adult couples. This was never the case with my parents as they were *always* home. Remember on *Sex and the City* when Carrie fears that her relationship with Aidan is stale and she basically asks him, "Why are you content with eating fried chicken on a Wednesday night? Shouldn't we be living exciting, unpredictable lives?" And he's just like, "I'm in my late thirties, have a Rogaine subscription, and maintain a quality credit score. I didn't come this far nor work this hard to be fraternizing with strangers in stovepipe jeans at trifling-ass clubs. Quit searching for problems. We good." Basically, my parents are Black Aidans. Blaidans, if you will. They never really felt the need to go out.

To be fair, they did take us to Niagara Falls, to see plays, and to amusement parks, but they were not the kind of parents to plan family road trips all the time or go on vacations by themselves. Maybe that was partially due to them being the only two members of the village it takes to raise two precocious children and not having tons of expendable cash. But, honestly, knowing who they are, they could have had Rockefeller money when I was growing up and still would've been content with chilling at home and watching *Wheel of Fortune*.

One of my biggest career achievements will forever be when I served as one of the moderators on Michelle Obama's historic *Becoming* book tour. It was an out-of-body experience, stress inducing (I often had nightmares about screwing up so badly in front of her twenty-thousand-plus audience that I would be escorted offstage by her Secret Service detail), and inspiring. More on that later. On the night of my final stint with Michelle, she invited my parents to the last date of the tour in

Nashville, which was on Mother's Day, and said she would love to do a meet and greet with them as well as have them as guests at the after-party. I was shocked! Usually, when a person is like, "Lemme meet your parents," that person is a white woman with chunky highlights who asks to speak to the manager when she has nothing but complaints and a desire to get a coupon or refund for her troubles. I don't know what I did or how I did it, but I was humbled by the lovely offer. All I had to do was fly myself and my parents out and find us a hotel to stay at, and since the Mother's Day event was still a month away, I had decent travel options. Surely, a personal invite from MO would be enticing enough for my parents to travel? Y'all. *Y'all.* *Y'ALL*, when I tell you that they came through with some plant-based, room-temp bullshit, I mean it.

I swear on my collection of wigs that the first thing out my mom's mouth was, "Uh . . . I don't know. I'll probably be tired then. Let me get back to you." Come again? Octavia Velina Robinson (née Wyckoff), are you legit RSVP'ing with a lukewarm "maybe" by pretending you know a full *month* in advance that staying up past 9:15 P.M. on a Sunday night is too big of an ask? Just go to sleep a couple of hours earlier the night before you fly out, so you'll feel well rested! And even if you're fatigued from the flight to Nashville, guess what? Rise to the occasion! Drink some tea! Have a bite of coffee-infused chocolate! Hell, snort a line of coke for the first time in your life if that means you'll stay awake long enough to rub elbows with Michelle Obama, the Queen of Smarts and Defined Triceps. Like, what else did you have planned for Mother's Day? To watch *The Voice*? To eat a portobello mushroom and call it a "steak" because vegans can't resist doing the most with the absolute least? Speaking of "doing the least," my mom did *not* circle back to me about this invitaysh, so I had to hound my parents like a bill collector in order to get a yes, but not before they were dramatizing the specifics such as waking up early to head to the airport and dealing with a short layover. LORD! Why do people gotta act brand-new? None of us in the Robinson clan are above catching a connecting flight at O'Hare and dining on a Garrett popcorn tin to help pass the time, but sure, let's all act like we're Kardashians who are used to flying private.

Anyway, long story short, my parents had a blast. They met and took a photo with Miche (that's Michelle's nickname, bt-dubs). They stayed awake and had a great time watching Stephen Colbert interview her. And true to form, they were 1) predictably and laughably underwhelmed with the hotel accommodations even though I got them one of the nicest suites in the joint and 2) on the earliest flight out of Nashville the next day because they had no interest in sightseeing.

As much as I've inherited their penchant for being "over it" and wanting to stay home (when I'm out, I keep everyone abreast of the fact that I'm planning on leaving even though I just arrived, and I will definitely not say goodbye), I diverge from my parents on the topic of traveling. It always piqued my interest, despite my assuming that I must be unadventurous like my mom and dad. There was just one problem. For the majority of my adult life, I didn't have the financial means to find out if this was true or not. While many of my college classmates studied abroad over the summer, I worked odd jobs in order to afford to live in New York. I got older and my social media was (and is) littered with friends taking vacations, going on international trips for work, having destination weddings, etc. Meanwhile, my continual financial struggles throughout my twenties and into my early thirties meant that traveling was, best-case scenario, a fantasy, and worst-case scenario, a fast way to accumulate even more debt. On the rare occasions I did leave town, I did so by maxing out credit cards, and then, understandably, I began associating traveling with shame, self-loathing, and something that left me in a worse financial position than I started out in. Even worse, I projected onto others. I alternated between viewing their escapades as frivolous and a sign they have too much money and not enough sense, or feeling jealous that having the means to travel was a nut I couldn't quite crack. Still, money wasn't the only thing that factored in my remaining homebound.

As we all know, it's hard to envision something for yourself if you don't see evidence out in the world often enough. Even though Black people (and all people of color) travel, we don't often hear or see stories of any Black people, outside of the rich and famous ones, encountering different cultures, going on adventures, and having fun away from home; therefore, it was hard to imagine myself having worldly adventures. There are no seminal works such as the *Eat Pray Love* movie or the *On the Road* novel about Black people in the middle of an existential crisis or trying to find themselves against the backdrop of America. Rarely in the mainstream media is there the celebrated lore of travel informing Black people's creative expression the way that David Bowie's time in Germany led to the Berlin trilogy (*Low, Heroes, Lodger*) or how two drug-filled Las Vegas trips became the inspiration for Hunter S. Thompson's most famous book, *Fear and Loathing in Las Vegas*.

If anything, media frequently portrays POC life as the following: 1) rife with adversity due to skin color and/or lack of wealth, 2) that we're in homemade studios making mixtapes or playing sports, or 3) that white people invade our spaces in order to find themselves and learn to be grateful for their own lives because people of color make do with so little. If anything, the general perception of traveling for POC is getting out of poverty or the "bad" neighborhood they currently reside in. If we're lucky enough to do that, the reward is not a vacation or a chance to head to another country to have fun and fall in love / make life-changing friends, but to . . . land in a middle-class community, in which we're one of a few, or the only one, of our "kind." Supposedly, this new position as the neighborhood token is how us Black folk know we've done right in life. Assimilation in white-dominated spaces is the endgame, not our own individual happiness, which exists outside the purview of whiteness.

Y'all, I'm so starved for a Black-people-just-living-their-lives-and-traveling tale that I would settle for a short story about a Brooklyn-based AfroLatina using an E-ZPass to head into Jersey City for a Target run. My standards are *that* low! In all seriousness, we don't get shown enough how freeing, enriching, fascinating, influential, and informative traveling can be because, according to society, we're not supposed to explore or have full lives the way white people do. Instead, the most we should aspire to is middle-class suburbia, where we tolerate macro- and microaggressions that are the by-product of having "made it," such as a passive-aggressive neighbor who notices your grass is a few inches higher than usual, so they put a pamphlet in your mailbox as a gentle reminder about the neighborhood rules on acceptable lawn height. Yes, this did happen to my brother, Phil, and yes, the neighbor who did this to him is white.

Noncontroversial statement of the day: Maybe, *just maybe*, some white people have a bit too much free time on their hands. I mean, I thought the purpose of training to compete at the CrossFit Games and apple picking at an orchard for leh-zur (that's leisure for the unpretentious) was to eat up any and all spare time they had. Guess I was wrong because some white folks are committed to working an unpaid internship while studying at the University of Now Would Be a Good Time for Me to Mind My Own Business, But I'm Not Ready for That Conversation because keeping tabs on someone else's grass is . . . ignorant.

What I'm getting at is that these sorts of low-grade nuisances are what Black people are conditioned to "look forward to" instead of wanting to see and experience the world, which is often coupled with the myth that Black people have zero desire to travel. So given all these factors—my parents, my unstable financial status, and societal assumptions—I slowly became convinced that traveling wasn't *for* us, meaning Black people. Obviously, I was wrong. Traveling is for everyone; it can just be made more difficult for Black people. That's an understatement. It can be downright terrifying and life-threatening to travel while Black.

Green Book, the Oscar-winning film about interracial friendship, is based on the actual *Green Book* that was created in the 1930s. To be honest, I've never watched it, but I considered seeing the movie until at a press event, actor Viggo Mortensen sat beside costar Mahershala Ali and, as proof of the racial progress in America, Viggo barfed up, "For instance, no one says 'nigger' anymore." And I was like . . . but you said it. Just now, so this is kinda awkward. Also, has he ever been to a Kendrick Lamar concert? There's a whole lot of Scotts and Daves absolutely putting the stank on that word as they rap along to Kendrick. And finally, there are so many examples of racial progress that he could've chosen to make his raggedy-ass point. He could've mentioned the impressive gains Black students are making in graduating from high school and attending college. Shouting out Jackie Robinson for breaking the baseball color line barrier would have been a nice touch. He could have talked about how Black people don't have to park-our in church shoes off the front bumpers of Oldsmobiles anymore in order to get away from police siccing rottweilers on them, thanks to the Civil Rights Act of 1964 passing. Viggo had a plethora of options, but he went straight for "nigger." With the hard "er." Pass on him and this movie. But *Green Book*, the book? I'm in awe of its Black ingenuity.

In 1936, Victor Hugo Green, a Black postal worker, published the first edition of *The Negro Motorist Green Book*, which served as a guide for Black New York City dwellers to know which businesses they could patronize without suffering discrimination or abuse. Jim Crow was everywhere, not just in the South, so even certain parts of Harlem weren't safe for Black people. Word traveled about the book, and its popularity grew. Eventually, Green became the Pitbull of his time. (Why don't I teach American history at Howard University?) His book was so in demand that the following year, he released a national edition, thus kicking off a fifty-year-plus reign as the go-to—and, in some cases, lifesaving—resource that Blacks relied on for their everyday lives and especially when traveling throughout America. I mean, this book was a detailed catalog of Black-owned businesses around the country, ranging among hotels, restaurants, barbershops, gas stations, vacation hotspots, and more. At the guide's peak, *two million* copies of it were in circulation. Just think of the bravery of Black people during this time. Yes, they risked their lives and their safety to do things like getting their hair done and filling up their gas tanks that would, today, fall under the category of "errands to run on a Saturday." But what I marvel at the most is that in the face of the unbearableness of living in Jim Crow America, Black people still chose joy. They still chose to leave the confines of their neighborhoods to dig their toes in the sand at the beach, to take their kids to another state to try a different cuisine, to relax as every human being is entitled to. If you would have asked me any time before 2015 if I could be that bold, I'd respond "No." But then my former manager emailed me about an unexpected job opportunity that came at the perfect time in my broke life: a two-day trip to Budapest to teach a group of thirty-five designers from a tech startup how to be fearless via sketch comedy and improv.

That sentence is, indeed, word salad, but I had spent the previous two months eating sad salads because I broke up with my ex and then spent almost all my money to move into another apartment. I was in no position to be choosy when it came to work, but I did have questions. Are there Black people in Budapest? What do they eat in Budapest? And seriously, though, where the Black people at in Budapest? All the questions ceased to matter when my former manager told me what the compensation was: flight, hotel, AND three thousand dollars, which was ten times more than I had ever been paid for a comedy gig up until that point. Admittedly, Budapest was never on my list of cities I dreamt of seeing, but it was unlike any place I'd been before, so basically, it was the same as going to Paris, Madrid, or Tokyo. #Uhhhhh #HadIEverLookedAtAMapBefore #OrSpunAGlobeInSocialStudiesClass #NowIUnderstandChristopherColumbus'sConfusionAndNavigationIssues #HeStillTrashTho.

The point is, for this unworldly gal, Budapest was practically Shangri-la and I had to go there, except I didn't have a passport. I quickly put the cost of an expedited one on my credit card, and when I finally got my passport, I glowed like I had Fenty Beauty highlighter tattooed on my cheekbones, temples, forehead, nose, and chin. Just luminous from every angle because never again would I utter the sentence "I don't have a passport." Everything about the passport thrilled me. The slightly raised ridges and embossed gold lettering on the cover. The picture of my half-smiling face. The pages of the passport practically begging me to replace its brand-new smell and crease-free form with a slight odor, smudged ink, and wrinkles as signs of well-earned wear and tear. The idea that I could now become worldly. But it wasn't just the passport that I loved. I found each aspect of the trip pleasurable.

The mediocre airplane food on Air Berlin received a chef's kiss from me. When I arrived at customs to declare my reason for being in Budapest, I proudly declared, "I'm here on business! Teaching improv to a bunch of dudes in tech." Turns out the phrase "teaching improv" is not the icebreaker you'd think it'd be in eastern Europe. But there were so many victories along the way that made up for the occasional misstep. Walking along the Chain Bridge, which spans the Danube. Silently taking in centuries of art at the Museum of Fine Arts. At night, hanging with a couple of newfound and temporary friends as we stumbled upon a found bar aka an abandoned building that was transformed into a bar, but not in a gentrification way. A banged-up claw-foot tub functioning as a place to sit. Graffiti on the walls of a stairwell that wouldn't feel out of place in the background of an influencer's selfie. Karaoke blasting from multiple rooms. Hungarian words flying everywhere. I savored every second of this sensory overload. But nothing compared to the quiet hour or two I spent one afternoon sitting in a little café, eating pastries as I people watched. In the stillness, I didn't even care that after manager fees and taxes, I wasn't going to net much money. I had traveled. Internationally. For the first time. By myself, and it was amazing. I didn't know how I was ever going to travel again, but logistics and lack of money were no concerns of mine. I was far too entranced by the Budapest of it all.

Now, I recognize that I could've been heavily romanticizing my time there. But I swear it was so innocent and pleasant that any reservations I had about traveling abroad solo as a Black woman, while never fully gone, receded to the background long enough for me to feel safe. So because of that, my self-defeating belief that traveling was just not meant for me or other Black people was replaced by something more hopeful. Still, I'm Black. Meaning that when it came to traveling, I was somewhere between feeling the one extreme of blind optimism and the other of grizzled cynicism.

Since the publication of the final issue of the *Green Book* (1966–67), it *has* gotten easier and less dangerous for Black people to travel, although given the social uprisings of 2020, the L.A. riots of the '90s, and more, that is debatable. Too many Black lives have been extinguished for us to pretend that the ugliness of the 1930s, '40s, '50s, and '60s is firmly in the past. However, there's no denying progress has been made. The fact that a modern-day *Green Book* is not a *necessity* to travel is cause for celebration; however, leaving home for vacation or mundane purposes can be a roll of the dice, as Rhonda Colvin chronicled in her 2018 *Washington Post* article "Traveling While Black," noting everything from disproportionate traffic stops, tickets, and car searches, to first-ever travel advisories from the NAACP.

And as we have seen so frequently in the last few decades,

years, and months, discrimination against Black people knows no bounds. Being carefree while Black is not widely accepted. Eleven Black women in the book club Sistahs on the Reading Edge were reminded of this when they were kicked off the Napa Valley Wine Train for laughing and being too "boisterous." First of all, let's pause and give these women their flowers for having a Black-ass group name. This is the kind of name that lets you know they're "Before I Let Go" purists and will only rock out to the original Frankie Beverly and Maze version. Secondly, it's a *wine train*, not a "sip lukewarm water and snack on dry-ass pretzel sticks while sitting on your Wayfair couch" train. Every car on a wine train, at the bare minimum, should be noisy and messy like Studio 54 in its heyday: people loudly having a good time, sequins everywhere, and a nipple slip from Grace Jones.

Okay, okay. Look, I understand that people being loud in a public setting can be irritating. However, in a world that wants to embarrass, shame, or criminalize Black women for not operating within the confines of stereotypes—jezebel or strong/angry—I find it deliciously defiant and, more important, necessary for Black women to show public displays of happiness. Not only to normalize it for the outside world, but to remind themselves that they are entitled to feel and express the totality of their humanity, which includes joy. Unfortunately, the group, which included an eighty-three-year-old woman, were rudely confronted by staff for laughing too loudly and then escorted off the Napa Valley Wine Train by police. This resulted in two of the ladies losing their jobs. Eventually, Sistahs on the Reading Edge sued for $11 million in damages, and even though they settled for an undisclosed amount, I think it's clear there isn't enough money in the world to make up for instilling fear in Black people and escalating a situation, which so often results in murder at the hands or gun of a cop.

I've never experienced anything as debasing as being arrested for being Black, but more times than I care to count, I've been made to feel like a *National Geographic* subject if styled by Shopbop. Every time I've visited my boyfriend's sleepy hometown of Bournemouth, which is on the south coast of England, I am the only Black person there. And because I like to wear giant braids and bold makeup, I'm highly visible. Some would stare. Others would compliment me, which, don't get me wrong, is nice, but, ultimately, feeling eyes on you and being watched by white people, even if the outcome is a positive interaction, is draining. Knowing that I am under a microscope puts me on edge, thus making it difficult to relax and feel comfortable in my own skin. Instead, I'm hyperaware that I am the Outsider and alternate between feeling rebellious and trying to make myself small.

When I am not concerned with being watched in Bae's hometown, I am sometimes confronted by the ways people of color can be pushed to the margins, and disheartened by racially insensitive things that are glaring to me yet don't register as even a blip to others. Such as when I'm at a nice dinner in a fancy hotel and the only other POC present are the employees. Or when I'm visiting a person's home or a museum and see a casual or outright racist figurine that, because it's been a part of the culture for centuries, is deemed okay. Or like in 2019, when walking in an outdoor market, I clocked, out of my periphery, an older gentleman staring at me. He caught me on a day when I was feeling particularly audacious, so I locked eyes with him as if to ask him what his problem was. He apologized and followed up with a "Can I take a picture of you?" My mood shifted a little as I thought, *Oh, okay! I may be thirty-five, but clearly, it's never too late to be discovered and start a modeling career.* He continued, "I want to show my wife." *Wooooooow! Pretty bold move, but I guess my Diane-Keaton-if-she-attended-Thotchella look aka cream-colored linen clothing that covered most of my body, is the oat milk that brings all the boys (and maybe some wives) to the yard.* And then he finished his statement, "We've never seen a Black person before." Record scratch! GOOGLE IMAGES? RIHANNA'S INSTAGRAM ACCOUNT? A HYPE WILLIAMS MUSIC VIDEO FROM THE NINETIES?

Look, I understand the curiosity and desire to memorialize the moment of being relatively up close and personal with a Black person, especially if it's your first time, but no. Do you know how many things I've seen for the first time that I *didn't* take a picture of? A woman whipping out her toddler's penis so he could pee on the sidewalk at high noon. A man admitting I was right in a staff meeting. Myself when I texted someone "I'm on my way," and I was *actually on my way* and not still in bed, unshowered, with my sleeping cap on and crust in my eyes. I mean, get a grip and act like you've been here before. Act like you've seen a beautiful Black person before. If you haven't guessed by now, I wouldn't let the stranger take the picture, and he was disappointed.

Looking back on it, I could have asked him why he wanted

a picture. His answer could've been harmless or perhaps it would have turned into a situation where I'd have to do emotional labor and be the "Black experience" that he'd run home and discuss with loved ones and friends. And I just couldn't take that risk because, on that day, I just wanted to be a girl who was shopping with her boyfriend. I didn't want to stand out from the crowd, feel exoticized, or be a character in someone's mini awakening about Blackness. I just wanted to be unremarkable in every conceivable way, which is something, I've discovered, I desire most when I'm at the airport.

I follow every rule in hopes of drawing as little attention to myself as possible, as if that will prevent people noticing I'm Black or judging me for being Black. Well, it doesn't matter how much I try to render myself invisible, I'm still harassed. Like the time I was pulled out of line because one airport employee couldn't believe that I could afford business class. Once I showed him my boarding pass and ID, he let me back in line, and not even a minute later, another airport employee ran in my direction, questioning why I was in the line. Of course, everyone watched me be humiliated as they each tried to justify their assumption that I didn't belong. Another time, I, along with my coworkers, who are all white, approached the gate to board our flight. I was first and greeted the gate agent, then handed him my boarding pass. He announced loudly and rudely, "I'm sorry, we're only boarding *business class* right now, so if you want to wait your turn . . ." Oh, so you think that because I didn't have the *strenf* to cover up my hyperpigmentation this morning that I'm going to let you loud-talk me like that? Bruh, Black women *invented* loud talking. #Know-YourRoots #HenryLouisGatesJr.

Seriously, Black women know when a person is trying to be messy, so we match their energy by pointedly increasing our volume, thus turning the tables on them, so they can now be the ones who are embarrassed. Which is why when the old white couple in front of me turned around to see how I was going to react, I blew my invisible harmonica in the key of "I Got Time Today" and let out an "I *am* in business class, so I don't *need* to wait *my turn*, but it's *good to know* that *you* don't think *I* can afford *business class*. Well, I *can* and I *did*. So listen to *your* scanner hit *my* boarding pass with a confirmation beep. *Beep*." Y'all, I ain't never been on key a day in my life, but in that moment, I was harmonizing like a member of En Vogue. The gate agent stuttered, trying to get out an apology as I walked away. It was nice to give him a taste of his own medicine and yet . . . it wasn't enough to mask the demoralized feelings that lingered.

There have been moments when I wondered if traveling is worth it. Is it worth the headache or the energy of having to defend myself? Is it worth being on my best behavior at all times when I know it's still not enough to prevent someone exercising what they believe is their inalienable right to publicly shame me for existing? Is it worth the frustration of knowing I am being watched from afar, so that I can never entirely and fully feel comfortable? Well, yes, because I believe the tide is changing. The ignorant assumption that Black people don't or shouldn't travel and the endless attempts over decades and decades to make us feel unwelcome are simply not working. We don't feel defeated and we're not staying home. We continue loading up our Away suitcases and embarking on new adventures as writer Eugene Yiga notes in his 2019 CNN.com article, "How the Black Travel Movement Is Gaining Momentum."

Like most things when it comes to Black people, the tourism industry refuses to reflect reality and catch up to the changing times since the publication of *The Negro Motorist Green Book*. It's clear we're either an afterthought or flat-out ignored by the powers that be in tourism. Even as recently as a decade ago, I would be hard-pressed to find an online ad, subway billboard, or travel website that wasn't littered with smiling white faces, which is mind-boggling when you consider the following: There are nearly five million Black millennial travelers in the United States, and as a group, we spent $63 *billion* on travel in 2018 (up from $48 billion in 2011). Wow. Given those numbers, one would assume we'd be included in tourism ads. Unfortunately, quite the opposite is happening. The website Travel Noire, which caters to the Black travel experience, reports that less than 3 *percent* of travel advertisements focus on Black people. Da hell, Sandals, Travelocity, and Expedia?! We've been pumping all this money into tourism, and you companies can't put several Black queens and kings in all their shea butter glory in your ads? Not *one* spoken-word poet / doula / DJ in your commercials? Well, as Black people, we have demonstrated time and time again that we can be shut out, disrespected, and disregarded, but our dogged determination proves that nothing will stop any of our revolutions, such as the Black revolution, the Black hair revolution, and yes, our travel revolution. And I'm proud to be a part of this movement.

In the years since Budapest, I've made up for lost time and traveled either for work or pleasure any chance I could because every single time I returned home, the growth in me as a person was palpable. *That's* what travel is really about. Having nice pictures to post on Instagram or flexing your vacation wardrobe for strangers to see doesn't compare to the possible internal transformation that awaits us. Interacting with different people and cultures makes them real, as opposed to composites of half-baked assumptions, unnecessary fears, and misnomers that may have existed in your mind. You might see how there's more than one way to do things, or learn to appreciate an aspect of life that you never considered before, such as sleep. The go-go-go energy of New York that I've adopted as my own personal philosophy is always challenged whenever I leave the city. Like, oooh, corner stores aren't open 24/7 in case I get peckish at three in the morning while writing. People here rest. Huh. Maybe I should, too. And that's just the beginning.

I've done a retreat with my boyfriend and mingled with farmers; I've stood on the stage at Red Rocks and avoided haggis in Scotland. I loved the malls in Denver, and I want to go back to Copenhagen purely for Hija de Sanchez's tacos. My favorite part of the twenty-four-hour trip to Dublin that I took with Mai was her popping my Guinness cherry as we realized our flight was boarding, so we chugged half the pint before running to our gate. As a *Top Chef* aficionado, I knew I had to swing by Kristen Kish's Arlo Grey restaurant during my stand-up tour stop in Austin, Texas, and it was one of the most deliciously gluttonous meals I've ever had in my life. Clearly, plenty of my treasured traveling moments are food related and happened because being a stand-up comic requires me to be on the road. But, as it turns out, one of the best nights of my life was the result of a last-minute trip out of Brooklyn. A little backstory.

I'm an incredible gift giver. Okay, fine, I've messed up a time or two, but, overall, I have a 95 percent success rate, mainly because I do my research and I'm not afraid to be a little selfish. When it comes to research, I comb through peo ple's social media accounts and cross-reference with the folks in their lives to make sure that I'm on the right path, or I take mental notes when someone mentions something they want or would like to experience.

But the truth is that every once in a while, the gift is one that is not just for the recipient, but also a skosh for me. I know this sounds trifling, but hear me out! For some inexplicable reason, I can thread that needle, baby, between "Mother Teresa wishes she had the range of my selflessness" and "I'm too cute to not reap a little fun for myself out of this." Yes, that is a mess, but also, if you're reading this and thinking, *I've never given another person a birthday present that wasn't 100 percent for them*, you ain't telling the truth. Periodically, the lines of pleasure blur and mutual enjoyment is a by-product of the gift.

For example, if you've given lingerie as a present, that was for the other person and also because you want visual stimu-laysh. Or maybe the gift is a book. On the surface, that seems completely innocuous, as you bought it with the good inten-tions of "Oh, I know [insert xyz person] would just love it!" Um, unless that person is a bibliophile such as myself, all you did was give an already too busy person homework! Not only that, but you're probably low-key expecting them to follow up with a verbal book report, and every time you see them enjoying their life via social media, you're cussing them out for not documenting their reading of *Their Eyes Are Watch-ing God.* So, ya know, we all get caught up in the game of mu-tually beneficial presents. All of this, of course, is a preamble to justifying the present I got for British Baekoff: a trip to Mumbai to ~~see U2's first ever concert in India, which was also the last show of their *Joshua Tree* reboot tour~~ celebrate his thirty-first birthday.

In my defense (there is none), I was invited by some homies from #TeamBono (Ha! Like I've ever needed an invitation to go to one of their live shows), but there was one problem. I had already planned a staycation birthday weekend for Bae in NYC after months of us being on the road for our respective jobs. Between the two of us that year, we had flown sixty times for work, and the idea of being in one place for four days in a row, in which we were guaranteed to get eight hours of sleep nightly, felt downright revolutionary. On the flip side? It's a personal invite from U2 to see their final Joshua Tree show. Ever. For the rest of time. Like never again would we hear, live, "Where the Streets Have No Name," "I Still Haven't

Found What I'm Looking For," and "With or Without You" in that exact order. Okay, that's dramatic, but also truthful. That concert was going to be one for the books.

So, when I was asked to come to Mumbai, it was more than an invitation. I was being summoned to be a part of history (tbh, Black history), and take my rightful place next to Henrietta Lacks and Alvin Ailey.[1] Moving on. As much as I was looking forward to the weekend I had planned for Baekoff, I didn't want to miss out on a one-of-a-kind experience, so I FaceTimed him, told him the deal, and, without a moment's hesitation, most likely due to a trifecta of him understanding how much I love U2, that he does not care about his birthday in the slightest, and the fact that he loves to travel and experience the world, he responded with, "I've never been to India before. Let's do it." I couldn't believe it! I was so excited . . . then immediately, I felt guilty. He was tired. Hell, we both were, and here I was hijacking his birthday. I began trying to talk him *out* of dropping everything to go to Mumbai. He resisted: "How many times are we going to be invited to India? Let me know what shots I need to take and when the flights are booked." Even as I'm writing this, I cannot believe I'm

---

1. LOL. Can you imagine the USPS wasting adhesive technology on their stamps because my face was going to be on them during Black History Month thanks to my contribution to the culture being "Thirsty Black Woman Who Traveled Sixteen Hours to Be the Only Black Person at a U2 Concert"? But, also, this isn't my fault! The Obamas, Mariah Carey, Colin Kaepernick, and LeBron James have practically taken the last of notable firsts a Black person can achieve, so now I'm left with bargain basement options, so I'll take what I can get at this point if it means my mug is on a stamp that someone will use to mail out their holiday cards.

lucky enough to date someone so unbelievably generous that getting hepatitis A and typhoid shots and taking malaria pills counts as acceptable birthday pregaming. So, with help from my assistant, I quickly put together an all-new birthday itinerary, and off BB and I went.

It was a whirlwind trip (we could only be there for a few days before heading to the UK to celebrate Christmas with his family) and despite it happening two years ago, the memories are so vivid that I can close my eyes and it's as though we're back in the heart of Mumbai. The sparkle in Baekoff's eyes because no matter where we ate, there was a plethora of vegetarian options for him to choose from. The controlled chaotic driving, which could unnerve the average person, made me feel right at home as if we'd never left Brooklyn. Each step on uneven rocks in the Elephanta Caves was worth it because they got us closer to the sculptures of Hindu and Buddhist iconography. Our time at Zero Latency, a VR video game space where we shot zombies, was punctuated by my yelps and screeches because VR is too real for me, yet I'd happily do it again for my gamer boyfriend, who, in past relationships, was made to feel bad for playing video games. I miss the scent of our skin, which was a combination of our sweat, sunscreen, and lotion. I miss those spectacular Mumbai sunsets. Then, there's the U2 of it all.

Bono dedicating "With or Without You" to British Baekoff and me in front of over fifty thousand people is a once-in-a-lifetime and full-circle moment, since BB and I met at a U2 concert. Hanging out at the after-party and talking about big life shit with BonBon,[2] dancing our behinds off, and drinking wine, which resulted in our driver silently cussing us out because we'd previously said, "We'll only have a drink and then be back in thirty mins," and then we didn't leave the party until like five A.M., are moments I think about routinely because we wouldn't have experienced any of them if we stayed in NYC. And given what the world has been through because of Covid, the memories of before times, when we could go anywhere we wanted, are even more special. But the icing on the cake is that Baekoff said that trip was, hands down, one of the best birthdays of his life. Yay! My streak of great gift giving continues, and the roles were reversed for once since *I* was the one taking this well-traveled man somewhere *he'd* never been before, but that's not what's important. Cuddling with the love of my life in India was proof that traveling could help me surpass my wildest dreams or, in the case of Mumbai, the belief that I had as a child that because a place like Mumbai is so far away, it's not even worth hoping I could go there one day. Truthfully, being carefree, Black, and female at home, let alone abroad, was not something I believed was possible for me because society has proved otherwise, so I never dared to dream it. And if I hadn't started traveling in 2015, I would have continued not dreaming, accepting that all those stories, movies, and TV shows where white people go somewhere to find themselves, adventure, love, a different worldview than the

---

2. Dear reader, that's my nickname for Bono and he, for some reason, puts up with it. ☺

one they're used to, or simply to relax, were reminders of what I *couldn't* have, of the life that I would never be allowed to live.

And while Covid has put me and the rest of the world (except for the obscenely rich, who have been quietly and not-so-quietly bouncing around) on the bench, I'm looking forward to the day when I can bust out my passport once more and go to a different city to see a U2 concert. I mean, to experience different cultures and all the ways my worldview will be challenged and expanded. Heh. Okay, fine. It's mostly U2 and a smidge of everything else a foreign city has to offer. Kidding! It's a fifty-fifty split! I need middle-aged white man angst *and* adobo seasoning to awaken my butthole upon its exit out of my body to remind me I'm alive. More than that, I need to leave the protective cocoon of quarantine and reemerge in the world as a more confident Black woman traveler who refuses to shrink herself in an overseas country or put strangers' comfort ahead of her own.

Traveling shouldn't be an elitist or racist activity. It should be available to everyone who wants it because exploring the world changes you. It changed me. Relaxing outside the confines of my home renewed my spirit. Seeing people who look like me whose brains aren't wired like mine because they don't live under the white America gaze was awe-inspiring. I mean, learning shouldn't be limited to what we read in books, and evolving can't always happen when we're confined to our area code. Connecting with a person via food, music, conversation, cultural smells, architecture, and any other thing that's different from what you're used to can be life changing. And when Black people are told and shown that only white people and rich people are allowed to do this, we are also told and shown that only white people's and rich people's lives are worth expanding. That their stories are the only stories that get to be told. That they are the only ones who get to write them, with people of color—if we're "lucky" enough to be mentioned at all—serving as exotically beautiful, tragic set dressing.

Well, I'm writing my own story. I am a Black girl. I am a Black girl who travels.

Please Don't Sit on My Bed in
Your Outside Clothes

———~

If you're curious about what I'm like before I have sex—my
parents are reading this like, "I'M GOOD!"—just imagine
that local reporter you know and love who's dressed in the
uncool attire from New York & Company (aka anything not
from the Gabrielle Union capsule collection) and barely keeping it together as drunk and rowdy people repeatedly inter-
rupt her puff piece about that year's Halloween parade.
Despite how distracting the ruckus is, her confident gaze into
the camera and plastered-on smile serve as evidence that not
only can she handle the unexpected, but she invites it in. Her
even tone is proof she will get through this story like she has
hundreds of times before, leaving viewers dazzled by her ability to both be amiable and handle things like a pro. And for a
long time, leading up to sex, I felt as though I was that local
reporter, and the drunk and rowdy folk were the thoughts
jockeying for position in my overactive brain.

To be clear, it's perfectly natural for hundreds of half-thoughts, random notions, and unrelated tangents to fire off in people's minds due to the anticipation of what's about to go down. The problem for me is that most of these thoughts aren't particularly salient or helpful. In fact, the majority are half-formed, ignorant, reeking of self-doubt, or, worst-case scenario, funny, which can make me accidentally laugh out loud instead of focusing on sex. I swear to you, my brain always starts out fine: *I hope this'll be good.* Or *I hope I don't catch feels.* And *Why did I wear jeans so skinny that they require this dude to engage his core in order to help me take them off?* Ya know, basic stuff. Then it quickly devolves from there:

I really hope this motherfucker doesn't want me to put the condom on him because the only way I know how to do it is like a disgruntled Zara employee who got stuck on window-display duty and has to clothe twelve mannequins by herself before midnight. What if I were to turn on the "Baby Shark" song halfway through just to keep things interesting? Ugh, I'm such a slob. Do you think he notices that my bedroom looks like the FBI came through here with a search warrant? TBH, I'm not the biggest fan of his first name—too damn formal—so maybe I could test-drive some nicknames and see what he responds to? If he fumbles with my bra, I'm not smashing. J/K. He's hot, and just like the proverb "Each one teach one," which originated during slavery because Africans were denied the right to read, so that when an enslaved person did learn to read, it was their duty to teach someone else, I'm going to educate this mofo, so maybe this is my way of giving back? Aaaaaaaand now I'm thinking about slavery. Great. But also, does teaching this dude how to unhook a bra make me a philanthropist? Okay, maybe not a philanthropist, but at least on the path to having a street named after me, or a Tuesday in August declared Phoebe Robinson Day, or being given keys to the city. Like, all I want is to hold a comically large pair of scissors, cut a ribbon, and have people applaud me. What exactly do I have to do in order to make that happen? Have city-approved plans to construct a building? Start a brick-and-mortar business? Okay, bitch, you need to focus on the task at hand. A few beats pass. Should I give Emily in Paris *a chance? That's it. You're allowed one last thought and then it's game—I really wish I focused on squats at any point from middle school to my middle thirts, so I could have built up the thigh strength to ride the D for more than 8.6 seconds.*

Y'all, I'm aware that last one is a touch specific, so I'll explain. Recently, as I was descending into the squatting position over my boyfriend's penis, about seventeen thousand of my hip bones snapped, crackled, and popped, and I had so many questions: Did someone light some kindling? Is a box of carpenter nails tumbling down the staircase I don't have in my apartment? Like, why do my hips sound like the breaking-glass sound effect at the beginning of WWE's "Stone Cold" Steve Austin intro music? And if you think it's any better in missionary position, it ain't! As I'm lying down, there's a fifty-fifty chance that Bae moving my thighs up to my chest will sound like me when I'm at my parents' house for the holidays and it's three A.M. and I ever-so-delicately touch the plastic lid on the store-bought cake and crinkle noises reverberate for half a minute.

In summary: I AM OLD. And instead of fighting it, I'm leaning into it. So bring on the bags of Werther's Originals, having a strong opinion about how to fold fitted sheets, and writing in cursive. I know, I know. Calligraphy is making a comeback as a relaxing adult activity, but if you're out here writing whole-ass letters to friends in cursive, you are, at the very least, pre-menopausal aka your puss puss needs a Ricola and a cup of Throat Coat tea to stay lubed up. But back to the matter at hand.

Despite all the thoughts that pop into my head pre-sex, there's one that reigns supreme. Prior to British Baekoff, almost every time since I started having sex, I would think, *Please don't sit on my bed in your outside clothes, please don't sit on my bed in your outside clothes, please don't sit on my bed in your outside clothes*, as if it's an incantation that would magically make my suitor of the moment suddenly be mindful of the germs that his clothing is harboring and put a pin in the passion for a few minutes so he could take off what he's wearing, fold it all neatly, then wash his hands before coming to bed.

Now, I suspect this whole "threat of outside clothes contaminating household furniture" is, to put it lightly, a cultural thing because "Please don't sit on my bed in your outside clothes" is a directive I've said to almost every white being entering my space. White parents. White friends. White dogs. That said, when it comes to men, race doesn't necessarily matter. It seems that for all men, particularly the straight ones, this fear that I have isn't top of mind for them, although if a Black dude is on the receiving end of this request, he's not surprised. He simply responds with some variation on, "Yep, got it. My grandma used to say this to me all the time when I was growing up." And if you're still not convinced that this is a cultural request because you don't have enough empirical data aka no friends of color, then I will appease you by chalking it up to being a Robinson special.

Now, I gave you a sneak peek into who Ma and Pa Robinson are as people in the previous essay, but that amuse-bouche isn't enough. Oh, how I wish you could spend some time with them, but that isn't in the cards because they have zero interest in meeting anyone new for the rest of their lives. I mean, they treated an all-expenses-paid trip to meet Michelle Obama like it was an offer to shovel cow dung on Old McDonald's farm, so you're foolin' yourself if you think my parents will view hanging out with you as anything other than precious time they could spend driving to and from a Redbox kiosk to rent a DVD. Yes, my brother hooked them up with a Netflix account. Yes, I got them HBO Max. Yes, they pay for Hulu. But apparently, it's not enough and they need to waste gas and pollute the planet so they can get the latest direct-to-video John Cena movie. Honestly, I wanna tell on them to Greta Thunberg so she can give them a stern talking-to about how they're contributing to climate change, so they will stop going to Redbox to rent wack movies. But I digress. The point is my parents are delightful and you will never meet them, so the next best thing is me sharing three key facts that'll give you deep insight into Phillip and Octavia Robinson.

Number one, they *love* keeping track of how long it's been since they were last sick the way an alcoholic counts the days of their sobriety. No matter how much I remind my mom and dad that this information isn't worth bragging about, that no chip awaits them to mark their achievement, they'll find a way to work it into conversation.

"Mom, I'm having trouble with my taxes. Can you download your accountant wisdom into me real quick?"

"Well, it's funny you mention 1099 independent contractor forms . . ."

"I mean, I didn't—"

"Because it's been *1,099 days* since influenza last felled me."

Secondly, the parental units are incredibly giving and selfless people. A present from them is usually the item you mentioned months ago that you since forgot about, but they never did. When the family fell on hard times while I was in high school, my mom walked several miles to and from work every day because they decided that losing their car due to being behind on payments was better than pulling me out of private prep school halfway through junior year. And as many parents were having to deal with the reality of homeschooling their children while working from home during Covid-19, my dad volunteered to homeschool my charmingly precocious niece to help lessen the stress my brother and sister-in-law had due to their demanding jobs. I know that saying "Feelings aren't facts," but I feel like my parents are fucking amazing and there's no convincing me that isn't one of the purest and truest facts.

And, finally, the third piece of information to complete this sketch of my parents is their unwavering belief that there should be a deep divide between the outside world and the holy cleanliness of their home. Growing up, there was never this bipartisan, reaching-across-the-aisle, "both sides of the argument are valid." To them, outside is a hellscape full of unhygienic people and trifling surfaces whose sole reason for existence is to disrupt the harmony they've painstakingly created. Since I can remember, after each week of us coming and going from work, school, extracurricular activities, parties, dates, and study groups, my parents would do a deep clean of THE ENTIRE HOUSE, including dusting, mopping, and washing the baseboards. This is a task that, to this day, they still carry out like clockwork every seven days.

Just to do a quick study in contrasts, after eight months of quarantining in our apartment, Baekoff and I hired cleaners to get our home back on track. Once they were finished, they told him how dusty our apartment was. Admittedly, that's mostly my fault because he's very neat and I'm a slob kebab, but they ain't know that! All they knew was they spent the previous four hours wishing they were wearing eye goggles because the amount of dust kicked up made them feel like they were in that sandstorm scene from *Mission: Impossible— Ghost Protocol*. While they were annoyed, they weren't stupid, so they basically waited until the wire payment and tip went through like a heist and then, with some bass in their voices, they low-key cussed us out with such pinpoint accuracy that it felt as though these three Russian queens took ESL specifically to tell my boyfriend and me that the air quality in our apartment wasn't suitable for their precious lungs! Meanwhile, the baseboards at my parents' crib are pulling a Mariah Carey by going "Dust mites? I don't know her" every damn day. In summary, if my parents are the epitome of the phrase "Cleanliness is next to godliness," then Bae and I represent "Unkemptness is next to a pile of unfresh drawers in Beelzebub's walk-in closet."

Clearly, Phil and Octavia strive to keep a sanitary home, and they aren't going to let anything get in their way. Not even their kids. And not even each other. When my brother and I were younger and we'd come indoors from playing outside, there were no greetings, nor inquiries about how playtime was. Our parents were straight up like "Do not pass go. Do not collect two hundred dollars. Y'all are funky. Take a shower." Daring to sit down on the couch after coming home from school was just inviting them to ask us if we knew how many trifling people we interacted with. If you guessed that the answer was "all of them," you are correct. And when my brother and I wanted to prove our independence by sitting on the beds in our respective bedrooms, our parents' Spidey senses would tingle, they'd catch us in the act, and they'd make us change our clothes. As for how our parents treated each other, on numerous occasions, I've seen my mom rebuke a kiss from my dad because he smelled like "outside."

While my aversion to the outside invading my home isn't on par with my parents', the decree of not sitting on my bed in my outside clothes is one I've been living by since I moved out of their home. And I can't tell you why. Perhaps it's just that the lesson stuck with me, and I'm sure there are others my parents wish made the cut. Like the fact that they are very passionate about wearing house shoes. Whenever I come home to visit, my parents marvel at how I can walk barefoot from the bedroom to the kitchen to get breakfast. And I want to be like, "Am I breaking some rule of decorum, because, Mom, you've been wearing that same floral nightgown since I was a child, and thanks to all the years of wear and tear, it's as sheer as Dita Von Teese's hosiery, so I think you can handle my bare-ass feet on your floors." So, house shoes? That concept didn't really take. But the no-outside-clothes thing? Stuck to me like glue.

Even in college, which was difficult to enforce because the average dorm room's furniture consisted of a desk, a chair, and a bed that typically served as a communal seating area. I'm sure in my friends' eyes, I was the equivalent of Nurse Ratched, but whenever I considered loosening up, I couldn't get the image of them sitting on the New York City subway and then coming to crash on my Target brand Room Essentials bedding. But, still, every once in a while, a friend would wear me down, so I would offer up a corner at the foot of my bed, which I thought was generous. Looking back on it, forcing grown-ass folks to sit with 90 percent of their butt cheeks hanging off the edge of a bed as I starfished on my comforter was rude as hell. But! Not as rude as the one time a crush of mine came over to watch a movie with me, made a beeline for my bed, and sat squarely on one of my pillows. *Oh, hell no.* Y'all, pillow sitters are quite the bold type. #OnlyOnFreeform. Like, I'm talking "former president of the United States Bill Clinton, a well-read and highly intelligent man who wanted to do anything but cop to his affair with Monica Lewinsky, so he stalled his impeachment hearing by asking for clarity on the meaning of the word 'is'" kind of bold. Because when you are POTUS, attended Georgetown University and Oxford University, and lived long enough to be an AARP member, to feign an inconceivable amount of ignorance and think everyone around you will fall for it is a level of confidence I want to aspire toward. And I believe that is the nerve my crush had to think it was okay to put his denim behind on my pillow. Did I say anything to him about it? Naw, I liked him too much. But did I tell every single friend about this unsanitary nightmare? Abso-fucking-lutely.

All these years later, multiple friends from college have reminded me about how strict I was about outside clothes. BEING TYPE A IS FUN AND NOT AT ALL EXHAUSTING FOR MYSELF OR THE PEOPLE AROUND ME! But also, my personality must've been straight trash if this whole "no sitting on my bed in your outside clothes" made it into the Phoebe Robinson highlight reel all these years later. So you know what this means: A fair percentage of the eulogies at my funeral are gonna be doo-doo because I was boring as hell for a very long time. Of course, I could make up for lost time, make a bunch of new friends, rack up some fresh experiences such as skydiving and getting a tattoo. But honestly, I'm just gonna waste money on legal and notary fees so a lawyer can draft a will that won't contain any info about what I'm bequeathing to whom, but will just be the following declaration they must read aloud: IF PHOEBE TOLD YOU THAT YOU COULDN'T SIT ON HER BED, YOU CAN'T SAY SHIT AT THE FUNERAL. JUST WEAR BLACK, EAT A SAD-ASS THREE-BEAN CASSEROLE, AND NAIL THE MOTHERFUCKING KEY CHANGE WHEN YOU SING PUFF DADDY'S "I'LL BE MISSING YOU" AT KARAOKE IN HER HONOR.

The point is, as much as I try and fight it (and I'm not trying that hard, trust), not allowing anyone to sit on my bed in their outside clothes is a rule I live by, and is a defining part of my personality, it seems. And I think everyone is like that. We all have guiding principles that govern our lives in big ways and small that don't always make sense to other people. Those guiding principles can become set in stone out of habit, or because something just resonates with you on a deep spiritual level and you don't feel complete without it. Whatever the case may be, it means something to you, so you hold on to it. And potential petri dish concerns aside, this outside-clothes business is something that, no matter where I am when I express this mandate, makes me feel connected to my parents and all their lovable quirks. And like they're in the room with me. Most important, as you age, you're more cognizant of your parents aging as well, and that may cause you to look fondly on all the lessons, tips, and oddities they passed down to you over the years. And I know for a fact that my parents love doing that with me and my brother, sister-in-law, niece, and nephew. Whether it's a note, an email, or a quick word, they want to leave us with every bit of knowledge. I like that. Even when I don't want to hear it. Because at least I know they care.

Well, dear reader, even though we've yet to meet, I care about you. I want you to live a deliciously rich, highly specific, and wonderfully weird life. And I would like to help. You know those people who don't have kids, so they want to impart wisdom to any- and everyone they meet, especially other people's children; meanwhile, the parents are making faces that say, "Please do not listen to this person that I'm unfortunately related to by blood"? Well, I'm going to be that auntie for y'all whether you want that or not. And the first thing I'm imploring you to do if you haven't already (and especially because of the coronavirus of it all) is to never again sit on your *own* beds in your outside clothes. I brought this up on social media and people were telling on themselves, revealing their trifling ways, and trying to find loopholes like they're a rich celebrity who wants to get out of paying taxes:

- *I'm sorry. What are "outside clothes"? Are they not just clothes?! I can sleep in the same clothes I wore that day, wake up the next morning, and wear them out again. (I love social media for showing us all the different ways people live.)* I don't. This is no way to live and I ain't need to see it. Wish I was like Guy Pearce in *Memento* because I would intentionally forget to tattoo this fuckery on my body, so I could one day forget it. But I can't, so I'm left to be haunted by the thought of someone GOING OUTSIDE, BEING AROUND THIS DIRTY-ASS WORLD, AND THEN COMING HOME AND GETTING INTO BED.
- *So wait . . . say I get up in the morning and decide I want to pop out and get a coffee. I'm supposed to change into full "outside clothes" to go across the street for my coffee and then back into my pajamas when I get home? And then later when I need to run to the store or take out the garbage, I'm supposed to change into new outside clothes and then back into my pajamas when I come inside again? WHAT KIND OF MADNESS IS THIS??? I get up in the morning and get dressed for the day, no matter how many times I go outside during the day. My pajamas only go on when it's time to sleep.* Oh, boy. This. Is. Rough. And no, we're not "hanging

tough." #MomJoke #NewKidsOnTheBlockForever. For real though, I'm at a loss for words. If you're going outside multiple times a day, just have an "outside clothes" outfit by your front door that you change in and out of and then put it in the laundry bin at the end of the night. Why are we acting like that's *not* an option? Why are we behaving as though changing in and out of PJs is akin to doing high school trig?

- *Okay, yes, but: Let's say BonBon comes over to hang out with you, and he casually sits on your bed wearing his outside clothes. WHAT DO YOU DO?!* Call him a Lyft to take him to JFK Airport and kick his ass out. I am too old to be playing games with someone damn near twice my age. And he too grown not to know that if he wanna sit on my bed, he needs to bring a day bag and change clothes in the guest bathroom once he gets to my home.
- *I've never heard of outside clothes! I just wear my same clothes everywhere.* What the fuck? You never heard of them?! Bitch, did or didn't Mr. Rogers, as soon as he stepped inside his home, take off his red cardigan and shoes? Quit acting brand-new. You know what? We need to start redlining heauxes and if you don't have outside clothes, around-the-house clothes, and in-bed clothes: YOU. CAN'T. VOTE.

As you can see, many people out in the world (and maybe even you) need my gahtdamn help, so I'm assembling some of my most precious knowledge, opinions, and hot takes that I've accumulated throughout my life and sharing them with you. You can let me know in thirty years or so which of these have stuck with you:

PHOEBE-ISM #1:
RICH PEOPLE AIN'T ALLOWED
TO POST NOTHING KITCHEN-RELATED
ONLINE NO MO'

This might sound strange, but I secretly enjoy being humbled. Maybe it's just the masochist in me, but I believe that once my bruised ego has healed, I can see that the offense was to keep me in check. I'll give you an example. I have a personal assistant named Zoe who is smart, literally looks like a model, and is eleven years younger than me, so yes, I feel as old as fuck around her and, of course, my director of operations aka Mai, whom I already told you about. They're lovely human beings without whom I would not be able to keep my multiple businesses running. They're also the yin to my yang because I'm an entertainer who is fine with taking up space with my loud presence and they are . . . how do I put this? "The Sound of Silence" is their nash anth. They're quite comfortable leaving me hanging after I tell a joke. So, usually, during our hour-long videoconferences, they just stare blankly back at me after 80 percent of my jokes. The 20 percent that do elicit laughter typically end abruptly as if there's a conductor just off-screen signaling the end of a concerto. At first, I was like, "Da fuq?" but now, when they don't laugh at a joke, it reminds me to feel grateful I'm not surrounded by sycophants, and instead, I work harder until I truly give these shy queens something to laugh about. They keep me humble, which is a good thing. Another moment that keeps my feet squarely planted on the ground? When a rich friend or celebrity gives the world a sneak peek at how they're living.

The kitchen British Backoff and I have is the first grown-up kitchen I've ever had in my adult life. Instead of a ragtag group of plates, bowls, and saucers, we own a complete matching dish set. Coasters so that our coffee table no longer has condensation rings that make it look like a distant cousin to Michael Phelps's back after a cupping session. We even have an Instant Pot, dishwasher, and a SodaStream. Although these may seem like run-of-the-mill staples that I should've possessed before I entered my midthirties, owning them makes me feel like Padma Lakshmi minus the bank account and looks.

Then one day, I Marco Polo'd[1] with a close American friend who now splits her time between London and Greece with her rich husband. On the day she Polo'd, she was in the middle of Greek holiday prep at their vacation home by the ocean. I know her life sounds perfect, but just like all of ours, it isn't. She's been through it. Anyway, since I've never been to her vacation home in Greece, she wanted to give me a video tour. In NYC, an apartment video tour consists of just holding up

---

1. Essentially, the Marco Polo app is the video version of text messaging, in which we all can live out our direct-to-camera *The Real World* confessional dreams and communicate with friends and loved ones on our terms with no pressure on the other party to have to respond right away. Holy hell, we're a noncommittal generation.

your iPhone and going, "There. That's it." Not the case for her. They have a butler's pantry. A second kitchen. The dishes the average person daydreams about cooking but then settles for ordering from Seamless for dinner? She actually makes them! As she was going through the tour, she zoomed in on the bone broth she was making because she had a hankering for it. Usually, when a person has a hankering for something, it's a bag of chips or a burger, ya know, a desire that can be satiated in thirty minutes or less. Bone broth takes like *nine hours* to make. That is the Kama Sutra of hankerings.

As much as I tease, I know deep down that she means no harm. A world that includes multiple homes and making bone broth simply because she's in the mood for it is her normal and she'll be the first to deliver an incredulous look to me mid-convo that connotes, "Yes, I know this is slightly ridiculous, but this is my life now, so let's laugh about it." So I don't mind when she dips in and out of #UnrelatableContent because her self-awareness is on point. The same cannot be said for the average celebrity or an influencer, especially during the first wave of coronavirus-related quarantine. It seemed as if every day, a different famous person was posting sixteen-, eighteen-, twenty-ingredient-long recipes that they *swore* us plebs could replicate. Look, I get it; the old adage goes "Sharing is caring," but sometimes the sharing felt as if we were using our 5G to be a witness to a show called *Look How Much I'm Thriving* that none of us asked for.

One time during the 'tine, this celeb, who shall go unnamed because I do love this person a lot, was walking us through a dinner we can all make at home. They started listing ingredients like water and I was like, "Ooo, relatable," and got suckered in. Yes, I'm a simple bitch. Anyway, as this person was listing ingredients, they started sharing their tip about where they get their spices and began with, "Williams Sonoma has—." Nope! I'm out. If the company sounds like a law firm, I'm not purchasing my seasoning from there. Generic store-brand parsley flakes taste just as good (they probably don't, but just go with me).

Even though I was out, I couldn't turn away from this cooking tutorial because my gut instinct told me it was going to get absurd. And 'surd it did become because this celeb mentioned chipolatas. If you don't know, cuz I didn't, a chipolata is a small spicy sausage used chiefly as a garnish or hors d'oeuvre. Wayament, we out here using sausages as a *garnish*?!?! Oh, so you *rich* rich. When you're that rich, shouldn't you spend your evenings moonlighting as a vigilante à la Bruce Wayne? Before I could ponder that question, this heaux was like, "And next, you'll want to add in some fresh prawns." LOL. Who had fresh prawns on deck in those times or any other? Possessing fresh prawns on a regular-ass Tuesday because there's a chance you may need them is definitely not what the governors meant when they asked us to go to the grocery store and stock up on provisions. Like, as I was fighting to get the last of the Angel Soft two-ply, I saw a chick running past me whilst carrying a carton of eggs like she was on Team Jamaica in the 4 × 100 relay race at the Summer Olympics. And here was this celeb basically acting out what would be their last meal before their castle was stormed during a coup. WE ARE NOT LIVING THE SAME LIFE.

You know how bands are typically four or five people, so when you see Edward Sharpe & the Magnetic Zeros, which has ten members, your brain overloads from all the questions: Are their residual checks just fifty-seven cents each? Have they ever decided on dinner in under an hour? Who is having sex with whom? What?! That's a reasonable question. I mean, you telling me that Fleetwood Mac only had five people and they all fucked one another, but Sharpe & Zeros are just settling for hand hugs? Anyway, this level of confusion is what I feel when I see these recipes that have a laundry list of ingredients. So new rule: If your recipe requires more than twelve ingredients, do not share it under the guise of something we can *all* do because that's a lie.

I understand these famous people meal tutorials aren't done maliciously. Usually, they just seem bored (and are most likely motivated by the high they get from the attention and social media worship). Still, these videos tend to show how out of touch these folks can be. Acquiring all the ingredients for these meals requires shopping at multiple markets and stores, which is most likely done by someone who is paid to shop so the celeb can spend their time dealing with more pertinent matters. It also means having hundreds of dollars to spare so they can have what the average person would consider a "dinner of their dreams" on a lazy Monday night. So while the attempt may be to remind the public that celebs are just like us, the truth is they're not. That's why I want these celebs to stop pretending and just own it. Like if one of them opened their cooking video with, "Even though for many years I was living paycheck to paycheck, I got money now, so

I'm a bougie bitch and I'm about to make an expensive-ass meal in my expensive-ass kitchen. Don't worry, I will definitely be indicted for tax evasion in about seven to ten years and be brought back down to earth and purchasing Hunt's brand tomato paste right along with ya, but until then? I'm putting saffron on everything. These grits. My tits. *Everything*." At least that would be honest. Unsanitary but honest.

PHOEBE-ISM #2:
IT IS ABSOLUTELY IGNORANT YET COMPLETELY ACCEPTABLE TO WEAR BLUE LIGHT GLASSES OUTSIDE YOUR HOUSE

In many ways, I've unwittingly spent my whole life working toward my dream aesthetic: manager of a college bursar's office. Y'all know who I'm talking about. She's usually a fifty-something Black woman who walks around by dragging her feet, glasses dangling from the glasses chain hanging around her neck, a rubber spiral keychain living on her wrist, and she always has a folder in her hand that she intends to file throughout the day, but never does. You take one look at her and you just *know* her sweet potato pie tastes good as hell and that she ends all her conversations with, "Well, I'mma let you go," and then continues talking to you for another thirty minutes. This woman is my Kwanzaa future that I'm tired of waiting for to arrive. Deep down, I wish I was already fifty-seven years old, so some young whippersnapper would show me a picture of Jason Momoa and I could respond with, "Mmm, that's a

good-looking boy. Yeah, I like that right there." I mean, techni-
cally, I can and *do* do that now, but it's not the same. When
you're AARP age, you can be as vocally horny as you want
without judgment. In fact, it's cute. Endearing. Encouraged,
even! As an older person reveals their lusty thoughts, a gaggle
of heauxes from *Grease* seems to appear out of nowhere with
a refrain of "Tell me more, tell me more!" in a key of Cialis.
Because life is long and hard, the least people can do is grant
elders time to indulge in the harmless fun of objectifying celebrities they will never meet.

However, when you're in your midthirties and mildly
attractive, a few people think you're actually plottin' and thot-
tin'. Case in point: When I posted on Instagram about Lenny
Kravitz's shirtless October 2020 *Men's Health* cover and how I
wished to be baptized in the jojoba oil he uses to keep his locks
on point, someone commented, accusatorially I might add:
"Don't you have a boyfriend?" Yes, HEAUX, I do! And? I ain't
got a shot at banging Lenny Kravitz! The commenter acted like
I was talking about hooking up with my next-door neighbor
named Dave. It's Leonard Albert Kravitz. Everyone, including
my boyfriend, would smash Lenny Kravitz. So me saying that
I would hypothetically hook up with a celebrity I have ZERO
ACCESS to, by the way, is not a sign I'm trying to cheat, but an
expression of fact. The sky is blue. 2 + 2 = 4. I would toss my
NuvaRing in the trash if I was about to bone Lenny Kravitz.
All straight-up facts. And if these internet strangers are too
busy to write on my posts about hot celebs, they'll just tag British Baekoff in the comments as if to say, "Have you seen what
this bitch is out here doing?" The answer is: yes. Like I said, life

is long and so are relationships, so me spending twenty minutes waxing *ho*etic about a famous sexy dude is twenty minutes that my boyfriend has without me in his grill, asking him to do unpaid IT work around our apartment. Truthfully, you haven't lived until a British person's query of "Have you tried restarting your computer?" is *drenched* in condescension, covered in panko bread crumbs, and baked at 180 degrees Celsius. But I digress. The point is, I have always aspired toward rocking the managerial look, especially the glasses part.

Growing up, kids were teased for wearing glasses, made to feel as though their less-than-perfect vision was a weakness, but to me, glasses signaled someone who is smart, respected, studious. A person who has all the answers. So when I got older, despite my 20/20 vision, I decided to give glasses a whirl. Meaning in high school, I went through a stint of wearing fake eyeglasses in class while taking notes on *Gulliver's Travels*. Can I do a spin-off of Barack Obama's book *The Audacity of Hope* and call it *The Audacity of Nope* in which I chronicle this goofy-ass mess? Like, despite all the messaging I received from movies and TV shows in which the female character is considered a babe only *after* she would "de-glass," my sixteen-year-old behind was like, "Lemme have my mom drive me to Dillard's—LOL—so I can get some unsexy and fake glasses to pair with my turtleneck dickeys and show off how interesting and learned I am, which will surely be the key to unlocking my virginity." Ooooh, boy. I think it goes without saying that my virginity remained locked and dead-bolted for quite some time, but at least I helped Dillard's stay in business. Anyway, I quickly realized that fetishizing wearing eyeglasses was ridiculous. I outgrew this phase and have carried on life sans eyeglasses. Until Covid-19 happened.

Suddenly, I was on Zoom, staring at my computer screen several hours a day. The glare and strain took their toll and soon I was getting headaches. Then a friend turned me on to blue light glasses, which, allegedly, are supposed to make the effects of staring at a screen all day lessen or disappear. And because I have good taste, I chose a couple of frames that fit my face perfectly. I received so many compliments on my Quay blue light glasses and snazzy eyeglass chains during Zooms that I started wearing them when I wasn't at the computer. I'd throw them on while reading a book, eating lunch, and doing dishes. I'd call Bae into the room, just so I could dramatically take off my glasses and say, "Objection, Your Honor." He would shake his head, but he couldn't deny the cuteness.

That's when I thought, *Well, if I'm looking this good, then everybody needs to see this.* While everyone is masked up and scurrying away from one another to keep their distance and/ or rushing to get back home, the outdoors and every store became Quay Blue Light Glasses Fashion Week for me. What Naomi Campbell did for Versace by strutting the catwalks in Milan, I was going to do for blue light glasses by sporting them in Target as I searched for Preparation H for my boyfriend. And honestly, that sounds about right. Naomi is synonymous with couture and I guess I am synonymous with . . . troubleshooting tender buttholes while donning Angela Lansbury in *Murder, She Wrote* cosplay.

Yeaaaaah, that's not really how I envisioned my public life with blue light glasses going down, but to be complimented on my hipster frames while holding a box of Preparation H gel has gotta mean *something*. Normal societal code is that when you see another human shopping for something terribly personal, you pull a U-ey and hope the twenty-five knots of wind gust from said U-ey doesn't alert the person that you hightailed it outta there to avoid secondhand embarrassment. However, this stranger saw the Preperaysh and soldiered on toward me. Maybe they really did like my glasses that much and just had to let me know, or maybe they felt pity over what they imagined my butt emergency to be and wanted to give me an ego boost. Whatever the case may have been, the point is that the kindness from a stranger has to be a testament to just how damn good I looked with the glasses on. So, I'm committing to rocking my blue light glasses out in public with chunky glasses chains and all as I inch closer toward my destiny as a horny middle-aged office manager.

PHOEBE-ISM #3:
FOR THE LOVE OF GOD,
WEAR MATCHING UNDERWEAR

I don't have the evidence to prove this theory, but I believe that people who wear mismatched underwear every single day of their lives are the same people who are the worst teammates to have in a game of Pictionary. Much like a game of Pictionary where teammates are given quality and obvious clues and, in return, they provide terrible answers, ad campaigns, runway shows, and store mannequins constantly give women a visual guide on how to succeed at wearing coordinating underwear without really trying; however, time and time again, these folks put on underwear all slapdash like the Lyft XL that's picking them up from their *Eyes Wide Shut* orgy went from "arriving in ten minutes" on the app to "Sahit is here" within seconds. I. Just. Don't. Get. It. Is the mismatching a cry for help? Are you hoping it will keep you in the running of being one of *Glamour* magazine's Female Disruptors of 2021? Do you honestly not care that your skivvies don't go together? I mean, how can you not??

Now, I'm aware this stance of mine screams "peak type A" or is maybe inspired by that irrational fear some have about dying whilst wearing clashing Underoos. I mean, if morgue attendees launch into a Comedy Central roast at the mere sight of my corpse wearing a bra that does not go with the pair of boy shorts on my body, then consider me their muse. At that point, I'm dead, in Heaven, and chilling with Aretha Franklin and her hat from the 2009 Obama inauguration, so say what you want about my body.

In all seriousness, there's no grand reason for my staunch belief in matching Underoos other than wearing matching underwear is . . . the . . . obvious thing . . . to . . . do? Think about it. When Rihanna throws her Savage × Fenty Fashion Week shows, the models and celebs waltz down the catwalk in coordinating ensembles. When you're shopping online for underwear, the companies respect the price of your Wi-Fi enough to not waste your money by showing you images of models wearing a lacy bra with saggy granny panties. And the mannequins in the GapBody section aren't doing their job if they're dressed like it's laundry day. Clearly, the Universe (as well as good old common sense) is, at every turn, showing us just how easy it is to achieve this. Like all we have to do is command + C and then command + V what we're looking at onto our bodies. Except people act like this shit is impossible.

If I tell a girlfriend that I always wear matching underwear, the common response is, "Who has the time?" Literally all of us. It absolutely takes the same amount of time to pick out a matching underwear set as it does to Choose Your Own Adventure it. The other refrain I get is, "Well, no one is gonna see it, so it doesn't matter." Just because you're not planning on having sex with anyone that day doesn't mean no one is seeing it. Bitch, *you* see it! You know and control what you have on beneath your clothes. Put some effort in! Dress to impress yourself and feel good. And I'm not talking fancy underwear either.

I know there are some people who wear *only* designer lingerie, and unless you're in the Pussycat Dolls and you're on call to show up at house parties and over-sing while scantily clad, no one's asking for all that. The basics will do. And before you accuse me of being a privileged gal whose underwear buying is easy, rest assured it's not. I'm a 36A. Plenty of bras don't come in that size, or if they do, the majority are padded like a Casper memory foam mattress so I can appear to have a C cup because I'm not "womaning" properly unless I possess a heaving bosom. Out of principle and because there's nothing wrong with having small tatas, I refuse to wear padded bras. So if an underwear set doesn't come in my bra size or have a nonpadded option, I just don't get it. Sure, this is quite limiting, but I would rather 90 percent of my underwear sets have me looking like

I'm about to go to volleyball practice—#SportsBraNaysh—than to look like I put on underwear in the dark. And if wearing coordinating undies for yourself doesn't move you, then fine. Dress to impress others. For the potential that today might be the day you catch some strange, and if making a good first sexy-times impression is *still* not enough to motivate you, then perhaps you're a lost cause?

Like when people are on the heaux patrol and still aren't wearing matching underwear, I feel like Gordon Ramsay on *Hell's Kitchen* when the cheftestant perfectly cooks the entrée and dresses the plate beautifully before bringing it up to the pass to be served. Gor-Gor gives the plate a once-over, turns, and screams, at no one in particular, "WHERE'S THE LAMB SAUCE, YOU DONKEY?" Like, you put in all this effort into delivering sexy banter, you're rocking an outfit that shows off your body perfectly, yet you select your underwear the way people pick groceries on *Supermarket Sweep*: grabbing whatever the fuck. That ain't no way to live. So, for the love of God, wear matching underwear.

PHOEBE-ISM #4:
TRULY NO ONE CARES THAT YOUR
IN-BOX IS DOWN TO ZERO
SO SHUT THE HELL UP

I SAID WHAT I SAID. I'm so over people bragging about answering all their emails in a day like this is some great achievement. Calm. Down. You're not going to be rewarded with a campaign of your face on a box of Wheaties. There's no blue ribbon waiting to be pinned into your lapel. It's just *emails*. Even worse than those people who behave like they are the Simone Biles of Microsoft Outlook are the people who go, "I can't go to sleep at night unless my in-box is at zero." An unanswered email has you so distraught that you can't go to bed? Allow me to introduce you to my new email signature: "I'm getting a FULL EIGHT HOURS of sleep because I'm not responding to your bullshit right now and I feel GREAT about it," which is accompanied by a thumbnail pic of me deep in slumber. Is that extremely petty and aggressive? Yes, but sometimes these heauxes need a reminder that if "Black don't crack" under the stress of Jim Crow, then it for damn sure ain't gonna crack because Matt's trifling ass is emailing me (and cc'ing the main person at my job I *don't* like) at 6:43 P.M. for clarity on a project I obviously don't give a fuck about. Trust and believe I'm getting my proper eight hours of sleep every night, I'm waking with no visible signs of aging, and I'm waiting until he hits me with the "Hey . . . just circling back about this" email two days later before I respond.

PHOEBE-ISM #5:
EATING A COUGH DROP IS FOR EVERY OCCASION, NOT JUST WHEN YOU'RE SICK

Everyone has their own "old person" thing—wearing a jacket when it's not even cold outside, taking naps, getting to the mall right the fuck when it opens, etc.—and I guess a steady diet of cough drops is mine. It's not like I have a nagging cough, I don't wear out my throat from all the talking I have to do for work, and I'm not constantly sick. One day, I just woke up and decided to turn Halls Defense assorted citrus flavor cough drops into around-the-clock amuse-bouches.

At first, I started small, like the eight-piece packages that you buy at the checkout counter in a gas station, or the twenty-five-piece when I just wanted to have some around the house in case I got a tickle in my throat during the winter months. It has now escalated to me ordering multiple two-hundred-count value packs online and eating about thirty of them nightly before bedtime. This is ignorant enough. The worst part is when Bae and I have decided to go to sleep. We'll turn off the lights and television. Kiss each other good night before rolling back over to our respective sides of the bed. A full five minutes of silence will pass. He is clearly falling asleep and then he'll be awakened by the sounds of me slowly unwrapping one last bedtime Halls and putting it in my mouth.

Why is it that when it's absolutely silent and you go to unwrap something, the wrapping paper is made out of trees and Sonos technology? I mean, where's the shiplap to drown the crinkling out? Oh, *all* of it is in Waco, Texas, thanks to Chip and Joanna Gaines renovating everyone's houses to Luke Bryan music on *Fixer Upper* from 2013 to 2018? Well, *thanks* for that. Anyway, British Baekoff is now awake from my Halls unwrapping and we laugh. Back to quiet . . . until a few minutes later, I'm equal parts drowsy and terrified that I'm going to fall asleep, choke on the cough drop, and die. So, I turn my mouth into a loud-ass trash compactor as I crush the mostly undissolved Halls between my molars, thus awakening him once more. I. Do. This. Every. Night. You know when you watch the local news and someone is arrested for murdering their spouse over something trivial such as changing the channel? Baekoff and I have jokingly decided that if thirty years from now he murders me, it's because he refused to let another night's sleep be interrupted by my cough drop chewing. But at least I died living my truth and you should, too, so keep on keeping on with doing those tiny little things that annoy your partner.

PHOEBE-ISM #6:
DOGS AREN'T MY BEST FRIEND.
WE HAVE HUMANS FOR THAT!

I know, I know! This is blasphemous to express, but I gotta live my truth. I don't get the hype about dogs, to which folks see that as a challenge and say enthusiastically, "Wait until you meet my dog!" I do, and still nothing. I am not moved. My heart has not expanded. I'm still just me and thoroughly un-impressed by it all. Yep, I saw them do the thing where they shake your paw and get a treat. Uh-huh, nice party trick. And yes, their ears perking up when they know they're about to go for a nice long walk is cute, I suppose. Them wanting to cud-dle up beside you every time you sit on the couch is . . . a bit thirsty? Don't you want space? No? Okay, guess I'll just stand over here, third-wheeling it.

Before I go any further, now would be a good time to state

that I'm not anti-dogs. As a Black person, I have to make this clear. Thanks to yet another ignorant stereotype about Black people, it may seem that because I'm not down with dogs slobbering all over my face I must want them to vanish from existence like this is the end of *Avengers: Endgame*. False! I'm just a Black person who happens to not care much for dogs. And before some of you get too excited, I'm not a cat lady either. Like, this isn't a cats vs. dogs situaysh. I'm disinterested in it all, to be honest.

I never had pets growing up nor did I yearn for one. I was content with my Sega Genesis, my TV shows, and tagging along with my older brother on whatever ill-advised adventures he wanted to embark on. Believe me, I'm surprised, too, because I was definitely a kid who, if her classmates or friends got something, I was asking Ma and Pa Robinson for that very thing. Cable? Def. American Girl doll? You betcha. But if someone got a dog, I was #TeamHardPass. I've just never desired having a pet in general, which the average person seems to accept, but in the same breath will be like, "But *dogs*, though. You should get one." Thankfully, I'm allergic to any and all pet dander, which was my Get Out of Jail Free card, meaning I didn't have to interact with anyone else's dog, and it was an easy way to shut down conversations where I was being gently encouraged to change my mind and get a dog. Then hypoallergenic dogs became all the rage once I became an adult and all of sudden, my Get Out of Jail Free card was viewed as an excuse, or as a sign that I lack the belief that I, too, can fulfill my destiny as a pet owner.

It goes like this. I tell people I'm allergic to dogs, so I'd rather not. *But my dog is hypoallergenic. It's fine!* Bitch, I'm trying to be polite. Even if I could handle being around pets without an itchy throat, a runny nose, watery eyes, and routine sneeze attacks, I. Don't. Want. To. Touch. Your. Dog. Why do people act like because their dogs are hypoallergenic, it's a game changer for my respiratory system and I'm all of a sudden gonna want to snort a line of labradoodle fur straight up my nostrils? Sometimes, a dog lover will take it a step further and offer advice on how I can easily change my entire life to accommodate the thing I do not want. *Oh, you know what you could do? Get a hypoallergenic dog, and if it's still a problem, you can just take allergy medicine every day for the rest of your life. That's what my wife / husband / mother / cousin / best friend does, and that way you can still experience the transformative love you'll get from having a dog.* That . . . is too much.

I'm actually quite fine with not experiencing profound love if it requires this much effort. I mean, I stopped shaving above the knee about four weeks after my boyfriend and I started dating. I'm pretty sure a big part of love is people agreeing that putting in sustained effort is not really what they signed up for. Like the goal is to find your partner in crime who is also done trying. So if I'm low-key phoning it in with my soul mate, what makes you think I'm willing to resign myself to a life of taking Claritin in the hopes that I can breathe out of *both* nostrils for twenty-three minutes a day? *But when you get home from work, they're RIGHT there, so happy to see you.* I can think of few things more annoying than my big toe barely grazing my entryway rug and having someone getting all up in my grill with their excitement. *But they're your best friend.* My best friend is a grown-ass woman who, like me, knows how to handle her tequila, supported my questionable fashion choices throughout the years, and loves talking shit via text message when we're both in our respective business meetings. Fairly certain a rescue dog can't top that. Honestly, the *only* thing that is remotely appealing about having a dog is when people tell me they have to bounce from a party or a work event in order to get home. That's tight. I mean, the main joy of going out is coming the fuck back home and having a built-in reason that you can use anytime you want to leave (and that no one will make a fuss about) almost makes me consider having a pet for half a second. But then reality kicks in and reminds me of the plain and uninteresting truth that everyone refuses to accept: Dogs simply aren't my thing and that's okay.

That's it. There's nothing gnarly lurking in the shadows. I'm not emotionally closed off. I cried at *Marley & Me*; I feel things. I'm also not against being responsible for another living being, nor is my not wanting a dog because I'm a contrarian. I'm not secretly waiting to meet the one dog that's going to convert me into a dog lover. And finally and perhaps most important, I don't judge others whose lives *are* enriched and enlivened by having a dog. We're all entitled to need or not need certain things, people, experiences, journeys that will help us feel as though we've lived an overflowing, juicy, love-filled life. Me not having a dog is not an indictment against anyone else and their choices. I don't think you don't have taste because you have a dog; I think you don't have taste because you're walking your dog while wearing toe shoes, which is certainly the "fetch" of footwear. Get a grip. Oh wait . . . don't, actually. That's how you ended up in this footwear nightmare.

PHOEBE-ISM #7:
IT'S NOT TRUE LOVE IF . . . YOUR PARTNER DOESN'T GET WEIRD WITH YOU

After British Baekoff and I started dating, I constantly talked about how I wanted to finally go to Paris. He, being from the UK, is fully over Paris. He would always respond with some variation of "I could take the train to Paris anytime I wanted. The people are rude, The streets are dirty. It's overrated and not special." Okay, well, it is to me! A two-hour train ride from London got you to Paris. I'm from Ohio; a two-hour ride from my childhood house got us to Cedar Point Amusement Park. Clearly, our lives were drastically different growing up. And because BB knew that, he set aside his ill feelings about Paris and took me there during a summer vacation to visit his mom.

Baekoff and I were there for only two and a half days, but it was heaven. The food was delicious, the architecture was incredible. Romance was in the air. But the pièce de résistance? There was a bidet in our hotel room!!! Y'all, I lost my damn mind. He did not. Baekoff had used a bidet before, so he was very business-as-usual about it, even though he was amused by my childlike wonder. Honestly, no matter how many times one uses a bidet, how can they act chill when their bumhole is being shot at with a water gun like they're a carnival game and a stuffed Sheriff Woody doll is the reward? Anyway, I had never used a bidet before, let alone seen one IRL, so I wanted him to help me though this journey, so he offered to stand outside the bathroom door. But that wasn't enough for me. I made him stand in the bathroom, mere inches from me, with our eyes locked, as I peed and then used the bidet. DATING ME IS A SWEET TREAT! Could you imagine your partner forcing you to lock eyes as they're relieving themselves and then you had to go whisper sweet nothings in their ear over a shared croissant? Well, British Baekoff did it and did it with aplomb. In fact, the other day, I asked him how he felt about being a party to my bidet experience and he responded, "I felt undeniably closer to you." Nothing I appreciate more than a statement from the love of my life that I can't tell whether it's a compliment or a sad realization. Gotta love a man who can keep you on your toes! Anyway, the point is Baekoff just knows that sometimes I have to do things in my own little strange way. And holding a staring contest with him while I bidet'd for the first time in my life was one of those things, unbeknownst to both of us. What can I say? I'm a good improviser, so I can go with the flow. Oh, you thought improvisation is only for jazz and the Upright Citizens Brigade Theatre? That's just being small-minded.

Wow. I covered a lot and I probably have way too many opinions, but I've made it this far in life, so I must be doing something right. Thank you for letting me be your surrogate auntie. It's been an honor to overshare about my sex life, and if we were in the same room, I'd give you a handful of Halls and fifty dollars for your troubles and send you on your merry little way. Anyway, I hope you learned something and next time we hang out, I promise to be 3 percent less ignorant. Oh! One more thing: If you still have any questions about this whole sitting on your or anyone else's bed in your outside clothes, send them my way. I'm honored to be the Dr. Ruth of interior hygiene.

We Don't Need Another White Savior

I f, when you read that title, you did so in the melody of Tina Turner's "We Don't Need Another Hero (Thunderdome)," then you're my kind of person. Even if you didn't, you bought this book, so all the royalties I'm about to get (I'm talking them sweet, sweet FDR dimes and George Washington quarters) will help me continue to be able to afford some Calvin Klein bralettes—#JusticeForTheBoobDeficient—so you, too, are also my kind of person.

And since you're *all* my kind of peoples, may I be frank for a second? To be a person of color, especially Black, and live in America is to be born with the title of this essay in your bones, in an "I think, therefore, I don't need another white savior" kind of way. Shout out to René Descartes and the Descartes estate for letting me put the Bad Boy Remix on that centuries-old philosophical proposition. In all seriousness, rejecting the messiah complex energy that many white people can, intentionally or unintentionally, exude is innate within Black people, and rightfully so. Given (loud-as-fuck stage whisper) *slavery and literally every single thing after it*, being on guard is the safest and most sensible thing a Black person can do. So we tread lightly, especially when we encounter well-intentioned or newly enlightened turned know-it-alls, because one of two outcomes usually happens.

At best (but is it a "best"?), it's virtue signaling, which is rooted in easy, surface-level solutions to problems that are intrinsically complicated and difficult to solve, but, hey, at least these solutions let the world know these folks are on the right side of history. And at worst, the results can be self-serving. The actions reinforce the narrative that the only way to fight racism is to center whiteness and have white people swoop in to "save the day" by speaking on behalf of Black people in a "we know best" kind of way, which history has shown (e.g., white chefs attempting to lead the "soul food fusion" genre) is typically in direct opposition to what Black people actually want (in that case, proper seasoning), and also removes Black people's agency and disregards the knowledge and experience Black people have accumulated from their decades upon decades of antiracism work. And while both of these aforementioned outcomes are nothing new, in 2020 they appeared in record numbers. This is understandable given the way our society functions; however, I'm deeply concerned and more than a little frustrated that these signifiers of "progress" don't lead to changes that benefit Black people in any real, tangible way. And I know I'm not the only who feels this way, especially since we're all still living in a post-traumatic fog of the events of summer 2020 while enduring more harm with the string of violent 2021 attacks on Asian Americans and Pacific Islanders.

Simply put, summer 2020 was a gut-wrenching, soul-crushing, blood-boiling, debilitating, and scarring season that galvanized not just America, but the world. Racial uprisings happening against a backdrop of a global pandemic is something that no one should live through, and as heartbreaking as it was to have footage of George Floyd's murder circulating all over social media and news outlets,[1] it created a collective fury. While the jury is still out on whether that passion will bring about substantive change, there's no denying that it was a historic summer. A groundswell of outrage, marches, and demands to defund the police mixed with a "Well, the world is on fire, so I *gotta* do something" energy was a chaotic combination that birthed something no one expected and very few wanted: social justice "warriors." These weren't the sjdubs of the past or recent past—Kimberlé Crenshaw (professor of law at UCLA and Columbia Law School), Alicia Garza (cofounder

---

1. Truthfully, a whole essay could be devoted to the damage that occurs from videos of Black people being murdered going viral. On one hand, these videos are what it "takes" for the nation to pay attention to the blatant injustices, abuses of power, and results of systemic racism. On the other hand, the circulation of these videos reinforces the notion that Black life is a wholly traumatic experience, that death by the hands of, usually, white authority figures is a fate that cannot be avoided, and I wonder what the cost is mentally and spiritually when these videos are used as a means of raising "awareness," when Black people are forced to compartmentalize at work in order to engage in small talk to their coworkers and bosses as if Black people aren't being slaughtered. What are the nuanced results of repeatedly being fed the narrative that Black people are victims? At what point are these videos no longer "news" and just propaganda to uphold patriarchal subjugation? I reckon that we crossed this threshold a long fucking time ago.

of Black Lives Matter), Rashad Robinson (president of Color of Change), and Marsha P. Johnson (trans activist and one of the prominent figures in the Stonewall uprisings) just to name a few—but a new breed. A breed that was comprised of many who were for the first time acknowledging systemic racism's existence and/or that antiracism is not just labor to be done by Black people, but work that *everybody* needs to participate in, and boy, did they participate.

You ever watch a group challenge on the OG *Project Runway* when host/mentor Tim Gunn would take the contestants to Mood Fabrics and give them thirty minutes to shop for materials? The designers would barely confer with one another, instead running off in different directions only to come back together when time was up to see what everyone bought, and it was an utter shit show. Just a whole bunch of chartreuse, gold lamé, zippers, rhinestones, and tweed, and then when the last straggler, who was overwhelmed by having too many options, finally arrived at the cash register, all they had to show for their frantic efforts was a spool of periwinkle-colored thread. When I saw that, I was like, "Oh, *that's* the bitch who's going to be sent home at the end of the episode. Southwest Airlines. Middle seat. Luggage will be lost, even though the person didn't check any bags; Southwest will find a way to lose their carry-on suitcase somewhere in Des Moines, Iowa. #TheLordWorksInMysteriousWays." Point is that chaotic, throwing-anything-at-the-wall-and-seeing-what-sticks mindsets are kind of how some of these reactions to 2020's social uprisings came off. Nothing but frazzled energy and barely formed ideas and solutions driven by a slight desperation to not get caught "making a mistake," and this concern, of course, overshadows what should be the focus: Black. Lives. Mattering. In all the ways. In case you don't remember, here's a sampling of what we got:

- Corporations released carefully constructed statements of "committing to diversity" and sent out newsletters with JPEGs of Black people in them. Uhhh . . . Black people had to die in order for y'all to dump some Shutterstock pics of them looking at pie charts in a Mailchimp newsletter template about the company ecosystem? I mean, thanks for blessing our eyeballs with that dose of melanin, but really, just employ Black folk, so you're not typing the following into Google: "Yikes, I really forgot to hire Black people for the past thirty years, so can you show me images of bootleg Daniel Kaluuyas that I can use, which should be a sufficient make 'em up for my . . . 'oversight'?"
- Remember when that one woman's protest in Portland, Oregon, for Black Lives Matter consisted of her sitting butt-ass naked on the ground and spreading her legs, and so many people were like, "Yaaaas! Pussy power," nicknamed her Naked Athena, and proclaimed, "This is how you use your body as a shield." Oh, word! Would've been nice if someone told King Shaka and the Zulu Kingdom this. Maybe they would've put down their handcrafted wooden shields and instead instructed the Zulu women to open their legs like the suitcase from *Pulp Fiction* and blind the colonizing

Brits with their poonanis, and then the Zulus probably wouldn't have lost the Battle of Rorke's Drift and the Battle of Ulundi. 😐

- Or how about that time in Cary, North Carolina, when a group of white religious leaders and several community members, during a Black Lives Matter demonstraysh, washed the feet of Black religious leaders and served up a prayer repenting for the sins that Black people have had to endure at the hands of a white supremacist society? 😬 I mean . . . okay? I feel like . . . Black people never asked to . . . have their moisturized feet dried out by . . . Pert Plus 3 in 1 Shampoo + Conditioner Plus Body Wash? Again, totes preesh the effort, but this ain't it.

- And then there were the panels. Oh! We cannot talk about these uprisings without mentioning the explosion of panels. Y'all, there is nothing some media folks love more than sitting in a velvet Wayfair chair with a glass of San Pellegrino water and asking people of color to talk to / educate audiences in exchange for a tote bag, a room-temp turkey club sandwich, and reimbursed Uber fare. This past Black History Month, I got more than my fair share of the annual "Heeeey, being Black is something, huh? Care to talk about it in a forty-minute block between a segment on beauty secrets and a talk delivered by a popular twentysomething white actress on how she found her voice?" Y'all, for real, if a white chick named Heather is hitting me up anytime between February 1–28,[2] I already know the deal: It's because she just watched a movie from iTunes' "Black People Shit (Mostly Slavery & Learning Poetry / Starting a Dance Team at an Underprivileged High School)" section OR she wants me to talk about why the Black experience should be recognized. Sigh. Ya know I can talk about other things besides being Black and performing the "Blackness Is Hard" Masterpiece Theatre that people just *love* to eat up, right? I have opinions on so many "non-Black" things! Like Mel C was the best vocalist in Spice Girls and we don't talk about that enough. Whenever your boss tells you they don't have money to give you a raise, that's usually bullshit. And I don't care what anyone says, rare steak is disgusting. See?! Tons of things I can talk about.

- Oooh! How about *alllllllll* those other times I saw online and in "extra special" episodes of TV where folks were asking how to make Black friends? I just. Y'all. I can't. Like if this is what we're going to do, I'd rather go back to people not giving a fuck. Are we really asking in the 2020s how to make Black friends? While I'm certain this question is asked in earnest and in an effort to change, it's just . . . bizarre. Like, comically so. I don't really know

---

2. Leap years don't count because mofos are like, "Black History Month ends at 11:59 P.M. regardless!" and roll up to work with shamrock glasses they bought from Duane Reade in anticipation of St. Patrick's Day, which is a full fortnight and a quarter away.

how to help middle-aged white people who think forty-eight years old is a good age to start befriending Black people. It's like waiting until you're sixty-two to begin building generational wealth because it just dawned on you that you'd save a lot of money if you start couponing. It's kind of too late, no? Furthermore, making it known that you want to start being around Black people can come off like, "Here's a new pet project I can dabble in! Got any tips?" That's why I think the better question would be, "Why did it take countless horrifying deaths to see Black people as human instead of simply as trauma porn?" But if you are still curious as to how to make some amigos negros, maybe these tips will help. Like try and be their office Secret Santa. Go to an Anita Baker concert and flawlessly sing along to her performance of "Caught Up in the Rapture." That'll surely turn heads and help you make some fast friends. Win an award and then spend the majority of your acceptance pretending to be "embarrassed" that you won and proclaiming how a Black person should have won. J/K. Don't do any of that goofy shit. Just speak to Black people. And no, I don't mean during transactional exchanges in which they are in subordinate positions to you—waitstaff, receptionists, makeup artists—although engaging in respectful small talk with the people providing you a service is always appreciated. But what I'm suggesting is sparking up conversation with folks you meet in line, at happy hours, networking events, while at the gym, etc. I mean, it's really not that complicated. Don't be weird about it and it will happen. But honestly, trying to add Black people to your friend Rolodex is *soooooo* beside the point. You don't *need* to be Black people's friend in order to fight for their humanity. And if you think you do, I guarantee all that will end up happening is that the handful of Black people you know will, in your eyes, become the exception (#BlackExcellence) to the rule (Black people are a problem that needs fixing). And this leads me to my next point . . .

- Black people who encourage this kind of nonsense, stop. We don't need to co-sign foolishness. For example, the whole "Speaker of the House Nancy Pelosi and Minority Leader Chuck Schumer rolled up to the Emancipation Hall in the U.S. Capitol to introduce new federal police reform legislation while rocking kente cloth in a 'solidarity with Black people'" fiasco. Lol. Wut?! WHY DIS HAPPEN? WHY WERE THEY SMILING THE WHOLE TIME WITH A "NAILED IT" ENERGY? WERE THEY NOT ON A GROUP SLACK WITH MAXINE WATERS AND CORY BOOKER, WHO COULD HAVE LET THEM KNOW THIS IS NOT THE MOVE? HOW DOES CAUCACITY TAKE NO DAYS OFF? Look, I know the Congressional Black Caucus provided the kente cloth as a symbol of working together to make change, but nah . . . Nance and Schooms can exist in their white experience and do them while Black people are in theirs, and the two groups can still find common ground. That'd be like if British Baekoff wanted to show his solidarity with my experience of having periods, so he'd shove a tamp-tamp up his urethra for five days. I'd be like, "'Kay. Doesn't change the fact that I bleed and have horrible symptoms once a month. And now that you pulled this stunt, instead of me nursing myself with a heating pad, we gotta make a trip to urgent care, so there goes my Saturday!" Point is, we, as Black people, don't need to be handing out ill-advised assistance so white people can assuage their discomfort, and white people need to use their critical thinking skills so that when presented with a bad idea, they can say, "I'm good. I'll keep wearing my Talbots and Brooks Brothers suits and do the work instead of jumping at the chance to make an empty gesture."

Before I move on, we have *got* to talk about one more thing: ITakeResponsibility.org. It announced its arrival in a two-minute-plus video chock-full of and only featuring very privileged white actors who shot themselves exclusively in black and white like it's a whack-ass French New Wave film to show they are "really sad and care deeply," but not *too* deeply, because half of them are lifelessly reading off a sheet of paper.[3]

---

3. Why was it so poorly acted by such a talented crop of people? Y'all have careers that have lasted decades, won you awards, and paid for your mortgage and your plant-based diet provided to you by your private chef. Like BIIIIIIIIIIIITCH, you were in *The Devil Wears Prada*. Is this how the fuck you did a chem read with Meryl Streep? You just did this trash-ass acting, wilting her fresh AF blowout with the hot air you lifelessly blew out your mouth? Get. It. Together. You shouldn't have to *act* like you care about Black people. Just *do*, and do it not in front of the cameras for brownie points.

It's like they JUST REALIZED IN 2020 that racism, unchecked microaggressions, and Black people being murdered is HAPPENING and they want to now speak out because Black people are their neighbors (Bitch, where? Not your zip code), are their friends (lolz, I saw your Christmas party pictures you posted on social media, and the only Black people in attendance are faintly in the background, serving potato croquettes), and are their family (your immediate and extended family is literally just blond hair, blue eyes, and white skin, but go off on how we all fam). And [in infomercial announcer voice]: That's not all!

Some of them were wearing nonprescription Quay glasses to prove they're serious. (Wild, mate! Get it? Because Quay is an Australian brand?) There was melancholy piano music playing in the background (I guess none of them know how to use GarageBand to compose a better score or use a free song that's in the public domain). And when you go to the website, there's a *drop-down menu* where you can select generic "boo-boos" you've committed, including but not limited to "saying 'I don't see color,'" "denying white privilege," and "not being inclusive." Then after you do that, you go to a *second* drop-down menu, where you can select an option on how you're going to make it better, e.g., "demand police accountability" or "donate to families." Really?! They out here giving the "up, up, down, down, left, right, left, right, B, A, start" cheat codes on what racism is and how to do antiracism work? Noooooooo, biiiiiiiiiiitch. That's lazy, trifling, and insulting to the antiracism educators, activists, organizers, and organizations who don't have the luxury of using a crib sheet and instead must show up prepared with knowledge, lived experience, and a dedication to the cause because they understand the gravity that one false step in their execution means they will be disregarded and, more important, they grasp the severity of what it means for a society to build itself on the foundation of racism and white violence.

Whew. I don't know why, but I Take Responsibility in particular is the one that always gets me worked up. Even now, months later, as I'm writing this, I'm agitated, enraged, and absolutely confounded at the sheer audacity of its existence. That these celebrities heard but did not listen to what Black people wanted and raced to put together something so shoddy and tone-deaf. Actually, I take that back. I can think of several reasons why it upset me then at a guttural level and why it still does now.

By June 2020, when this campaign launched, I felt emotionally and mentally drained. Watching yet another video of police murdering an unarmed Black person put me in a headspace that wouldn't allow me to process celebrities "taking a stand" while saying nothing of substance. Then and now, the I Take Responsibility video is emblematic of how a movement can be co-opted by wealthy whites who are too concerned with *optics* instead of actually dismantling systemic racism in America and all over the world. When I laid eyes on that clip for the first time, it was on a day when I just wanted to go *one hour* without the bullshit. And seeing this video and its absurdity made me laugh until I cried on the phone with a friend and also infuriated me because this kind of self-flagellation happens time and time again and none of it is for Black people. And, in some way, these kinds of actions can make us feel even more alone and invisible. I know I probably shouldn't speak on behalf of the entire Black community, but I'm pretty damn sure they would all agree with me that the video and #ITakeResponsibility initiative aren't for us. This then raises the question of who they're actually for.

Like most people, the events of summer 2020 were not only difficult to process, but made me examine my own life. Interracial dating during and post these uprisings, especially when the significant other is white *and* British aka Patient Zero, was tricky, heh. Certainly it was not a situation either British Baekoff or I could have prepared for, so at times, for me, it kind of felt like when you see those high school basketball bloopers where someone on the home team absentmindedly steals the ball from their teammate and then scores a basket for the away team. Not that I view my boyfriend as my opponent; he's my partner always. However, I would be lying if I didn't admit there were fleeting moments in which living through last summer while quarantining with a white person felt . . . strange. Like we weren't on the same team because when we leave our home he is white and I'm Black. And I don't mean this in some Pollyanna "We're so in love that it never dawned on us that because of the color of our skin, racism could enter our love bubble" way. Rather, what I mean is that it's one thing to have sociopolitical discussions with our respective families or vent my frustrations about a microaggression that transpired at work, but it's another to spend several weeks together with a motorcade of NYPD vehicles patrolling up and down the street you live on at all hours of the day and night. And while they may claim that they're just doing their job, I know the unsaid truth: Their presence was designed to make sure I didn't feel completely at ease in my home or neighborhood, whereas to Baekoff, the motorcade was absurd and an abuse of power, but he did not fear for his safety, did not have paranoid ideations that maybe he's next while making a cup of tea, and did not speculate if the police were doing the very same thing at that moment in his brother's neighborhood, the way I did about my brother. All of these anxious thoughts I had were absorbed by my body on a molecular level, and they weren't in Baekoff's. And I wondered all the ways it would be different if they were.

My curiosity didn't stem from him doing something wrong. It's as though this internal question of "what if" Immaculately Concepted me. Like, what if I were quarantining with a Black person? Would our bodies sync up so as to share the burden of the secondhand trauma we were witnessing? Every so often last summer I wanted—no, needed—to wake up, roll over, and be able to commiserate with another Black person. Share an oh-so-heavy exhalation with someone who just got it. BB didn't. I mean, he saw the pain all over my face, but he didn't *know* it. It wasn't familiar and deep in the marrow. And instead of either of us fighting that reality, we accepted it. Not once did Baekoff ever *try* to do anything. Never did he attempt to *fix* it all, and believe me, my baby loves to fix shit.

Sometimes I catch him, shirtless and in shorts, just strolling up and down our apartment hallway like a principal after the first-period bell has rung, except Baekoff isn't making sure students aren't missing class, he's checking to see if it's time to re-caulk and seal the bathroom. I mean, who stays on standby for some routine caulking? Even the Property Brothers would tell him to calm the hell down. Anyway, British Baekoff loves making home repairs so much that every single time he bends over while fixing something, I get an eyeful of ass crack. And not just a sliver. It's a hearty amount. Like the length of a golf pencil that you'd use to fill in the bubbles on a multiple-choice test. I swear, every time I see his ass crack, I flash back to freshman year of high school and a *Beowulf* exam. Jokes aside, I see this man's ass crack all the time and I don't know how that's possible. He wears pants or shorts or underwear, yet it's always . . . out. Like the neighborhood Black uncle who's always on the porch and telling everyone to let their mom know he said hi. Between you and me, sometimes I won't tell Baekoff if something's broken around the apartment just so I can go ninety minutes without our Philips Hue lights refracting off his butt and blinding me. I can accept a lot of things in a relationship, but attacking me with a self-created solar eclipse made out of ass cheeks and Con Ed electricity when I don't have my sunglasses handy is not one of them. I digress. The point is my man likes to fix things, be-cause that's his love language, but even he knew his helpful nature was no match for what summer 2020 wrought.

So he followed my lead. Held me when I wanted to cry. Reminded me to take breaks from the news for my mental health. Listened when I needed to vent and stopped talking when I told him that I couldn't have any more discussions about George Floyd on a particular day. And, even though he couldn't go to marches with me because of the potential of him getting arrested, which would lead to his automatic deportation, he would check in via text frequently to see how I was doing and if I felt safe. When he didn't understand something, he wouldn't burden me with the task to teach him, but instead looked up the information to fill in the blanks. And most important, he didn't post on social media or bring attention to himself so he could get virtual pats on the back. He did things privately, such as having one-on-one conversations with his mom and friends back in the UK. He made donations to various organizations and he didn't even tell me about them half the time because, again, he wasn't trying to get brownie points. In fact, the only reason I know this is because I'd walk past our office and see him on a bail-fund website, typing in his debit card number.

I'm not sharing all this to show that my white boyfriend is the *right* kind of white boyfriend. It's that he and I both knew that intangible limitation—he'll never be able to fully understand what I and every Black person go through when these kinds of murders happen and are broadcast all over the world. He didn't attempt to overcompensate, making sure *I* knew that *he* knew he's one of the good ones. He did almost everything *but* center himself as a white savior who was previously ignorant, but is now all-knowing because he read two books and highlighted a bunch of pages. He was doing the bare minimum, which wasn't cause for celebration and was what every white person, famous or not, should have been doing, on those days—and there were many. But it appeared these simple tasks were either inexplicably difficult for plenty of white people to do or, more accurately, were an option they lacked the presence of mind to realize even existed. Baekoff declined to participate in performative allyship, and that was a much-needed salve.

Performative allyship or performative activism rose in popularity during the uprisings and protests following George Floyd's murder, but the concept has been around for several decades. It was first featured in Barbara Green's 1997 book about the Federation era of women's suffrage in Australia, entitled *Spectacular Confessions: Autobiography, Performative Activism, and the Sites of Suffrage 1905–1938*. Other notable mentions were in 2015 articles for *Hyperallergic*, a Brooklyn-based arts mag, and *Atlas Obscura*, another online magazine and travel company. One *Hyperallergic* article examined the Greenham Common Women's Peace Camp and the tactics some of the women used to protest nuclear weapons: "They decorated [a] fence with pictures, banners, and other objects. They blocked the road to the site with dance performances. They even climbed over the fence to dance in the forbidden zone."

Hmm. Doing some Laurieann Gibson choreography—#BoomkackNaysh[4]—to show your objection to a social or

---

4. Laurieann Gibson is a music video director and choreographer for top acts including Beyoncé, Lady Gaga, and Alicia Keys. In 2005, Gibson rose to prominence on Diddy's seminal MTV show, *Making the Band*, and became known for the way she taught steps at hyper speed to ratchet up the drama and then, in post, the editor punctuated each "boom" and "kack" with a door slam sound effect, which was foreboding, I guess, as the music industry closed its doors on all the bands who tried to make it. #JusticeForDanityKane #JusticeForDiddyDirtyMoney

political matter isn't inappropriate or self-indulgent in and of itself. Art and movement can be a powerful tool for expression and something that can reflect the feelings of the masses. Keith Haring's "Ignorance = Fear/Silence = Death" poster, Rosie the Riveter, and choreographer and Scripps College educator Suchi Branfman's film *Undanced Dances Through Prison Walls During a Pandemic*, which was a dance protest by people incarcerated at the California Rehabilitation Center, a medium-security state men's prison in Norco, California, in response to a prison lockdown that left them in near 24/7 isolation with no change in the foreseeable future, are all examples that come to mind.

However, what the Greenham Common Women's Peace Camp did comes off as though they were using the nuclear weapons as a backdrop to have an arts-and-crafts day capped off by a performance. It not only screams "Pay attention to me and my demonstration," as if highly visible "activism" is supposed to serve as evidence that they did their part, but it also says "My demonstration brings me pleasure." Look, I'm not a purist who believes that antiracism work should be one giant, endless slog chock-full of misery, setbacks, and heartbreak. That's not sustainable for anyone. I believe enjoyment can be an act of protest in a world that wants to exert power and crush folks under their thumbs. The problem is when the act of performing and the endorphin high that comes with it end up being the sole objectives, as opposed to a by-product of antiracist work.

Jeff Ihaza, a writer for the now-defunct website the Outline, perfectly encapsulated this point when he wrote about performative allyship back in 2017:

> One of the most crippling tendencies of modern liberals is their obsession with being seen, whether it be at a protest wearing a fuzzy pink hat alongside Madonna or in viral tweets totally owning the president. This preoccupation with optics is more often than not frighteningly self-centered. . . . From "performative" activism to a fixation on clever protest signs, modern liberals know better than anyone else how to cash in on a political movement, but they know very little about how to harness the power of one.

Although I'd take it a step further. Performative allyship is more than being keenly aware of the camera aka the world and presenting an idealized, if somewhat ineffectual, version of yourself. It's also the pacification of the idea of whiteness, which means that by design, the work that is done is to soothe and protect whiteness, not dismantle it. Much like on sitcoms when a baby cries and a first-time parent quickly runs through options ("Bottle? No? Binky . . . that's not it either? Okay. Want me to pick you up and walk around? Still not it. Shoot . . .") and settles on whatever is the quickest solution to get the crying to stop and keep the baby safe (*"Baby shark, doo, doo, doo, doo, doo, doo*— Yes! It worked! Whoo! Oh, sorry. Less celebrating and more singing. Got it. *Baby shark* . . ."), the same holds true for performative allyship and whiteness.

When the concept of whiteness is unsettled in myriad ways, ranging from progress via antiracism work to merely someone pointing out a microaggression, easy solutions such as Band-Aid brand, months after George Floyd's murder, announcing their Band-Aids are going to be made in darker shades, or Matt James becoming the first Black *Bachelor* in the show's franchise, are offered up by our so-called allies to make whiteness feel good that something has been done, while the policies and underlying structures remain mostly undisturbed so as to allow whiteness and its benefactors to maintain the status quo.

This happens because whiteness is actually one of the most fragile things in the world, right up there with butterfly wings, glass, and dudes when it comes to dating and rejection. For real. I know the societal narrative is that women are allegedly delicate little flowers who are too emotional, and songs such as Carrie Underwood's "Before He Cheats" and Jazmine Sullivan's "Bust Your Windows" certainly help reinforce the idea that women can't let anything go, but, y'all, any time at the end of the night at a club or a bar, when a woman doesn't give a guy her number, instead of cutting his losses, he's out here acquiring JG Wentworth's services in order to get a structured settlement for the three vodka sodas he bought her throughout the evening while *still* applying uncomfortable pressure in hopes of wearing her down and getting the number. Because rejection or anything that doesn't positively reinforce his fragile sense of self cannot be accepted. Same for whiteness.

That's why calls for substantive changes such as defunding

the police are generally met with pushback, requests to slow down and let bureaucracy do its thing, or deflection tactics, which, even if there are good intentions baked within them, are not really meant to bring about long-lasting results. The call to action to buy books written by Black authors and Blacking out the *NYT* bestsellers list comes to mind. As great as it was to see so many talented writers get the attention they deserve, it was still a little unsettling that the majority of books being amplified and receiving a boost in sales were antiracism books. Which are valuable, of course, but the fact that for many white people and non-Black POC, learning about Blackness means reading about how Black people survive (or don't) trauma and pain often suffered at the hands of white people reinforces the idea that whiteness is central to what it means to be Black and that Blackness = pain, hardship, and devastation.

While all sorts of these performative maneuvers have been around in various forms, so they're nothing new, social media has made it so that performative allyship has the ability to spread farther, wider, and faster. What performative allyship didn't expect was that we'd keep up with it and put its actions under a microscope, in real time, and analyze it. And the results, while brand-new to some and unsurprising to others, should be alarming to all: Performative allyship is often born from "not knowing," an utter astonishment that participants' understanding of society is in stark contrast with how it has always really been.

Last summer, social media became, more so than usual, a

place to dump any and every emotion, and I noticed a trend. Among the heartbreak and anger, similarly themed comments cropped up from many white people: "I didn't know it was like this," "I cannot believe this is happening," "This is not the America I know." Huh? This is the same America since 1619. The same America that had Japanese internment camps. The same America that ravaged Indigenous peoples. Just like how all of Pitbull's songs sound the same (MISTAAAAAAAH WORLLLLLLWAAAAAAAAAAAI!), this tune of oppression, violence, gaslighting, and inequality is the same dusty-ass song America has been playing for centuries. So how could anyone be surprised by the events of summer 2020? Given the history of Black people being murdered by white people, not just privately, but in highly public ways—from lynchings during the Reconstruction era to Lamar Smith, a farmer and civil rights activist, being shot dead on a courthouse lawn by a white man in broad daylight while dozens watched in 1955—how was it possible that so many were shocked that police officer Derek Chauvin kneeling on George Floyd's neck for nine minutes and twenty-nine seconds is something that could happen in America?

James Baldwin once wrote, "To be a Negro in this country and to be relatively conscious, is to be in a rage almost all the time." I would like to add to that quote:[5] To be white in America is, in some ways, to not be conscious at all, rather to be in a state of constant awakening; a state in which grace and

---

5. LOL. I know that me building on top of a James Baldwin quote is like putting ketchup on filet mignon, but go with me here, please. ☺

patience from others is requested and expected, yet others' hope that the "newly awakened" would remain just that, awake, and retain information that would inform their behavior going forward is deemed unrealistic. And so, without fail, many revert back to their old ways, dip out of consciousness again only to be awakened once again when another tragedy happens. This *Groundhog Day* cycle of awaking from ignorance only to forget and be jolted to life again is not only unsustainable, but impossible. To not know this is the America we've all been living in means one had to intentionally avert their eyes and ears, because it's all around us. In Cathy Park Hong's searing and essential book *Minor Feelings: An Asian American Reckoning*, she writes about the fantasy of white innocence, which has troublesome ramifications and is a luxury that's not afforded to any other group in America:

> Innocence is, as Bernstein writes, not just an "absence of knowledge" but "an active state of repelling knowledge," embroiled in the statement, "Well, *I* don't see race" where *I* eclipses the *seeing*. Innocence is both a privilege and a cognitive handicap, a sheltered unknowingness that, once protracted into adulthood, hardens into entitlement. Innocence is not just sexual deflection but a deflection of one's position in the socioeconomic hierarchy, based on the confidence that one is "unmarked" and "free to be you and me." The ironic result of this innocence, writes the scholar Charles Mills, is that whites are "unable to understand the world that they themselves have made." Children are then disqualified from innocence when they are

persistently reminded of, and even criminalized for, their place in the racial pecking order. As Richard Pryor jokes: "I was a kid until I was eight. Then I became a Negro."

And since we are living in the aftermath of summer 2020, with the time-honored tradition of promises that *this* time will somehow be different, I have to ask, "How?" Ma'Khia Bryant, an Ohioan teen, was gunned down by a Columbus police officer mere *minutes* before the guilty verdict came in for Derek Chauvin. What makes this death even more heartbreaking is that 1) she called the police because she was being bullied and a knife was her only self-defense, and 2) several Columbus police officers chanted "Blue Lives Matter" at the scene of the crime. Perhaps when I was younger, I could have taken those promises at face value and believed them. Been convinced that change was coming around the bend despite the absence of evidence. But I have lived too long and seen too much. As someone on the cusp of forty,[6] it would be foolish of me to have faith and "trust the process" based on nothing but verbal intent.

I mean, what is the knowledge that's being absorbed this time that wasn't years prior? Much if not all of the information circulating now isn't new. It has been percolating for decades, written, explained, and monologued by many Black people,

---

6. I know! I don't look like it. Lol. But also, I'm not, as Mai vehemently reminds me. I'm only thirty-six, which she says means I'm firmly in the midthirties camp. But the other day, she and I spent twenty minutes texting about the various stages of my foot peel (complete with me sending her pics of my feet with the "live photo" option turned on in case she needed to see the peel in motion) and the best moisturizing heel socks and foot repair ointment creams to treat cracked heels. I mean c'mon! That alone should be enough to legitimize my on-the-cuspishness-of-forty claim.

ranging from the famous to those sitting on stoops and in backyards. Many of these murders ("executions" is probably the apt word to use here) have resembled countless others from the past. So this renewed vigor, which is the first I'm seeing in *my* lifetime, where is it coming from? Why is there such a Tracy Flick from *Election* level of intensity that overshadows and obfuscates? What is driving this emboldened outspokenness when previously, Black people's needs were met not with solidarity or the open hearts of this era, but deafening silence? Enter white antiracism educators.

Y'all, the amount of white people posting selfies of themselves holding Robin DiAngelo's *White Fragility* last year, talking about all they learned, and recommending others read it if they wanted a good primer on how racism and antiracism work, had me cocking my head to the side à la Whitney Houston in that Diane Sawyer interview and saying, "Show me the receipts." For real. Show. Me. The. Receipts. If they're crisp like a bag of pork rinds and not yellowed like they were excavated from an 1897 time capsule, I'm going to need you to stop this performance because you just *learned* what antiracism was. If folks who worship at the altar of Robin and other white antiracism authors don't have this same level of enthusiasm for Black antiracism educators such as Ijeoma Oluo, Ibram X. Kendi, and Austin Channing Brown (just to name a few), the same amount of revelations when reading their work, and the same desire to amplify their writing to other white people as they do Robin or even Tim Wise, I'm going to need them to stop and take a look at the subtext in that message they're conveying: 1) that the Black people experiencing the pain are not to be believed, but a white person who has a degree in *studying* the pain and will never actually *experience* it is now the authority/expert, and 2) the package in which previous antiracism thinking was presented aka by a Black person is not as palatable as when the teaching is presented to me by a white person. That, in and of itself, is a problem, if not one of the major hurdles, to antiracism work.

Ya know, I distinctly remember the outrage when, in 2017, former vice president Mike Pence and a cavalry of other white male politicians looking like a painting of the Last Supper (at Red Robin Gourmet Burgers and Brews) sat around deciding the state of women's reproductive rights. Yet, where is the uproar over the fact that DiAngelo, Wise, and others of their ilk are considered the leading authorities and are the ones who the majority of white people will listen to over the everyday Black activists who have been doing this work for decades? There wasn't any. Don't believe me? Let's use DiAngelo as an example and look at the trajectory of her book and career since the *New Yorker* labeled her "the country's most visible expert in anti-bias training."

At the time I'm writing this, *White Fragility* has been on the *New York Times* bestsellers list for ONE HUNDRED AND THIRTY-FOUR WEEKS. That's two and a half *years*.

By comparison, Ibram X. Kendi's *How to Be an Antiracist* has been on the list for forty-six weeks. Granted, his book was published a year after hers, in 2019, but the ratio is glaring: DiAngelo's book has been on the list practically since publication, while Kendi's has been on the list for only half of its book life. Admittedly, neither her popularity nor her work in this field happened overnight. She earned a BA from Seattle University, then an MA and PhD from the University of Washington. She then went on to write books, teach, and coined the phrase "white fragility" in a peer review in 2011, and she has been doing anti-bias training since at least 2007. She has put in years of effort, but there are a couple problems: her rates and the fact that anti-bias training actually doesn't work. First, a word about the money issue.

Let me be clear: If there is a demand for what you can supply and it's not illegal and won't kill anyone, I commend your entrepreneurial spirit to give it a go and turn that into a business. Furthermore, I happily encourage people, especially women, POC, and the LGBTQIA+ community, to ask for what they think they're worth, because it's in the best interest of the employer to underpay for services rendered. So, yes, get yours. Make sure that you're being paid enough to cover your rent/ mortgage, bills, and unexpected expenses. HOW. EV. ER. When I read what DiAngelo's rates were for public speaking engagements as well as for running antiracist workshops, I was like, "Call me Robin Hood and slap some green control-top pantyhose on me because I'm about to rob this chick because she's *rich rich.*"[7]

In all seriousness, it gave me pause because of the lack of financial parity for people of color in every single professional arena in America. Various publications such as *The Daily Beast* have reported that Robin DiAngelo got paid $12,750 for the

---

7. Kidding! I do not condone robbery of any kind even if it's to give back to the financially insecure.

same conference keynote speech that Austin Channing Brown was paid $7,500 for. The disparity is infuriating, especially when you consider that DiAngelo only addressed what her salary range actually was after the conservative website *Washington Free Beacon* raised eyebrows by reporting on her rates for several speaking engagements. Then she took to her website, writing on her accountability page (lol) that while her average rate was exaggerated by the *Free Beacon*, she did admit the following: "my fee has ranged from pro bono (zero) to upwards of $30,000, which is well within the standard range for a bestselling author who is in high demand." Riiiiiiiight. Let's be real, it's not about the amount per se, but the fact that $30K is not the standard or attainable rate for 99 percent of Black antiracism authors and teachers, who have been in this field just as long as she has, but their complexion is wrong, so for her to seemingly pretend otherwise is disingenuous.

I mean, we all know that except for probably Kendi and author/journalist Ta-Nehisi Coates, Black antiracism educators aren't getting close to that rate, and we for damn sure know Black *female* antiracism educators aren't getting anywhere near that rate. You can't be teaching antiracism while not advocating for financial parity for the people of color beside you who have been teaching the same things your work is parroting to audiences who have no desire to hear it from the mouth of a Black person. It's so wildly problematic and patently absurd. And to make matters worse, DiAngelo started donating 15 percent of her after-tax income "in cash and in-kind donations" only *after* it got out how much she earns. So, the alleged leading voice on white fragility and white guilt seemingly was trying to make amends . . . out of white guilt? But that's not even the worst part.

When a white person is considered the leading voice in how to be antiracist, it creates more harm and mental anguish for Black people because they are proven right yet again that there is no conceivable way that, even when armed with years of education and personal experience, they can be seen as authorities on antiracism, or the many ills that stem from a racist society, including advocating for government policies and legislation, addressing racial disparities in poverty, jobs, mass incarceration, and housing, and how the police system was designed, as Olivia B. Waxman wrote in her *Time* magazine article "How the U.S. Got Its Police Force":

> In the South, however, the economics that drove the creation of police forces were centered not on the protection of shipping interests but on the preservation of the slavery system. Some of the primary policing institutions there were the slave patrols tasked with chasing down runaways and preventing slave revolts. . . . Many local sheriffs functioned in a way analogous to the earlier slave patrols, enforcing segregation and the disenfranchisement of freed slaves.

All these varying ways of oppression and more need to be addressed with Black people in the room and leading the conversation. Of course, we know that it's not "representation matters," but "quality representation matters." Just because one is Black does not mean one is qualified to spearhead antiracist work, any more than because I'm Black, I'm Rihanna's heir apparent. I'm not because I can't sing, but, more important, I cannot tiptoe across an NYC sidewalk grate in stiletto heels without falling. Like, Jesus may have walked on water in *chancletas*, but idk if She has the range to pull off what Rih did! Anyway. The point is that when qualified Black people are left out of the conversation and their contributions are ignored, so that only white people are in the room, it fills white consumers of antiracism teachings with the sense that they are to become the white saviors who will swoop in and save the day, and that attending these white-run workshops is the first step they need to take in becoming the social justice warrior, which no one asked for, by the way. And, as it turns out, these antibias seminars are, across the board, ineffective in the first place. Per a 2019 article in the *Harvard Business Review* by authors including Adam Grant and Angela Duckworth:

> Evidence has shown that diversity training can backfire, eliciting defensiveness from the very people who might benefit most. And even when the training is beneficial, the effects may not last after the program ends.

The workshops ain't working, y'all. And like I previously stated, it's not just Robin. It's the entire industry of White People Educating Other White People on How to Be Antiracist When None of Them Know What It's Like to Be on the

Receiving End of Systemic Racism. Enough is enough. We cannot continue watching Black people be slaughtered and be on the receiving end of micro- and macroaggressions, while trees are chopped down so white people can turn them into books, highlight the pages, and not change one iota of their behavior. The days of Racism Is Bad 101 have long been over, but we are still stuck there.

I mean, what is the point of the lessons, the seminars, the books, the real-life deadly consequences of racism if it's not going to be transformed into action? What purpose does knowledge serve if nothing changes? Knowledge and learning, truth be told, are the easy parts. Reading, highlighting, and posting prompts on social media for robust discussions in the comments section can be fun and get the adrenaline pumping, but ultimately wind up being nothing more than empty exercises the majority of the time. I can think of two main reasons why.

One, many performative allies operate as though racism is this abstract, philosophical debate that doesn't have stakes in *their* world. The corporations need to step up. The executives need to do better. These celebrities should be canceled for [insert racially insensitive comment]. This white person is so unbelievably racist in a viral cell-phone video. These books are teaching me about past racism and discussing hypotheticals. The racism is always somewhere other than where anyone is. Like, what is racism? Fucking Nickelback CDs? The band has sold more than 50 MILLION ALBUMS, but *nobody* owns a copy? LOL. Okay. Similarly, there is no audacity to perform racism in any and all of its ugly forms without a system, meaning people to support it. So somebody's out here "racisting," but if folks can't even acknowledge the ways in which they intentionally and unintentionally hold up systems of oppression, how can they change their behavior? Simply put, they can't.

So what ends up happening is the cycle of white guilt, which leads to the task of self-improvement, then goes back to white guilt because change isn't happening fast enough or at all. And as we all know, guilt is never a good motivator to rectify behavior, but a license to wallow in the pity, which leads to more guilt about their participation in systemic racism, which is now combined with them feeling bad about the fact that they feel bad. Basically, white guilt is a *Cathy* comic, y'all. Like, that bitch always has a sob story. Constantly caught up in the drama without realizing she's a key architect of the spectacle that is her life. Always getting fired and acting like she doesn't know why. It's like, "Cath, Jamba Juice let you go because you were making smoothies to bring home to your cats."[8] #ThisConcludesMyAntiRacismSeminar #CanIGetPaid40K?

The other reason why most of performative allyship is ineffective is that folks move in extremes and go from zero to one hundred as an antiracist. One day, they were unaware how pervasive racism is, and the next, they're flooding their social media with information, showing up at marches and protests, screaming about supporting Black businesses. WHERE DID

---

8. That is a real plot from the comics. Normally, I choose a side, but I'm Switzerland this time because cats need a balanced diet.

ALL THESE WHITE PEOPLE COME FROM?! I'm serious. You ever throw what you thought was going to be an intimate get-together and it turns into a full-fledged house party, and a bitch who *was not invited*, but showed up with napkins and red Solo cups, now acts like they call the shots and pay *your* property taxes? That's how this aggressiveness in being antiracist comes across sometimes. And while I'm sure a decent amount of it is well-intentioned, intent doesn't matter when it's causing more harm, and from what I can see, as the number of non-POC participants in antiracism increases, so does the "May I speak to your manager?" energy. The revolution cannot and should not be Karenized. That vibe wants fast results, placation, and constant positive reinforcement, and recontextual izes easy wins as major victories, so that when the wins don't happen quickly, or happen at all for the weightier and messier issues, disappointment and frustration settle in, threatening to dissuade future efforts.

To me, lacking patience and expecting results immediately for both the micro and macro issues that plague America shows a complete lack of understanding of how pervasive and fundamental racism is to the foundation of our society. Truth be told, systemic racism will most likely not be dismantled in our lifetime. While I would like things to change so that all my Black brothers and sisters and I can live in a better world, I know that's not the ultimate goal. The ultimate goal is that those who come after me will not have to experience even a tenth of what I have. Achieving that goal requires a level of acceptance in the face of glacial progress, and that is, in part, what prevents burnout and allows one to stay the course.

Too often what we're seeing is people blowing off steam at the first sign of adversity and then not rolling up their sleeves and jumping back into the fray. And that combination of impatience and losing interest because massive change has not happened since they decided to get active, when there have been people on the front lines for years and decades doing the exhaustive work to dismantle racism, is the opposite of staying the course. It's participating in a trend, in a moment. This is not a trend. I repeat: This is not a trend. We have to undo every single institution—both big and small—in our country. And if the expectation is permanent change, then we must understand that the system cannot change unless the people in it, particularly the ones who benefit from it in myriad tangible and intangible ways, change as well.

A key part of that change is people putting ego aside and thoroughly examining themselves. They must acknowledge and reckon with their participation, both passive and active, in systemic racism instead of presenting themselves as having been on the right side of history. That preoccupation with their own vanity is nothing but participating in the Woke Olympics. That is of no use to Black people and not what we need. We deserve folks digging deep and committing to changing their mindset and their behavior, or else history will repeat itself. We need folks willing to do the work even if they may never see the fruits of their labor. We need folks to stay the course. So even though it's been over a year since the global social uprisings and the police have not been defunded, stay the course. If after a couple of tough conversations with a loved one, that person has not changed their beliefs on racism,

Black Lives Matter, and more, stay the course. When minor wins happen, celebrate if you want to but remember: Stay. The. Course. This country and the people in it will not be easily resolved or fixed. This will be one of the great fights of our lives, as it has been for generations. So stay the course. Do the work.

By the way, "work" is more than dismantling government institutions. Work includes, but isn't limited to: looking at your team/employees and hiring people of color in more than underpaid, subordinate positions. Speaking up at your schools when the course curriculum doesn't include queer and POC history. Same goes for who is doing the teaching. If it's all just cis white teachers, that's detrimental to every child's education and understanding of the world. If they never see Black people or other POC in positions of authority, how can they ever see themselves as leaders? Then there's housing. Moving out of communities that have Black people in them OR moving into predominantly Black communities, gentrifying them, and displacing Black people makes it mighty hard to say we're all family. How about patronizing Black-owned businesses other than Rihanna's and Beyoncé's?

While doing this work, remember the work affects Black people. What happens out in the world, both the good and the bad, reverberates throughout our lives. Please don't turn anti-racism or Black people into a pet project. We are human beings. So when one looks at the life of a Black person, what movie do they watch? Is it *12 Years a Slave*? Why not *Akeelah and the Bee, Brown Sugar,* or *Dave Chappelle's Block Party*? When wanting to understand the "Black experience," are the books being read starting and stopping at antiracism or are they expanding beyond narratives centered on racism, such as *Queenie* by Candice Carty-Williams (friendship and dating), *American Spy* by Lauren Wilkinson (espionage), and *You Should See Me in a Crown* by Leah Johnson (YA novel)? Falling in love, being a spy, and being a teenager are also a part of the Black experience. News stories about Black death and murder populate the news, but the stories about LeBron James opening a public school in his hometown of Akron, Ohio, quickly fade away because they do not fit the limiting narrative of what Blackness is. And if you really want a taste of what Blackness has to offer, look around you. Check out the Black kids playing in the street during summertime. Smile when you see a mother/daughter duo shopping at the mall. Feel secondhand joy when you see a Black family having a good-ass time together. Listen to Black people in the workplace when they have really good ideas. Don't save us. *See* us.

Bish, What? That's English?!:
A Tale of an American Dating a Brit

～

One of my favorite things about dating a white person from the UK[1] is that I get to introduce him to so many things in Black culture that helped form who I am. Exposing him to blassics aka Black classics in music led to mixed results: "Confessions Part II" by Usher ("too ignorant"), "How Many Licks?" by Lil' Kim (a lot of "oh mys" and "oh, dears!"), and "Breakdown" by Mariah Carey featuring Krayzie Bone and Wish Bone ("love the slow, thrusting beat" #Eww). Thankfully, my

---

1. This might be a deep cut, but fans of *The Real Housewives of Atlanta* will remember what I'm about to refer to, but even if you've never seen the show, you should still get it. Anyway, in an episode of *RHOA*, all the ladies and their boos were on a group trip when Marlo Hampton tried to get clarity on salacious rumors about Kandi Burruss (read: Marlo wanted to be messy as hell while everyone was eating shrimp scampi). Once the rumors were repeated, Burruss, Kenya Moore, and Porsha Williams took turns saying, "Who said that?" "*Who* said that?" "*Who said that?*" for approximately twenty-seven minutes. Well, that's literally what every colonized and formerly colonized group on the planet said when they read "One of my favorite things about dating a white person from the UK" before finishing the sentence.

TV show selections garnered universal reactions: He loves *black-ish* and *Living Single*. And then there's seasoning. Like the saying goes: Bring a Brit seasoning and he'll go, "What's this? I prefer my food to taste like sadness." But teach a Brit how to season and his taste buds will rejoice like Whoopi Goldberg's choir singing "Joyful, Joyful" at the end of *Sister Act 2: Back in the Habit*. Look, I could go on listing all the things he has received an education on thanks to me, but I want to focus on one particular night when I asked Bae if he'd ever seen *Waiting to Exhale*. "What's that?" he asked.

Shocked, I immediately sat up in bed and said, "Oh, we're watching the movie. Like right now." I searched for the film in my iTunes library while trying to make sense of his cluelessness. "You know what? You've probably seen it, but just don't remember it by name. Like the scene where Gloria flirts with her new neighbor, Marvin?" This was met with a blank stare. "'Kay, but the soundtrack! It's full of bops!" All I got back was a shrug of the shoulders. "Fine. At least we can agree that the cast is unbeatable. Whitney Houston, Angela Bassett—"

"I have no idea who that is."

And with that sentence, I was so mad that I saw red, green, yellow, and all the other colors that make up kente cloth. I know Bae is from the UK, but how can he not know *the* Angela Evelyn Bassett? The icon who trained at the Yale School of Drama. The legend who has seemingly portrayed every important Black woman in history—Tina Turner, Betty Shabazz, Katherine Jackson, Coretta Scott King, and Rosa Parks—and still has never won an Academy Award. #TheDisrespect. The superstar who, in her nearly forty-year career, has never been the subject of torrid gossip or disgraceful controversies. And while we're at it, let's get shallow because she is one of the most stunning women of all time. Screw Helen of Troy and her face that launched a thousand ships, because Bassett's melanated beauty made thousands of Black women and girls appreciate their own beauty, and her arms were most likely responsible for dumbbell sales for the whole of the nineties.

Clearly, I worship at the altar of Angela Bassett, and I needed Bae to understand how pitiful his life has been for never having seen her act in anything. So I queued up the movie, fully prepared for him to bask in the glory of all things Bassett and . . . um, yeah. We need to talk, y'all. I mean, yes, she is incredible in the movie and it goes without saying that this film is iconic. I still remember when Oprah had the cast—Bassett, Houston, Loretta Devine, and Lela Rochon—on her talk show to discuss the movie and how it was a celebratory moment of four Black powerhouses. But, if I can be honest, *Exhale* is wild AF.

Dear reader, if you haven't seen the movie yet either, all you need to know right now is the plot: It's a romantic drama about four women navigating their families, careers, and love lives, which are mostly littered with terrible men. But here's the thing. All the women in the movie talk about how men are no good, but these ladies are either boning married men or making #TrifeLife choices when it comes to men. Looking at it now, that feels like trash attracting trash, but that's not how I remembered it as I was building up the movie to British Baekoff, and it's also not how the movie presents itself either. Let's look at Whitney Houston's character, Savannah.

She's an ambassador for Side Piece Nation, as she's been

smashing the very married Kenneth (Dennis Haysbert) in the hopes that he will eventually leave his wife. Then one day over lunch, she ends the affair because he utters this white lie: "You're the most important thing in my life." Right. I mean, he's been lying this whole time to his wife and daughter, but this lie to Savannah is what's unacceptable. I repeat: This lie, not *adultery*, is proof he's a bad dude and would cheat on her if they ended up together. This, of course, is supposed to be a triumphant moment for Savannah. How do we know? Because she punctuates this kiss-off by dumping his gin and tonic on his pants, and he's all like, "Whoa! Hey! C'mon! Savannah! Hey!" Kenneth, calm down. It's a G&T. Gin is clear and tonic water can be used to treat stains. Basically, Savannah pretreated your clothes before you throw them in the wash. You *owe* her. ANYWAY! The point is I remember watching this movie at sixteen, slightly confused about who was the "good guy" in this scenario, but still going, "Yes, Savannah! You tell him! If he isn't honest about the little things, then it's best you end it." LOL. Fast-forward to me being in my midthirties with this rule of thumb: If you consider cheaters a red flag, then as soon as a married heaux enters your life and offers to play a round of Pass the Peen, you tell them your name is not Milton Bradley so you ain't into games, then go home to watch *The Voice*. But Savannah's not the only character making suspect choices.

After a few meals of ham hocks and collards with her hot neighbor Marvin (Gregory Hines) and him fixing her leaky faucet (not a metaphor), Gloria (Devine) wants him to play stepdad to her college-bound son. I know grown folks can move fast in relationships, but it's only been a few months! You can't expect your new boyfriend to contribute to your son's college meal plan so he can have waffle fries on the regs. Hell, my parents were with me my whole life and didn't really wanna pay for my meal plan in college. They were like, "Sure you don't wanna get a RadioShack credit card and rack up debt with Odwalla juices and Rold Gold pretzels purchases like the rest of America?" I kid, I kid. But for real, Glo: PumpYourBrakes.DMV.NY.gov.

Then we have Lela Rochon's Robin. Her journey begins with her being a married man's mistress and then she decides to get serious about love . . . by smashing Michael, a coworker who *just* got promoted to her team. Despite a *very* mediocre dicking, they go on Zillow and look at three-bed, two-bath fixer-uppers when, at the most, they should be sharing a sad soup and tragic sal from Panera. Instead, they keep fooling around until, at work, Michael actually does his job and points out an important discrepancy in a report for a million-dollar account. This pisses her off, so she ends things with him. Robin, unless you and Michael got your MBAs at Risking It All for Some Strange University, you cannot expect your co-workers to endanger their livelihoods so your ego can remain intact. Anyway, Robin's not done making trash decisions because after dumping Michael, she then dates a cokehead before going back to boning still-married Russell and getting pregnant by him. Yes, this is messier than a truck stop restroom, but I saved the best mess for last: Bassett's Bernadine.

Her husband leaves her for his side piece, who's also a coworker, so Bernadine sets his clothes and car on fire (I'm here for it), rolls up to his job and WWE's his jumpoff's face into a West Elm desk (definitely reckless behavior, but I'm still here for it), and then she meets Wesley Snipes's fine ass and DOES NOT SLEEP WITH HIM (*this* is when a bitch decides to be pragmatic???). Yes, I know it's because he has a dying wife—yikes—but if this movie gonna be, in part, about thot life yet it won't have Wesley Snipes shirtless, I'm like, "Well, then why did Rosa Parks sit at the front of the bus if not so that generations later, we can ogle hot nineties Black dude sex symbols?" I mean, can a sis get a peek at one of his clavicles? A glimpse at half a bi and tri (that's bicep and tricep if ya didn't know)? A passing look at a quarter of a moisturized ankle? I mean, give me something! Sadly, the movie doesn't. All we get is Bassett and Snipes sleeping next to each other *comfortably* while fully clothed, which is how I know these folks are in really good shape. Seriously, who's out here rocking non-elastic clothing and can sleep for eight hours straight? Like Bernadine is wearing control-top hosiery in peaceful slumber. What kind of sorcery is this?! I do not know, but Bassett acted the hell out of this scene, all the scenes that came before it, and especially the one after it, when she gets a letter from Snipes, who writes that in the short time they spent together—two Moscow mules and some conversaysh—he has grown to love her! As she's reading this, she merely sighs sensually before moving on with her life. Talk about self-control! If I got a note like that, I would've been on the phone, trying to use my Capital One reward miles to purchase a flight out to see homeboy. I do not know how to play it cool. Anyway, as I'm harrumphing and talking at the TV over this missed opportunity for a steamy love scene, I noticed Baekoff wasn't chiming in. Turns out he was fast asleep. How could he???

Sure, it's not a perfect film, but the story lines are deliciously telenovela-esque, the 1990s fashion is still aspirational twenty-six years later, and Bassett's acting range is a thing to admire. Okay, maybe I'm biased because I first saw *Waiting to Exhale* in my teens, which, for most people, are formative years when things in pop culture can more easily work their way into your DNA. As a result, the movie will forever have a special place in my heart in a way that, even if British Baekoff did like the film, it just wouldn't in his. He's not a teenager watching this film for the first time, but a thirty-one-year-old man. The specific type of Black American woman experience shown in *Exhale* is something that he did not witness or grow up with on the south coast of England. This is a two-way street, by the way. There are things he cherishes that don't resonate with me. Take Paul McCartney and Wings, for example.

A year and a half into dating, he referenced one of their songs in conversation, expecting a moment of shared recognition. Unfortunately, for him, I missed the whole Paul McCartney and Wings train. "But I love Wings," he said, as if my not listening to them was a planned attack against him.

"First name 'Always,' middle name 'with'?"

"Ha ha," he said, mockingly. "The band. With Paul McCartney. Everyone loves Wings!"

"You are literally the first person who has ever mentioned them to me, and I've been alive for so many years."

"But it's Wings. They were huge, babe! Massive!"

He then uttered the word "Wings" about five thousand more times, rattling off song titles, none of which registered with me, before I said, "Hate to break it to ya, but I think they are more of a UK thing. Not that they weren't big here, but I think they're probably more beloved across the pond." He seemed to accept this before letting me know how much I've been missing out, which would be fine, except this impassioned defense of this band didn't track. I mean, this man claims to *love* Wings so much that we had a twenty-minute convo about them, but dude has yet to play any songs from their catalog in all the time we've been dating. Not a "Live and Let Die," a "Band on the Run," or a "Maybe I'm Amazed." But you know who has played some Wings? This bitch, because I accidentally hearted a Boz Scaggs song that Spotify put on one of my Daily Mixes, so then Spotify started slipping in all these other songs from the "financially comfortable white men who've never been denied a bank loan" genre and Wings' "Arrow Through Me" played and now I fucks with that song hard. Moving on.

As I'm sure you've picked up on, when people from different cultures and countries date, there is a learning curve for each person in everything from traditions to pop culture references. Not only that, but people outside the relationship are curious about how the learning is going. (DISCLAIMER: THE START OF THE NEXT SENTENCE IS FULLY ANNOYING, BUT ALSO, IT'S WHAT HAPPENED, SO LET'S GET IT OVER WITH.) The last time my boyfriend and I hung out with Bono (SEE, I TOLD YOU, BUT THE WORST IS OVER), he asked Baekoff and me what it's like dating each other, since it was the first time Baekoff had dated an American and I a Brit. We get this question a lot because when BB and I are together, we, without fail, turn into a comedy duo, playfully ribbing each other and telling ridic stories to the delight of those around us.

Also, the question comes up because movies like *Notting Hill*, *Like Crazy*, and *The Holiday* tend to reduce each culture to cutesy quirks and clichés: Brash American doesn't know the proper fork to use at dinner! Sheepish Brit stutters charmingly because he can't express himself! And I'm not saying that's not sometimes true, but that's not the whole truth.

Alright. Real talk: I always secretly hoped that I'd date a Brit because I was pretty into British culture growing up. Like the Hugh Grants. The Colin Firths. Knockoff Burberry trench coats that I buy at H&M. The Idris Elbas. Okay . . . when I write "British culture," I just mean "handsome and charismatic men who appear in some of my fav movies and TV shows like *Bridget Jones's Diary* and *Luther*. So I was a part of the problem. However, at the time of this book's publication, Baekoff and I will have been together about four years, so now seems as good a time as any to break down our observations about each other and our respective cultures since we began dating:

1. What better place to start than with the title of this essay: "Bish, What? That's English?!" Even though we both allegedly "speak English," we had trouble communicating with each other during the early stages of our relationship. He'd constantly say, "Stop yelling at me." I'd be confused and reply, "I'm not yelling. This is my normal voice. Besides, none of my friends think I'm loud." To which he responded, "*All* your friends are loud. Your entire family is loud. Everyone you know is loud. Every person I've ever met in America is loud."

Damn. Well, that settles that then. And what about on my end? When I first heard him speak, I thought to myself, *Oh, you just out here doing Kama Sootch aka Kama Sutra to the English lang?* I mean . . . is this what English is supposed to sound like?!?! And when I wasn't all hot and bothered over or envious of his accent, I wished I could rock one of those earpieces that former secretary general of the United Nations and Ghanaian diplomat Kofi Annan wore at UN meetings for language translations so I could understand what Bae was saying to me.

2. Remember the birthday trip with Bae to London I mentioned earlier? It was fantastic, magical, romantic. Blah, blah, blah. It was also eye-opening because I saw grown-ass adults wearing barrister wigs. I had no idea they're still doing that goofy shit! And when I asked him what the deal was with the wigs, he merely shrugged, as he had become so accustomed to seeing them that they didn't register to him as anything noteworthy. Before I go any further, if you're reading this and you don't know what a barrister wig is, lemme learn ya something. They look like shag carpets with a bunch of Little Debbie brand Swiss Rolls spray-painted white and hot-glued down the sides and back. Simply put, they ain't cute or chic, but that's not what we were taught in school, right? Like, we read about eighteenth-century aristocrats who were supposed to be of a "superior class," and we'd look at drawings and paintings showing them wearing powdered wigs and they were

considered the height of fashion. LIES! Those mofos were a bunch of Gigi and Bella Ha*don'ts* because they were filthy and funky. That's right, back in the day, folks were riddled with syphilis (dry heave) and lice (dry heave). So to cover up their hair loss, unsightly scabs, and rashes, their short- and long-term soloosh aka solution was to make wigs out of horse, goat, or human hair. And this tradition carried over to the judicial system because lawyers be fuckin'!

Kidding aside, wearing the wigs quickly became a sign of professionalism, and this tradition still hangs around hundreds of years later despite the fact that people's natural hair is highly visible underneath the wigs. Yikes. If you did that on *RuPaul's Drag Race*, you'd automatically have to lip-sync for your life; meanwhile, law yers are out here lawyering to *save* lives while looking like a sad-ass Halloween costume and smelling like Seabiscuit's haystack. And to make matters worse, barrister wigs can cost up to $1,350, while some judges' wigs top out at $3,800. Come again? Actually, don't because that's how we got in this mess in the first place. Hey-o! But for real, those prices are ridiculous. Very smart people are spending a month's rent or a mortgage payment to look a fool! UK, get with the times. Do like 75 percent of Black romantic comedies where, halfway through the movie, the lead cuts her weave out of her hair and decides to wear her hair naturally as an India.Arie song plays in the background. Ditch the wigs and show off your real hair, barristers!

3. Unlike many a Brit, Black women do not put their purses on the floor. Black women do not hang them from a door. Black women do not leave purses in the company of strangers. Black women probably wouldn't even feel comfy leaving them in baby Jesus's manger. In all seriousness, it is true the whole "no purse on the floor" thing is superstitious, as is the belief that the two shall never meet or else you will have money troubles. But that's not what it's about for me. Simply put, most places are trifling and most people are shady. Leaving my bag unattended is a surefire way for it to get dirty and/or stolen, as I learned the hard way when, years ago, I was dating my ex and we went to a party. "Hide your purse under that pile of coats," he said. "No one will find it," he said. "Everyone is chill," he said. Fast-forward a few hours to when I was ready to take me and my raggedy Forever 21 dress home, only to discover that my wallet with all my cards, ID, cash, and checkbook[2] were taken from my purse. I had to

2. I know we live in a Cash App, PayPal, Venmo, Apple Pay, direct-deposit-my-paycheck-to-my-City-National-Bank-account society, but once upon a time (ten-plus years ago), people, sometimes, still carried around checkbooks and wrote checks to pay for things. If the check was to a friend, you'd be like, "Don't cash this until when you look at the nighttime sky, you see Orion's Belt is slightly obscured by three clouds moving west at 11:57 P.M. . . . then wait three days after that and cash that shit." What's unsaid but understood in this request is "Look, I don't have the funds right now, so don't fuck up my life with a bounced check charge. Just wait. Puhleeze!" However, if the check was to a business, it's like, "Key Food, you and I both know what this is. I'm paying for cereal, milk, olives, and orange juice with a Betty Boop–themed check. Clearly, I'm not great at decision-making and I don't have money to pay for this ragtag group of grocery items. So if the check bounces, it bounces. I still got my Kashi corn flakes." #BrokeAndBougie

cancel all my cards, get a new checking account, a new ID sent to me, and borrow money from a couple of friends to tide me over. It was a disaster, but a lesson that has stayed with me to this day. In fact, on several occasions when I've done a stand-up show at a sketchy place, I've brought my purse onstage with me and opened my set with, "I don't trust none of you heauxes," and everyone, especially the Black women, laughed and nodded.

4. You know in *Ozark* when Ruth, the plucky criminal who often finds herself backed into sticky situations and one time, due to being overwhelmed by all the criminal activity going on, she said, "I don't know shit about fuck"? That's how I feel about the metric and Celsius system. If, as a kid, I knew I was going to end up with a Brit, I would have demanded that my teachers educate me on this. In middle school, we spent *maybe* one or two weeks on these measuring systems before our brains started hurting and we went back to U.S. units of measurement, which, if I'm being honest, I barely have a handle on. Horsepower? All I know is I've seen a GMC commercial or two where a pickup truck proves how much horsepower it has by racing against a herd of black stallions in an open field, which is exactly like zero point none of our lives. Anyway, the point is I'm now in my thirties, struggling to do Fahrenheit to Celsius conversions in my head so I can participate in small talk about the weather with my boyfriend's relatives during the winter holidays.

5. Speaking of small talk ... y'all. I assumed that because I'm from the Midwest, I *knew* small talk: "How are your kids?" "Have you been to Sam's Club lately?" "Can you believe the traffic on I-271 today?" "I love that dress. Where did you get it from? No way! And it was 40 percent off?!" That's some quality, foolproof stuff. Well, turns out (say it with me!): I don't know shit about fuck! Because Brits can easily spend a half hour in SmallTalkVille just yammering on about the weather, football aka what we call soccer, and what's on telly so as to avoid awkward silence in social situations; meanwhile, the average American is ready to wrap it up after five to seven minutes, and if there's some silence, oh well. Baekoff realized this the hard way. You ever ask the question "How are you doing?" and then the heaux had the nerve to tell you how they were actually doing? Well, until recently, my boyfriend was that heaux. He'd get excited at this query and chat away; meanwhile, the innocent person listening to him probably thought, *I know that if I could go back in time and not ask this man how he was doing, I'd risk bringing about catastrophic consequences as a result of this butterfly effect, but flap dem wings, boo, and get me out this conversation!* Anyway, the person and Bae would finish talking, and he would be slightly confused. I'd go, "Hun, just say you're good and keep it moving. No one has time for your pip-pip, tallyho cheeriness." But let's be real. Most people don't actually really care how you're doing, especially

in New York. It's just a thing to say when you're greeting someone / walking to and fro / getting waited on at a restaurant / participating in the social contract of "Doing the Least to Prove That I'm Not a Serial Killer," etc. I know that sounds harsh and unfeeling, but I argue that it's more of a matter of time and place. Us Americans can certainly pass the time with surface-level chitchat. We just don't want to do that all the time. And, more often than not, if we truly want to know how you're doing, we ask in a different way: "You good?" "You eat?" "You taking care of yourself?"

6. Formula 1 racing. The first time Baekoff turned it on, I was like, "Isn't this just NASCAR, but for people with investment portfolios?" Apparently, F1 is a huge deal: 1.9 BILLION people watched it on television in 2019, the official F1 podcast, *Beyond the Grid*, reached fifteen million downloads over forty-three episodes in the same year, and Netflix's docuseries *Drive to Survive*, which allows viewers to see what goes on behind the scenes (read: lots of petty drama) is an international hit. Clearly, plenty of people love the sport, and after watching *Survive* with Bae, I know how difficult it is to be a race car driver, and yet . . . the sport is boring as fuck! They drive around in circles wearing jumpsuits emblazoned with the names of cars I can't afford—Ferrari, McLaren—and everyone takes themselves so seriously. Between you and me, the only reason I watch

it at all (besides spending time with my boyfriend) is that Lewis Hamilton is hot, routinely beats his competitors, and is Black. Like Issa Rae said, "I'm rooting for everybody Black."

7. You know how when someone will want to drink and be like "Well, it's five o'clock somewhere" to excuse why they are drinking so early in the day? Well, that's how Brits are about sweaters. Excuse me . . . jumpers. Jumpers are all the rage for Brits and they will find any excuse to wear one. "Well, surely a leaf fell in Chechnya, so I best put on this here jumper in case it gets cold." My boyfriend is also like this. He's always dressed like the leader of a poetry group at the University of Manchester.

8. I'm down with a lot of British cultch—the sarcastic sense of humor is right up my alley, eggcups are adorable, and unnecessarily adding the letter "u" in words such as "colour," "honoured," and "humour" is a bit twee, but I'll allow it—however, British people and the whole "washing machines in the kitchen" thing is absolute nonsense. Part of me doesn't even want to bring this up, because sometimes Brits can be a *tad* touchy about the whole thing, like when UK TV presenter of home design and property shows Kirstie Mary Allsopp tweeted a few years ago that having washing machines in kitchens is disgusting, so she's dedicating

part of her life's work to eradicating this tradition, which resulted in an outcry on Twitter. Lol. Usually, a "life's work" is curing a disease, ending hunger, raising kids, mastering Busta Rhymes's verse in "Look at Me Now," but also, I get it, Kirstie! Doing laundry in the kitchen is low-key nasty. The kitchen now smells like a week's worth of funky drawers, sorting your clothes into color-coordinated piles means you have dirty clothes all over the kitchen floor, you're spilling Tide detergent granules everywhere, etc. This, to me, is an un-fresh hell. And this opinion, I am told by social media, is a classist point of view as plenty of people in the UK don't have a utility room to put a washing machine in, and placing it in a bathroom is usually a no-go due to many UK building regulations for wiring in a bathroom. Okay . . . and? Do what we do here in America: Put your laundry in cumbersome drawstring sacks, pack some Luna bars and trail mix, and take your ass on a harrowing journey to the laundromat and wash your clothes there. Is it annoying? Yes. Is it time-consuming? Obvs. Isn't it also much more sanitary and up to code to not wash my Thinx period panties next to an open bottle of balsamic glaze in my kitchen? Fucking duh.

Just think about it this way. If you went to Wolfgang Puck's restaurant and caught a glimpse of him shoving a pile of dirty gardening pants in the wash while he was dressing your beet and goat cheese salad, you'd be like, "No, *non*, *nein*" and leave. Yes, none of us are running restaurants, but we have people over! We're feeding friends, family, and children food that was prepared mere inches from unclean clothes, which, according to my research, is something Brits have been doing since the invention of washing machines, without question or serious pushback. Maybe I'm overthinking it, but that's highly unsanitary, especially when the prevailing thought is that Brits are overflowing with class and Americans are gauche as fuck. I don't think so. If I were Anne Hathaway's character in *The Princess Diaries* when Julie Andrews was gently reading her to filth for her lack of etiquette, I would've been like, "Bitch, please. I may be an ignorant American, but you probably have loose, dirty ankle socks lost underneath your refrigerator that smell like the women's locker room at Wimbledon. You truly cannot tell me shit."

9. The other day, Bae and I were enjoying a silent moment that couples share when they've been dating long enough to know that not talking all the time doesn't mean they're not compatible, they're just comfortable being in the presence of the other person. So there we were chilling in a very pregnant pause, when apropos of nothing, he lifted his head from scrolling on Instagram on his phone and said, "Walmart—I will never understand why anyone would want to buy clothes, a gardening shed, and guns all in the same place." Same, babe. Same.

10. You've seen it in movies, read it in books, or perhaps have been warned by a friend: Brits are stiff, dour, and unfeeling people. But as the legend aka Hollywood reminds us, it doesn't have to be that way. All it takes is for a plucky and loud American to show the sad, uptight Brit there's more to life than uttering "How dreadful" at things that are barely faux pas, that getting ketchup all over your face at dinner means you're carefree, and that rolling up your chinos, sitting down in a park, and reading to your partner is a sign you're not only opening up your heart and falling in love, but that you have transformed as a person! If the love Baekoff has for me ever inspires him to take me to the park and lie me down on the grass so he can read to me while ants use my scalp as the hosting site for their family reunion barbecue that's soundtracked by Kool & the Gang's "Get Down on It," I'd consider that a hate crime against the faux locks I had freshly installed in my head and yet another assault on womanhood that's masqueraded as romance. Call me cynical, but this sort of gesture reeks of pretension and feels distinctly like something men do *at* women, because way back when, men got together and decided these masturbatory and empty exercises are what women wanted instead of, I don't know, asking us?

Seriously, I imagine that back in the day, women were like, "What we really want are our rights. Can we look into getting us some?" And men just said, "Nah, you know what you *need*? To spend even more of your time having a basic-ass white dude talk at you. Lemme read you some Lord Byron. He had bars. Check out this sonnet." Aaaaaaaaaand that's how we ended up with this tomfoolery. I must say that after dating a Brit for the past four years, I don't necessarily disagree with the stereotype that they're a reserved people; however, I've personally observed that Brits generally choose to stick with either the safety and comfort of small talk (I've literally felt one of my eggs die inside me after a twenty-minute convo about *Wallace & Gromit*) OR at the first sign of a personal, substantive discussion, they shut down. And it seems the realer a situation and/or a topic of discussion gets, the more inclined Brits are to go with the latter option of closing themselves off.

Why? Maybe it's because the weather in the UK is cold and dreary, thus making folks more pensive and reticent to open up. But the weather in Seattle is depressing—it rains there on average 152 days a year—yet Eddie Vedder managed to make a whole damn career out of expressing *all* of his feels while sounding like a flooded carburetor. So what's up, UK? Why do y'all tend to hold back on revealing yourselves? There's probably a multitude of reasons, but I've learned that with Baekoff's family, they've never been a particularly verbose bunch. Emotions are just on a need-to-know basis and, apparently, how one feels about anything that's going on personally or professionally is not anything loved ones need to know? So when I started dating Baekoff, I must've seemed like I was a walking emotional open flesh wound with a fresh application of Neosporin as I kept him up to speed on every single thing I was feeling. Meanwhile, for me, he'd often come off like a tight-lipped *Downton Abbey* downstairs servant too scared to tell me that he accidentally sneezed on the tray of Yorkshire puddings for the Christmas party I'm hosting. Obviously, for things to work between Bae and me, we had to find some common ground. I've learned that I don't need to express all of my emotions and opinions all of the time; meanwhile, he has realized that behaving like an at-risk youth who needs me to get my Michelle Pfeiffer in *Dangerous Minds* on so he can open up to me for five minutes has made a bitch tired.

11. Tipping. It's not a thing that's done overseas because, ya know, people in the service industry make a decent livable wage there, unlike here in the States. So when Baekoff and I first started going out and would finish a meal at a restaurant, we'd get the check and he'd be like, "I see there's a line for a tip. So I guess we'll leave a couple dollars?" I'd respond, "I would rather subsidize our waiter's loan for their business on Etsy before I roll up out of here having only left a couple of dubs for what our waiter did during a stressful brunch service because 1) the minimum wage for folks in the service industry is horrible, and 2) everybody up in here would think *I* left that trash-ass tip because there's a

stereotype that Black people don't tip." While my boy-friend doesn't agree with the American system of people having to rely on tips because their baseline pay is offensively low, he understands tipping is a salve for those who are routinely disrespected by customers and overworked by their employers, not to mention that money is what helps them survive, so now my baby leaves a solid 20 to 25 percent tip no matter what.

12. Turns out I don't know how to make tea. I thought I did after being alive for thirty-six years, but I was wrong! I remember the first time I met Baekoff's family and had tea with them. I asked for green tea with honey. They handled this seemingly innocuous request the way I expected them to handle me being Black: colored pinwheels for eyeballs as they buffered, trying to process this information. Ya know, now that I think about it, maybe that's why Meghan Markle didn't get on with the royal family. Not because she's Black, but because she asked for Tazo brand tea with honey in it and that set the tone for her disastrous relationship with Harry's fam. J/K. It's definitely because she's Black. ANYWAY. The point is how I (and many Americans) drink tea is uncouth as fuck to Brits! And they are *not* shy about letting you know that. Every time I had tea, my boyfriend's fam would lovingly roast me about my "concoction." Lol. Store-brand honey and a raggedy Lipton tea bag do not constitute a "concoction." It's a day-two-of-your-period staple

that's good year-round. You know what's not good? The garbage they drink on the regs: Yorkshire Tea with a spot of milk.

If you've never had the displeasure of having Yorkshire Tea, I'll break it down for you. It tastes like the ends of boxed braids after your hairstylist has burned them with a lighter so as to seal and prevent them from unraveling while the braids are in your hair . . . but in liquid form. Yorkshire Tea is burnt, bitter, and b'not great (lol, I was going for alliteration and failed), yet Yorkshire or PG Tips, which is basically the same thing although British people think I'm mad for believing that, are the go-to tea beverages. Literally, Sri Lanks aka Sri Lanka and Assam, India (both former British territories), are like, "We have thousands upon thousands of flavors that are actually delicious. Wanna try?" And the UK is like, "No fanks, bruvs! We'll stick with the two teas that taste like worn-down car tires on a Ford Fiesta. Cheers!"

Okay, that pretty much sums up what it's like to be an American dating a Brit. Well, I'm sure I skipped over some cultural differences, such as meeting the parents. As we all know, in the States, introducing your boo to your parents is a big deal and typically reserved for when you're dating someone special; otherwise you're not going to waste your parents' time or one of their Sunday best outfits for a person you don't see some sort of a future with. It's kind of like on *Shark Tank* when a contestant comes on, makes a wild-ass evaluation of their company—"I'm asking for $200,000 in exchange for 5 percent of my company"—and is unwilling to negotiate, frustrating the sharks until one of them, usually Mark Cuban, gets so indignant and asks, "Why did you come on this show when you clearly have no intention of making a deal?"

The point is, whether they're business or personal, big-time meetings mean something, which is why it's rare for Americans to introduce their parents to partners they're not serious about. So, the first time Baekoff came with me to Cleveland for the holidays, everyone in my family knew this was my way of saying, "This is it. He's the One." Whereas when it was time to meet Baekoff's mom and I expressed nervousness about her liking me, he simply responded with, "I don't care if my mum likes you. She's not the one living with you. And she's not the one loving you. I am." Well, damn. It's like that? Oh. Okay. He then went on to explain that meeting the parents in the UK is more of a formality, like two people shaking hands when saying goodbye, as opposed to an approval-seeking or quality control process. Therefore, while it's nice to get affirmation from the parents, it's by no means a relationship-defining moment. So in the case of Mama Baekoff, he was fine if it didn't go well or if she didn't like me because as he (and the Brits) like to say, "On your bike, luv," which basically means "Go fuck yourself." Yeah . . . it's a bit extreme, innit?

But if that doesn't sum up British cultch, I don't know what does. All I do know is that I'm having the time of my life discovering all his cultural idiosyncrasies and vice versa. Sometimes they make us laugh, other times they open our eyes to a new way of seeing the world, and sometimes we may never fully understand them, yet they end up being a thing we inexplicably grow to love (witnessing Baekoff's excitement any time he has baked beans on toast makes me so happy). Whatever the case may be, dating each other has been one of the most enriching experiences of our lives in that whenever we go out and I'm rocking a brand-new 'do, he's lovingly on "edges duty," making sure my hair looks just as fresh at the end of the night as it does at the beginning, while I'm falling deeper into the Wings musical library.

They're really fucking good, you guys.

Self-Care Is Not a Candle
and Therapy Is Not a Notebook:
How We Are Doing the Most
and the Absolute Least at
the Same Damn Time

~~~~~

Whenever conspiracy theorists or folks skeptical of authority utter the phrase "Big Brother is watching," I'm like, "Hopefully in 4K Ultra HD! I mean, have you seen unremastered TV shows from the nineties? The film quality is hot garbage!" Kidding! But for real, when I hear this warning, I usually roll my eyes. Look, I agree that government surveillance is *no bueno*, but I'm in too deep! I have a phone, computer, multiple social media accounts, I use the internet, and I would let Big Bruth spy on me AND use me as a pawn to capture trifling heauxes in exchange for an overpriced sal. Like, if they told me I'd get a lifetime discount from sweetgreen, I'd go, "Drop a pin on your locaysh, boo, and I'll meet ya there in fifteen minutes like I'm Deep Throat with some tea to spill on Watergate."

Point is, the gubment's got my number and it's *fine*, okay?

Having them watch my boring little life is better than me pulling a Henry David Thoreau, who, at twenty-eight, moved to Walden Pond in Massachusetts (never heard of it) and built a cabin with his bare-ass hands (my ancestors built the White House, so I feel like I'm exempt from ever having to do anything architectural for as long as I live). Anyway, he did all of this because, as he wrote, he "wanted to live deep and suck out all the marrow of life" and being off the grid allowed him to do that. No. Fucking. Thanks. I'm into living sha-ha-sha-la-la-la-lowly on the grid with the modern-day comforts of Face ID and Gravity Blankets because life is not actually a delicious marrow, but a lukewarm *Fear Factor* smoothie that's comprised of wheatgrass, insects, and a splash of lemon. I will take two courtesy slurps then ask the bartender to keep the whiskey neats coming until the day I die. I am remaining firmly *on* the grid, so, Big Brother, put on your bifocals and enjoy the show! Now . . . with that said, I do have one small grievance: My phone needs to mind its damn business and quit eavesdropping on me, because every time I open Instagram, I'm presented with some goofy-ass ads, loosely based off something I've said.

One time, my friend and I were discussing beach season, and Instagram showed me an ad for a brand selling hydrating masks made to counteract dry bikini lines. Uhhh, my pelvic region isn't parched, but thanks for the concern? However, if it were, I'd simply drink some water, put a dab of Aveeno near my coochie, and keep it moving because I'm an adult. Then there was the time I mentioned to Bae that I was going to start bringing a packed lunch to work, and the next time I went on Instagram, there was an ad for a lunch box that looked like a purse and cost SEVENTY DOLLARS. Plus tax! Lol, I love how I write "plus tax" as if *that's* the thing that crossed the line. But for real, who's dropping a Ulysses S. Grant and a half to house their generic ham sandwich and bag of carrots? But these instances were just the tip of the iceberg.

I had recently started going to therapy to deal with, oh, you know, the dumpster fire that was 2020. My phone overheard me talking about it to a friend, and lo and behold, the next time I logged in to Instagram, a sponsored post appeared for a company called Bloom. The caption read: "Be your own therapist with cognitive behavioral therapy." Last I checked, I'm not a raggedy chair from a flea market that's begging to be reupholstered, so why in the Sigmund Freud hell would I attempt to DIY my life? One of the reasons for going to therapy is because one isn't capable of getting their shit together on their own, so they bring a highly trained outside source into the fold who can provide a much-needed analytical and objective perspective. So why is Bloom acting like my boo-boo-ass liberal arts college degree, the fact that I've seen the end credits— *not* a full episode mind you, *just* the end credits—of *Frasier* ("Tossed Salads and Scrambled Eggs" is a bop) and I have a therapy notebook app are, together, a sufficient stand-in for what a licensed professional can provide? Y'all, we both know it ain't. Think back to the last time you tried to be an impartial supervisor of your life. How did it go? I'll tell you how it went for me. Literally every single time I had to answer only to myself, I sent me to voicemail (the mailbox was full, naturally) and carried on with the bullshit.

Food diary? I'll eat healthy all day and then not record the

Rice Krispies Treat I had before bed because if I don't write it down, then the calories don't "count." Monthly budget planner? January 1, I'm on my "new year, new me" ish, so I'm keeping track of everything down to the penny, but by MLK Day, I'm like, "The $95.69 I spent buying emergency U2 concert DVDs? I'll just file that away in the old noggin and remember to deduct that from what I allocated for entertainment." Cut to me absolutely forgetting that purchase (I legit have the memory of Dory from *Finding Nemo*) and proceeding to blow more money on buying the *Die Hard* and *Rush Hour* movie collections from iTunes—#TrueStory—thus overspending in the entertainment category. Piano lessons? I bought a keyboard during Covid, certain that I would practice three hours a day and, by the time quarantine was over, I was going to be the next Alicia Keys. I kept that practice schedule for the first month, then I skipped a day, which turned into a few days, then a week later I'd get back on the wagon and then promptly fall off again until I eventually stopped playing completely. Suffice it to say, I'm not the next A. Keys. At best, I'm a mediocre wedding band pianist who only knows "Uptown Funk," "Livin' on a Prayer," and Lee Ann Womack's "I Hope You Dance," and I'm praying that everyone is too drunk at the reception to notice I put those songs in the rotaysh three times. Point is, self-discipline is hard. Accountability is harder. Therapy, at times, can be the hardest. And, at the rate society is going, actual and legitimate mental and emotional wellness is damn near impossible to achieve and sustain because the rebellious nature of self-care has been lobotomized and replaced with something far less complicated and much more tooth-less. Or at least that's how it seems. Beneath the soothing en-ergy of modern-day self-care lies a world full of deliberate flaws designed to get and keep us on the distractingly pleasurable hamster wheel of self-care so that we don't actually notice the ways society has failed us.

Self-care is, according to the *Harvard Business Review*, an eleven-*billion*-dollar industry. With that much money on the table, coupled with the societal shift toward obsessing about the self—e.g., constantly thinking about and tweaking the self—it's no wonder why what began as an earnest preserva-tion of the health of the individual, and, equally, of the com-munity (more on that later) has been reduced to *yet* another form of labor, which is right in line with our work-obsessed culture. Only instead of it being a nine-to-five day gig where you can clock in and clock out, caring for onself is an around-the-clock gig in which ABI aka Always Be Improving is less of a light suggestion and more of an addiction that's aided by technology and fueled by monetization. Charlotte Lieberman analyzes this in her *Harvard Business Review* article entitled "How Self-Care Became So Much Work." In it, she discusses how the dogged devotion to self-care and self-improvement is eerily similar to the oppressive energy that many of us put into our careers:

> Our focus is shifting away from the *actual* self—our bod-ies, minds, and spirits—and toward data *about* the self. With iEverythings around us at all times, we expect our

steps to be enumerated, our REM cycles to be recorded, and our breathing patterns to be measured. It's not enough to just feel better—we need our devices to affirm that we are doing the work. . . . This raises the question: Are we genuinely interested in feeling healthier and happier? It seems likely that the values driving us to be workaholics in the first place are also encouraging us to "optimize" ourselves by using metric-driven "hacks."

And if we're not accumulating data, we're spending money, which means that self-care is no longer accessible to everyone except the privileged. Furthermore, it's that being able to afford self-care is sometimes, in and of itself, *also* self-care. Disposable income then becomes visible proof to the world that you are working hard at your job so as to be able to work hard at your life. To be clear, I'm not saying this as a finger-wagging, omniscient narrator who's pointing out all the ways everyone else is wrong. I'm right there with you, stuck in pursuit of the instant-gratification trappings of shiny new things that, ultimately, end up having increasingly diminished returns.

In my estimation, I own fifteen notebooks / life planners, a couple dozen candles, three yoga mats, a few pieces of crystal, and subscriptions to meditation and self-affirmation apps, as well as buying myself a small bouquet of flowers monthly, and I consume self-help books the way some folks eat Pringles. My apartment is basically one introduction-to-crochet kit and several dream catchers away from being the equivalent of a fully stocked Etsy shop. As much as I am loathe to admit it, a massive part of me LOVES commercialized self-care. Each purchase gives me a hit of endorphins that scream, "Yes, honey! Keep gathering evidence that shows how you are constantly becoming the new and improved version of you." Then days (or truthfully, mere minutes) pass and I'm still the same me I was before I spent that money. Still saddled with the same issues. Still living in the same environment (some of it self-created, some of it not) that creates the anxiety that we're led to believe present-day self-care can fix, but, as we all know, it rarely, if ever, does. Instead, it keeps us locked in the same counterproductive cycle. Writer Shayla Love ruminates on this very conundrum in her 2018 Vice.com article "The Dark Truths Behind Our Obsession with Self-Care":

> At the time this issue went to press, there were 9.5 million posts on Instagram[1] about #selfcare, which is hundreds of thousands more than when I first started thinking about the topic critically. . . . But self-care has been appropriated by companies and turned into #selfcare; a kind of tease about the healthcare that we are lacking and are desperate for. . . . You can't actually treat an anxiety disorder with a bubble bath or a meditation app, and the supposition that you can is a dangerous one.
>
> If we lived in a world in which we were being properly taken care of, would self-care have the same appeal?

---

1. By the way, an article in the *Guardian* that was published the next year reported that the number of posts is now over eighteen million.

Furthermore, many of these things Love mentioned and more—unwinding for a couple of hours by watching TV, going on a walk, reading a book, drinking a glass of wine, calling a friend—should be the bare minimum. Utterly unremarkable to the point of being unmentioned. Which raises the question: If doing these lightweight activities is oft accompanied by a touch of pomp and circumstance so as to let everyone know we are, indeed, taking care of ourselves, isn't that a major red flag? Like, if you were dating someone and every week, they declared, "Just letting you know I'm not cheating. #SoupsMonogs," you'd most likely respond with, "Okay, Dick Van Dyke. How many chimneys are you sweeping aka who you fucking?" The constant need to make an announcement starts to feel a bit like that whole "the lady doth protest too much" thing. And when it comes to self-care, so many of us are that lady! We're screaming at the top of our lungs about how we're reclaiming our lives and taking care of ourselves, but I'm starting to question whether any of us actually believe that. If the numbers have anything to say about the matter, I think the answer is we don't.

Last year, ASD, the Affordable Shopping Destination, which is a fifty-plus-year-old consumer trade show that started as two associations joining forces to create a trade show and product expo group for the general merchandise market, began tracking the growing interest in self-care. They found that between 2019 and 2020, self-care-related Google searches increased by 250 percent. Mental Health First Aid, a program that teaches people how to "identify, understand, and respond to signs of mental illness and substance disorders," stated that "the most common mental illnesses in the U.S. are anxiety disorders, which affect 40 million adults (18.1 percent of the population)." And unless you've been living under a rock, you know that our healthcare system is an unmitigated disaster and that is, say it with me: by design.

Mental Health America, a nonprofit organization, revealed in 2017 that around 56.5 percent of U.S. adults who have a mental illness received no past year treatment, and 64.1 percent of U.S. youths who suffer from major depression never received treatment. Why? Well, as Love writes, "Another study in *JAMA* [*Journal of the American Medical Association*] found that in 2009 and 2010, only 55 percent of psychiatrists accepted health insurance, compared with nearly 89 percent of other specialist doctors. People on Medicaid have even worse luck: Only about four out of ten psychiatrists accept Medicaid, according to research published in *JAMA Psychiatry*. The only lower rate for Medicaid acceptance is for dermatologists." Ooof, pretty grim, and if you're hoping things are looking up now, you're about to be disappointed. Mental Health America conducted a report in 2021 on the state of mental health and found that the number of uninsured adults with a mental illness (5.1 million) increased for the first time since the ACA, the Affordable Care Act, was passed, with New Jersey coming in first with only 2.5 percent uninsured and Wyoming bringing up the rear with a whopping 23 percent who are uninsured.

This is a lot to take in, and I'm not sharing this data to bum us out, although seeing how dire the state of mental health is in America is certainly cause for despair. I'm bringing this information up (and believe me, I only scratched the surface) because clearly, there's a disconnect. Our mental health is worsening yet we're practicing self-care and improving all the time? The logic ain't logic'ing. As a society, we are struggling. Like *"The Wolf of Wall Street*'s Leonardo DiCaprio hopped up on bad quaaludes and crawling across a driveway to get inside his Lambo" struggling. What we're doing (modern-day self-care) isn't working. What we're *refusing* to do (treat mental health and health in general as a nonnegotiable pillar of society and operate with the understanding that taking care of one's self also means taking care of the community) also isn't working. So how did we get here? How did we lose our way when we had the blueprint of all blueprints? I'm talking about, of course, Audre Geraldine Lorde, whose revolutionary, highly political, and defiant execution of self-care unintentionally became the inspiration (and undefined catchall term) for our current crop of Instagrammers, executives, and celebrities, as well as for the average layperson.

To be clear, the idea of self-care has a long and storied history. It dates back to the ancient Greeks, which philosopher Michel Foucault examined in *The History of Sexuality, Volume 3: The Care of the Self*. In the 1950s, self-care came to be understood as simple activities such as personal grooming that allowed institutionalized patients to retain some sense of autonomy. A decade later, academics recommended self-care as a way for PTSD sufferers to combat their symptoms, and the solutions included things we tend to do today: meditation, eating well, sleeping, exercising, etc. With these remedies, coupled with all these white dudes such as Thoreau, Walt Whitman, and Ralph Waldo Emerson authoring the narrative of American individualism and specialness, it's easy to see how the seeds of self-care as it's commonly understood today were planted.

Nothing against these guys because they were mighty with the pen, but white men stay creating chaos with their semi-self-absorbed nonsense like overconfident Steve Urkels minus the apologetic "Did I do that?" energy. Seriously, these guys were just as narcissistic, if not more, as us 'lennials and Gen Zers. I mean, women get dinged for taking and posting selfies all the time, buuuuuuuut Walt Whitman wrote a poem called "Song of Myself." Obviously, he was not one to bury the lede on the fact that he's about to come with the bullshit, but the title is nothing in comparison to the fact that the poem has *FIFTY-TWO PARTS*. Fifty-two parts?! That is sooooooo many parts. In fact, it's too many parts! Ikea credenzas tap out at thirteen pieces. Say what you want about the Swedes, but they know how to get in and get the fuck out. Like, Walter couldn't have given us the Cliffs Notes version? How long does it take to say "I high-key fucks with myself"? Did we really need to trudge through beautiful language and imagery to read about him sounding his "barbaric yawp over the roofs of the world"? Bruh, take your yawps and wrap this shit up. We got places to be and people to see. This concludes my TED Talk. Come back next week when I drag F. Scott Fitzgerald for taking 218 pages to write about how the American dream is trash when *The Great Gatsby* could've been summed up in two words: "Duh, bitch!" But back to my point.

Self-care has kind of always been centered around individualism, so I don't want to pretend that it was this pure, enlightened concept that got sullied. However, we must acknowledge that its current iteration is inspired by a spirit of defiance even if that essence is often forgotten today. Self-care saw a resurgence in popularity due to another kind of trauma—racial injustice against Black people—and this new version was spearheaded by the Black Panther Party in the 1970s, which advocated for Black independence and infused activism and tactical resistance against white supremacy into everything they did. This time, self-care was less concerned with the usual personal upkeep of sleep and grooming, and more intent on being a rallying cry that marginalized people matter and are just as entitled to quality healthcare as their white counterparts, as Nicole Stamp writes in her article "The Revolutionary Origins of Self-Care" on the Canadian website Local Love:

> The Black Panther Party began promoting [self-care] as essential for all Black citizens, as a means of staying resilient while experiencing the repeated injuries of systemic, interpersonal and medical racism. . . . To compensate for this failing, the Black Panthers created free community healthcare clinics that tested for [sickle cell disease] and provided follow-up care.

Enter Audre Lorde. A self-described "Black, lesbian, mother, warrior, poet," she dedicated her life and creative work to fighting injustices ranging from racism and sexism to homophobia and capitalism. At the root of this work was an ideology that confronting these societal issues is for the benefit not of the individual, but for the collective. I mean, that's the only way to be a civil rights activist, correct? Like, you can't be a civil rights activist and be like, "Oh, now that we've gotten this far, I just meant I want rights for me. It's every person for themselves going forward." Like people working to get civil rights isn't akin to a group of contestants on *Survivor* forming an alliance in order to get themselves to the final four and then all bets are off. Could you imagine John Lewis telling Martin Luther King, Jr., to kick rocks with a selfish "time to get mine" energy after the Selma marches galvanized the nation? That would've been ignorant. Anyway, what I'm getting at is that Lorde and her work were for the liberation of herself *and* the people. That fierce passion for universal independence didn't weaken when she was diagnosed with cancer—first breast cancer in 1978, which lead to a mastectomy, and then the cancer metastasized to her liver—it only strengthened as she opted to take charge of her own treatment, which was yet one more revolutionary decision in a revolutionary life. She wrote her take on self-care in her 1988 book, *A Burst of Light,* and ended up revitalizing the concept when she said, "Caring for myself is not self-indulgence, it is self-preservation, and that is an act of political warfare."

Both the Black Panthers and Lorde saw self-care as a political act, one meant to protect the mental and physical well-being of underrepresented communities, namely women, people of color, and LGBTQIA+ folks, which the system purposefully neglected. If the system wasn't going to look after marginalized communities, then, damnit, the communities would look after themselves *and* each other. And because capitalism was one of the cornerstones of inequality and systemic oppression, it's only natural that the BPs and Lorde rejected capitalism and kept it out of the self-care conversation, which is why it's all the more disheartening that their version of self-care has been distorted by businesses in pursuit of the almighty dollar.

This retooling and commodification of self-care reminds me of when I first started going to dive bars during my college years. I thought drinking screwdrivers (a cocktail made from orange juice and vodka) was very adultlike, so I'd excitedly order one, only to be given what was basically Minute Maid concentrate with a splash of rubbing alcohol. Because it made me feel good and gave me the courage to grind on some barely-not-a-stranger's crotch,[2] I thought it was good *for* me in a way. And isn't "good vibes" a key tenet of contemporary self-care? Feeling good in the moment or working toward feeling good in the future seems to be the objective. And when we associate taking care of one's self with always being in a state of joy, are we actually taking care or engaging in activities that give us quick pleasure hits? Rewarding oneself is not the same as taking care of oneself. It's as Perpetua Neo, doctor of clinical

---

2. Many are up in arms about Cardi B and Megan Thee Stallion's comically raunchy collabo on "WAP" and their sensual dancing, because of the potential effect it could have on their young fans. I hear them, but I would like us all to remember that in the early aughts, the default go-to dancing across the cunch aka country in high school and college was literally teenage girls and women backing their asses into men's crotches and then grinding against them until their thighs tired out or a Bad Boy Records playlist ended, whichever came first. Like, we weren't even smooth with it. It was legit like, "Hi! Do you mind if I rub my butt against you the way Tom Hanks in *Cast Away* rubbed two pieces of sticks together to make fire for him and his bestie, Wilson, and then when the song is over, I'mma leave you to deal with your half chub while I go for a snack break and dip a Tostitos chip in a bowl of salsa con queso?" We *all* used to do this and went on to become Sallie Mae phone operators, essential workers, Apple Genius Bar employees, COOs, etc. So let's calm down, 'kay? The kids are alright.

psychology, puts it in an essay of hers on MindBodyGreen
.com, "I'm a Psychologist & Here's the Biggest Mistake I See
People Make with Self-Care":

> We all self-soothe. It gives us comfort and distracts us during difficult times, which can include things like taking a bubble bath, getting yourself a fancy drink at your favorite juice bar, or taking time off from work or child care.
>
> Self-soothing, however, does not help us move forward or remedy the situation. Or, it may lead to an emotional, physical, or financial hangover. Just as with overdrinking alcohol, any escape behavior can be used in excess, from shopping to eating to sex.

We've all been guilty of that mindset: I deserve to feel good because of all the energy I'm putting in at work / raising my kids / tending to aging parents / showing up for my friends, partner, loved ones / being alive. That's true! I fundamentally believe that we all deserve to feel good. But all the time? Even when self-improving? Doesn't growing and changing require some pain as well? For example, exercising can make you sore, but on the other side of that temporary discomfort is strength you didn't have before. To me, true growth doesn't exist without the breaking of the old and rebuilding it into something different and new. But when we're living in a world riddled with adversity that we must face head-on daily, it can seem, at times, as though the chance for happiness is slipping through our fingers, so we're going to take what we can get. We're going to get what society has been denying us in any form that we can because it's time for the world to pay up. At least, that's how I used to feel.

Over the past few years, I've felt I've given too much. Not in an "I'm an essential worker / doctor / great thinker of our time" kind of way, but in an "I'm a financially insecure free-lancer turned business owner who has had to learn on the job, which has cost me thousands upon thousands of dollars and I don't have a plan B / my parents can't bail me out" kind of way. My livelihood was predicated on the stress-inducing ex-istence of never knowing when or how much money was go-ing to come in. While that made me resilient and taught me how to persevere, it also made me feel a bit like a scrappy stray dog. And not the kind of dog in movies that gets adopted by an old, craggy dude in Levi's who refuses to go to therapy and instead magically heals himself because he has an animal he can feed Kibbles 'n Bits to. But the kind of dog that has "THUG LIFE" tattooed across its stomach and is ready to knucketh if anyone decides to bucketh.[3] Simply put, I was always in fight mode, constantly having to pick up the pieces and begin again. And when you pair that with my type A personal-ity, it's easy to see how I became a workaholic. Yes, I know. I've mentioned my type A personality and addiction to work throughout this book. If you haven't guessed it by now, they are two of the biggest themes of my life that were working for me until they weren't. Left unchecked for twelve years, they

---

3. I recognize that this Shakespearean spin on an early aughts Crime Mob hit may be confusing to some of the white readers. Now, y'all know how I feel when I'm in a room and a group of white people starts talking about Ben Folds Five. Lol. Was that a wild reference? Should I be more current? Hmm, nah, not my style.

mutated in ways I couldn't control, so while I was building the career I dreamt of, I also developed counterproductive habits, was in a constant state of burnout, and quietly felt trapped in the life I built.

Because even though my priorities shifted—I became an apartment owner, I could afford to fly home to visit my family and no longer wanted to miss important events because of job commitments, I started living and seeing the world—I stayed on the work hamster wheel since that level of intensity is what thrust me into the next phase of my life. Still, I knew what I was doing was no longer tenable. Something had to change. So what did I do? Much like I did with my career, I threw myself into self-improvement and contemporary self care.

You know when a TV show becomes a cultural phenomenon, so you decide to check it out, but you now have really high expectations? After binging the whole series, you're like, "Dat's it? I wasted a month's worth of eggs on watching something that is actually pretty average, and I'm not talking Kirkland brand eggs, but the ones that were chilling in my left fallope?" That's kind of how I feel about contemporary self-care. When I was finally financially able to participate in the world of #SelfCare, I was conflicted. For much of my adult life, I was on the outside looking in and believed that self-care was consumerism nonsense designed to take our money, which, if I'm being honest, was in part due to the fact that I was jealous that I couldn't afford to indulge in it. At the same time . . . having expendable money to buy face masks and bath bombs is nice, and using those products *does* feel good. And as much as I wanted to dig in my heels and dismiss these privileges as merely frivolous distractions, I couldn't. Turns out I do believe that pampering and substantive care can coexist. I came to this belief not because I'm wise, but because I ended up turning into Linda Blair from *The Exorcist.*

During the most stressful part of quarantine, when all my work was up in the air, I was so riddled with anxiety that one morning, while writing something—a script, this book, an email, I don't remember what—I promptly got up from my laptop, vomited quietly into a trash can (I didn't want to wake up British Baekoff), wiped my mouth, and then returned to my computer to work. BITCH, WUT? I was out here ralphing into a simplehuman trash bag all cuz of some emails and a Microsoft Word doc? I know I shouldn't judge myself harshly, but that was gahtdamn ridiculous. Vomiting should be relegated to morning sickness, the flu, and meeting Post Malone, I guess?[4] Anyway, I knew I needed help and immediately began therapy. A quick word.

"Hate" is a strong word, but I *hate* when folks do things like go to therapy, have a housekeeper or a nanny, etc., and don't acknowledge the privilege in being able to afford these expenses. It's like that time when, years ago, after months and months of saving, I bought a knockoff Hervé Léger bodycon dress during a 50 percent off sale at Macy's for my birthday party. I

---

4. Here's the tea. A few years ago at a meet and greet, a Texas fan threw up after smelling Post Malone. It became pop culture fodder for three days and then, apparently, everyone moved on as if Post smelling like BO and Costco corn chips isn't a hot-ass mess. Y'all, I know this is garbage, but when I reincarnate, I ain't tryna come back as a weeping willow tree or a hummingbird. I'mma see if I can come back as a white dude who "audacities" aka doesn't wash his legs in the shower and is still allowed to be famous and open a bank account.

was so excited and telling my friend, a fellow fashion plate and a comic who also comes from money, about the dress, and she responded, "Oh, I could never wear a fake Hervé Léger. You just have to buy the real thing." Listen, heaux! Not everyone can afford to spend thousands of dollars on a dress that looks like it's comprised of a bunch of seat belts from the Mitsubishi factory. So for her to behave as though buying designer clothes is everyone's experience showed how out of touch she was.

That's why I will never pretend that taking care of your mental health is just something everyone can do. It requires disposable money, which so many people don't have. So it's no wonder why people turn to candles and notebooks. What other recourse is there? The government isn't there for us. Mental healthcare isn't adequately funded, wrote Richard Frank, a professor of health economics at Harvard, because of "difficulty in defining mental illness, the lack of evidence on effective treatments, the high cost of covering mental healthcare, and the uncertainty in making actuarial estimates of costs." When people constantly encounter a system that doesn't believe them and won't use its resources to help them or spend the time necessary to find the most effective solution for bettering their mental health, and, most important, when people are unable to afford mental healthcare, *of course* they are going to look for solutions they can easily apply to their lives, hence notebooks, candles, blankets, etc. Damn, it's not just that the government isn't there for us, it's that many of their officials are actively working *against* us out of bias and greed. Either way, we're the ones who are suffering the consequences.

So I will never take therapy for granted or pretend that it is a universal experience. Rather, I'm forever grateful to have a therapist and that I don't have childhood trauma to unpack, but instead am wrestling with anxiety, poor coping skills, and workaholism. This is not meant to belittle my problems in comparison to others', but it's important to be up-front and honest. One more thing: If you're a person of color and in a position where you can start therapy, I highly recommend working with someone who is the same race as you. It was really nice not to waste a session explaining the "work twice as hard only to get half as much" concept with my therapist. She gets it. She's lived it. Now, with all that said, let's return to discussing my newish therapy journey.

In addition to learning how to deal with work-related stress, I wanted to deal with the stress of 2020, and finally, and perhaps most important, get a handle on the sense of lacking I felt, which I had hoped treating myself to takeout and buying more things would address. Despite all the self-care, the lacking persisted, so I drowned myself in work even more as a distraction and, as a result, I was connecting less and less with people. I was mentally rushing through every conversation, phone call, virtual hangout, agitated that I had to be fully present for someone else because *hadn't I already given enough?* Time, energy, vomit. Realizing how overworking was starting to make me selfish and unappreciative, I thought, *Well, I'll first work on myself, then eventually turn outward to restrengthen my relationship with the world,* but like Charlotte Lieberman wrote in that *Harvard Business Review* article, I was consumed with my "iEverythings" and tracking my progress. I was slowly becoming an island unto myself. *Once I'm done working on me, I will turn outward*, I'd tell myself.

But the work is never done, really, is it? And in striving toward excavating myself and analyzing all the pieces, I had forsaken connecting with others and communities. And I don't mean in the cliché New Yorker way of "I'm not talking to my neighbors," but in a deeper "I'm not caring for the collective" way. And I had misinterpreted that neglect as another self-related problem, so I burrowed within myself even more, not realizing that gravitating away from instead of toward others was exacerbating the problem. I don't know how I lost sight of the importance of community, especially when I consider the kind of family I come from.

By now, you're well aware of how amazing my parents are, but let me tell you about my brother, Phil Jr. Like my parents, he's imbued with a deep sense of community. He has spent much of his career working at various nonprofits and is now a state representative in Ohio. He's passionate about education, gun control, LGBTQIA+ rights. Basically, anything that's predicated on what will best serve the masses, he's a staunch supporter of. As far as my parents are concerned, you already know they're introverts and don't spend that much time with other people, but that doesn't mean they're #IsolationNation. Almost every business they started when I was growing up was rooted in, yes, money, so as to provide a better life for my brother and me, but also to provide a service to others. They understood the value of showing up. Whether it was them taking odd jobs to help pay for my high school education or my dad homeschooling my niece during Covid because he knew that would not only help lighten my brother and sister-in-law's workload, but that he could be a supplementary educational figure for Olivia, they know it's not about being a martyr. Caring about the collective and what's best for everyone instead of what would be best for himself (I'm sure my dad would love to just be straight chilling in his sixties) means that he's choosing to strengthen our collective, which will, by default, also strengthen him. He gets special time with her while also helping mold a citizen. And when my mom is not swamped with her day job, she's reading and playing with my niece and nephew as well. Taking them to the park so they can explore nature, painting with them to nurture their creative side, and so on. To my parents, their children and grandchildren are their community, because if they nurture and raise us right, they know we will pay it forward, and so on and so on.

Seeing how my parents and brother operate is all the proof I needed to suggest that perhaps it's time for me, and for all of us, to take a beat from modern-day self-care. For far too long, we've all been conditioned to focus on the "I" to the point that doing something that puts others first instead of the self is often met with suspicion. These efforts tend to be labeled as "virtue signaling," and while there is some of that, there are equally as many, if not more, people who genuinely want to contribute to the collective, but might not know how to get started. While some of that wariness is because we're an "iNation," I believe that much of that is because of the trauma all of us have lived through.

#MeToo. The Donald Trump presidency. The rise of technology and social media that makes it possible for us to see global atrocities in real time. The lives lost to the coronavirus. We are inundated with toxic behavior, violence, death, and fear, so self-preservation is understandably at an all-time high, which means that yes, a face mask does feel like taking care of oneself. It feels like it is a remedy in the face of a litany of information and destruction that is too much to process all at once, never mind actually do something about. And I think the only way out of that is for society to reprioritize the collective good, link arms, and figure this shit out together.

Ya know, this reminds me of one of U2's biggest hits, "One." Please bear with me because I'm not bringing them up arbitrarily. Although, don't tempt me because I'm down to talk about U2 all the time, anytime. Anyway. Inspired by the band's fractious relationship following the global success of the *Joshua Tree* album and the concert film *Rattle and Hum* not being received by the public in the way the band had intended, they returned to work on their album *Achtung Baby* and were flirting with the idea of breaking up. After months of trying to record in Berlin, "One" came together, by all accounts in a thirty-minute burst of inspiration, and rejuvenated the band. They then used this song as the centerpiece to build the rest of the album around. In the book *U2 by U2* (even if U2 isn't your favorite band, if you're into creatives openly and honestly talking about their process, I highly recommend this book), the band talked about how people interpret the song completely differently than U2 does, which explains why it's often played at weddings. Bono elaborates:

"One" is not about oneness; it's about difference. It is not the old hippie idea of "Let's all live together." It is a much more punk rock concept. It's anti-romantic: "We are one, but we're not the same. We get to carry each other." It's a reminder that we have no choice. I'm still disappointed when people hear the chorus line as "We've got to" rather than "We get to carry each other." Because it is resigned, really. It's not: "Come on everybody, let's vault over the wall." Like it or not, the only way out of here is if I give you a leg up the wall and you pull me after you.

I mean, if this song and the idea of showing up for one another saved the band, then why can't the idea save the world? Okay, that was a little cheesy, but I couldn't help myself! In all seriousness, *we*, you and I, are in this thing called life together and we're each other's only hope in making things better.

So let's get radical again. More than that, how about someone or *someones* in mental healthcare and politics get radical with us and help us save ourselves by moving away from capitalism and quick fixes and only focusing on self-soothing and not enough on the community and moving toward a society that cares for and about us? A society that shows us they care by making mental healthcare as accessible as charging stations for our phones. A society that listens to and believes people of color who, like Audre Lorde, want to take control of their health. A society that encourages us to push past surface-level pleasures and dig deep, all the while ensuring that they will be there on the other side of the pain and discomfort, waiting for us. If we could have that, maybe, just maybe, we all could get on the road toward becoming happier individuals. And . . . ?

Okay, fine, we could also buy a candle and a notebook because even though a candle isn't self-care and a notebook isn't therapy, they sure do look lovely in our homes. What can I say? I like pretty, unnecessary things, which I will be unpacking with my therapist right after we discuss my allegiance to yacht rock. It's not something I'm proud of, but I love me some Michael McDonald and so does literally every Black person, so I guess we all need some ther-ther. 'Kay, probably not what the Black Panthers had in mind when they advocated for free healthcare for all, especially Black people, but let's roll with it.

4C Girl Living in Anything but a 4C World:
The Disrespect

⁓

Folks will say, "People who do CrossFit are so strong," and I'm like, "Suuuuure? Yeah, they can do legless rope climbs and handstand walks, but call me when they're able to detangle 4C hair after it's been in mini two-strand twists for three weeks *without* their hands getting tired; otherwise, I. Am. Not. Impressed!" Similarly, I remember after the premiere of *The Last Dance*, the ESPN docuseries about the legendary Chicago Bulls, Michael Jordan was praised for his mental fortitude. I mean, I guess? Don't get me wrong, leading a team to six NBA championships is no small feat, but has he ever spent a morning as a Black woman trying to emulate Solange's thick and wavy Afro only to end up looking like Frederick Douglass on a Black History Month stamp and, as tears welled up in his eyes, let out a deep sigh and resigned himself to give off Freddy Dougs's "Y'all done messed up when you taught me how to read" energy everywhere he went that day? No? Then I'm not that blown away by what Michael Jordan achieved.

And when people go on and on about Apple's innovation under Steve Jobs, all I can think about is my vast wig collection, as well as the natural hairstyles I rock that allow me to look like a different Black woman every day. On Monday, popping on a pixie cut wig means I'm giving you vintage Toni Braxton. Tuesday is when I'm switching it up with a beachwave shoulder-length bob like I'm Kerry Washington on the red carpet. A giant curly wig on Wednesday has me living out my Tracee Ellis Ross fantasy, while Thursday, I'm serving you bone-straight Naomi Campbell, and by the weekend, I'm wig-free and sporting Fulani braids à la Issa Rae at the Met Gala in 2018. To do all of that in *one* week? *That's* ingenuity, bitch.

Look, my intention isn't to minimize the achievements of others; rather, I hope to shine a light on what's being overlooked. I understand that to some, Black hair is too inconsequential to be regarded as anything noteworthy, but I beg to differ. It's not *just* hair, and what we have done and continue to do with it is anything but unimportant. It's culture defining, influential, and often one of the many outlets we use to express ourselves. Why else would societies work so hard to ostracize and shame Black people and their hair if they and it didn't contain an awe-inducing level of confidence, glory, and power, which in the eyes of the insecure is seen as a threat? Just take a look at history.

Before colonization was rampant in Africa in the fifteenth century, each tribe had their unique set of hairstyles that would represent financial and marital status, religion, age, and more. So, in a glance at someone's hair, one practically got all the information they needed about a person and the beliefs they held. Fast-forward to the transatlantic trade. Knowing the significance of and how much self-esteem was rooted in African hair, owners of enslaved people shaved their captives' heads so as to dehumanize them and erase their identities. Because of or in spite of (take your pick) this degradation, enslaved people, as they had always done, found ways to be resourceful: cornrows.

The average person, when they hear the word "cornrows," may think of them as the foundation for a protective style to be placed on top or for a fun, easy on-the-go 'do, or may remember that brief and embarrassing time the media tried to "rebrand" them as "boxer braids" because white UFC fighters such as Ronda Rousey sported them in the Octagon. What in the Alicia Keys on the cover of her debut album *Songs in A Minor* was that white nonsense? Thankfully, the term "boxer braids" died a quick death and didn't overshadow cornrows' historical importance: Enslaved people braided escape routes in each other's hair as a means of communicating with one another without getting caught. Enslaved mothers would also braid seeds and rice into their children's hair, so that they could have something to eat when (and usually if) they got separated from their parents at slave auctions. Then there's the tignon laws in Louisiana, which were passed in 1786 by Governor Esteban Rodríguez Miró to stop the rise of interracial relationships by preventing Creole women of color from drawing attention to themselves in the streets of New Orleans. As Virginia M. Gould (author and lecturer at Tulane University) noted in an essay in *The Devil's Lane*, the governor hoped that forcing women to wear a head covering would control those "who had become too light skinned or who dressed too elegantly, or who competed too freely with white women for status and thus threatened the social order." And as we all know, the discussion, hatred, and imitation of as well as being intimidated by the beauty of Black hair is not a historical relic. It's an ongoing issue that's prevalent in today's workplace and beyond.

In July 2019, California became the first state to pass the CROWN Act, which updates the definition of "race" in the California Fair Employment and Housing Act and the California Education Code to be "inclusive of traits historically associated with race, including, but not limited to, hair texture and protective hairstyles." Thanks to this act, employers and authority figures at schools are prevented from enforcing discriminatory rules of grooming against people of color, like in 2018, when a sixteen-year-old New Jersey high school wrestler named Andrew Johnson was presented with the following ultimatum by a white referee before a match: cut his dreadlocks because they didn't "conform" to the rules or forfeit the match. We all know what was really being said: The locks were a symbol of Johnson's Blackness, so really, the problem was that, to the referee, Johnson himself did not fit within what the ref defined as acceptable, so like most Black people, Johnson had to make a choice: either reject a part of himself in order to participate in a world that doesn't want him OR suffer unfair consequences simply for not obeying white, patriarchal authority. What a choice to be thrust upon anyone, especially a teenager. He made the painful decision to have his locks cut, which, I can imagine, was because he didn't want all his practice and training to be for naught. If that wasn't bad enough, this wasn't done in private. Instead, a white female trainer for the team cut his hair off *in front of the entire gymnasium*, a cruel and intentionally humiliating act. And we all know that trainer gave zero fucks about making sure his hair looked presentable when she cut it, but instead had him out there looking like Zahara Jolie-Pitt circa 2009, before Brad Pitt knew what Carol's Daughter was. But in all seriousness, just *three years ago*, this was acceptable punishment for a Black person not shrinking themselves, and the only reason this case of abuse made a ripple is because someone filmed the incident and the video went viral.

Thankfully, since then, New Jersey joined California in passing the CROWN Act and so did New York. The New York City Commission on Human Rights created guidelines to impose penalties on those who discriminate, harass, demote, or fire people for wearing the following hairstyles: "natural hair, treated or untreated hairstyles such as locs, cornrows, twists, braids, Bantu knots, fades, Afros, and/or the right to keep hair in an uncut or untrimmed state." While this does bring about a sense of relief, the reality is much more sobering because California, New York, New Jersey, Virginia, Colorado, Washington, Maryland, Connecticut, New Mexico, Delaware, and Nebraska are actually the only eleven states who have passed the CROWN Act. Sure, others including Kentucky, South Carolina, Georgia, Michigan, Illinois, and Pennsylvania are

Phoebe Robinson

"considering" passing similar legislation, but they haven't. Yet. That means in *thirty-nine* states, it is fair game to discriminate against and jeopardize Black people's safety, mental health, financial security, and comfort simply because our hair is different, which brings me back to my #JokesNotJokes feelings about the astonishing, completely original, and immeasurable impact Black hair has had on not just Black culture but globally.

When you analyze the decades and centuries of psychological and physical harm and trauma Black people have experienced because of our hair, as well as the high-fashion creativity (CreativeSoul Photography with their series AfroArt), beauty (Diana Ross's entire hair oeuvre), envelope pushing (Grace Jones's flattop fade), and overall cultural contributions of their hairstyles to the zeitgeist (Bantu knots, Jheri curl, etc.), I conclude that Black women, in particular, need to be acknowledged and celebrated in a major way, and not just light-skinned Black celebrities during Black History Month. I want some year-round shit. Monuments erected that depict wash day, which is really a several-day odyssey. Like, if I had to spend the past eighteen years living in New York City and seeing that trifling statue of Teddy Roosevelt's raggedy self on a horse flanked by an African man and an Indigenous man, then we are loooooong overdue for a sculpture of a Black woman making a stank face while reading the back of a bottle of conditioner. This sculpture shall be named *Just Use a Dime-Sized Amount of Conditioner? Bitch, Where?* Every weekend, there needs to be a Jamaican Carnival–level celebraysh, but instead of bountiful booties and free-range titty meat on display, it's YouTube hair tutorial stars, who can no longer hide behind video editing, and instead must publicly struggle to style their hair while on parade floats.

That's just the beginning. I want more. Such as products created especially for us, like memory foam cooling pillows specifically designed to soothe our tender scalps after getting box braids, so we can sleep peacefully. A course at Barnard College called Shrinkage Tried to Stop Us from Being Great, But the Heaux Lost. Monthly swag bags delivered to our homes that are full of candles, journals, Sally's Beauty Supply coupons, artisanal cheeses, head wraps, and Cajun seasoning. I mean, BW deserve so much, y'all; at the very least, we should be secure knowing we will not ever make wack shrimp étouffée because we ran out of spices. But it's not just gifts and grandiose displays of appreciation that I'm after.

Putting Black women of all shades at the forefront of these hairstyles is not only instrumental in Black women seeing ourselves reflected in the media, but also allows the BW in front of the camera (and behind the scenes) to achieve the financial and career gains that culture vultures such as the Kardashian clan and fashion-week models make when they sport a poor facsimile of the hairstyles that on Black women are often denigrated as ghetto and ugly, can cost them employment and dating prospects, and may, perhaps worst of all, gaslight them and make them question their self-worth. All of this damage can take years, decades, and even a lifetime to be undone *if* it can be undone at all. I should know because, somewhat to my surprise, I am one of those people who is still doing the laborious work of overcoming what I've been conditioned to believe about my hair.

I remember the first night I served as the moderator on Michelle Obama's *Becoming* book tour. Yes, I'm aware 1) of the whiplash that just occurred from that segue, and 2) that the previous sentence is as down-to-earth as when, in the middle of the 2020 quar, Martha Stewart posted on Instagram about the summer house (built in 1776) on her farm that she converted into a library for her book collection. You know, I bet if the enslaved people who most likely constructed this home knew that it would one day *only* house, among other books, Joan Didion's entire oeuvre, some Glennon Doyle self-help, and a first edition *One Fish, Two Fish, Red Fish, Blue Fish* for Stewart's grandkids to read, the slaves would have surely screamed, "WORTH IT!" In all seriousness, while most of us are just hoping to one day afford a home that will house our *bodies*, M. Stew is devoting an entire property to her books and treating them with the same loving care Beast gave the red rose he kept in the protective glass cloche in *Beauty and the Beast*. Needless to say, this is not the most relatable thing Stewart has done, but neither is my launching into a story about my time with my Forever First Lady. However, I'm not bringing up Mrs. O (again) as proof of how cool I am by association, but because it wasn't until a couple years after that night with Miche that I realized my hair issues weren't a thing of the past as I had led myself to believe. Turns out I wasn't "cured," as I implied in my first book, *You Can't Touch My Hair: And Other Things I Still Have to Explain*, which if you don't have, you might need to purchase in order to understand my relationship with my hair.[1] Or I could just tell you now. After all, this isn't the Marvel Cinematic Universe, in which it's wise to watch *Thor: Ragnarok* before *Avengers: Infinity War* in order to fully understand Thor and Loki's complicated relationship. Okay. Long story short: I assumed that simply because I listened to neo-soul, stopped perming my hair at eighteen, then wore dreadlocks for five years that I must've defeated any insecurities or self-defeating talk about my hair.

This is not to say that I was lying when I wrote about my hair journey in 2016. I wasn't. I believed I had healed myself. Coupled with that naïve optimism, I'm a writer. I *live* for the hero's journey of overcoming an obstacle once and for all, and in this case, learning to have an unwavering love of my hair was the neat and tidy ending I wanted. But this isn't a two-hour movie or a three-hundred-page novel. Life is messy and complicated, so why was I prematurely celebrating like a HBCU marching band during halftime in a Grambling State vs. Louisiana-Monroe football game? Just mentally high-stepping, blowing a whistle rhythmically while doing a *Matrix* backbend and wearing a highly coordinated uniform. I blame nineties / early aughts talk shows that I watched growing up for my presumptuous "mission accomplished" attitude.

---

1. LOL. Suggesting you buy one of my other books while you're reading this one is similar to that college professor putting their *own* work on the class textbook syllabus. I used to make fun of those teachers for being what I perceived as tacky, but now that I'm older, wiser, and have bills to pay, I get it. Y'all think I was going to suggest you read something from Mark Twain? Does his estate *need* more money at this point? NO! But I do! So buy *You Can't Touch My Hair* in paperback, audiobook, and Sanskrit. J/K, there is no Sanskrit version of my book. Can you imagine a translator wasting their time and education attempting to figure out the Sanskrit equivalent of "peen"?

I may have been a preteen/teenager when many of these shows—*Ricki Lake, The Phil Donahue Show* (I watched reruns), *The Montel Williams Show, The Jenny Jones Show, Sally Jessy Raphael, Oprah*—were at their height, but I gobbled them up as much as if not more than the stay-at-home mom demographic these shows were tailor-made for. I *loved* watching them so much that I even checked out lesser fare such as *The Geraldo Rivera Show,*[2] *The Jerry Springer Show*, and of course, *The Steve Wilkos Show*, which was a spin-off show for Jerry's . . . bodyguard. Riiiiiight. And folks have the nerve to be mad at Black people wanting reparations when white mediocrity is routinely rewarded? Like someone in the Robinson clan probably knew somebody who knew someone who was definitely Harriet Tubman's work wife, and I can't get a weekly check for $49.95 in perpetuity as the U.S. government's way of saying "my bad for slavery," but Steve got a talk show (that's been on the air for FOURTEEN YEARS, by the way) while wearing stonewashed jeans and having the personality of a slice of Pepperidge Farm brand bread? Lol. Okay, society, you have some 'splaining to do.

Moving on! The point is that if you were an adult who held a note card and microphone while standing in front of a studio audience, I was tuning in, especially if the episodes centered around guests who discussed how they overcame a hardship or sought the help of a Dr. Phil type who'd provide

---

2. Look, the nineties were a much more innocent time, so I will not allow y'all to judge me for this because no one could have predicted that Geraldo would devolve into taking naked selfies and claiming Donald Trump as a friend.

easy and snackable advice in five-to-seven-minute segments. The audience applauded, the person sometimes agreed to take the advice, cut to commercial, and we all carried on with the illusion that all problems can be neatly resolved. If we were lucky, months later, these talk shows would treat us to follow-up conversations in which the in-studio audience (as well as us viewers at home) would pass final judgments on the guests' progress or lack thereof with cheers or groans. This sort of pass/fail way of grading people is not limited to just TV. It's ingrained in society.

We live in a world that loves an act three resolution: hero saves the day, woman figures out the key thing that's missing in her life, a person gives one grand speech that undoes all the damage from their toxic behavior. Therefore, the takeaway is, no matter how big or small an issue is, a person can magically fix it after a couple of tries. Meanwhile, life is routinely ding dong ditching us, so that when we open the door, our same ol' problems are like [in Killmonger's voice], *"Hey, auntie,"* because old habits and mentalities die hard. I learned this sobering truth ~~in my early thirties~~ last week, which raises the question, "Why?"

Why don't we discuss what growth and change actually are until we're older and perhaps a bit disillusioned? Furthermore, why do we not openly share this information so others can avoid a similar fate? And why aren't we explaining to kids that working on one's self is a continual and daily recommitment to behaving differently than before? As we know, young people are capable of handling more than we think they can, therefore, a little heads-up is only fair. Because, it seems, real life not resembling the fantasy is where many of us get into trouble. We end up frustrated or self-flagellating when we revert to bad habits (as we'll inevitably do). This pattern of unmanaged expectations leading to disappointment could be prevented if we were taught early on that nothing's wrong with us if we don't magically undo decades of learned behavior in one try. Young people can handle hearing that, and the fact that we're too scared to give it to 'em straight probably says more about our PTSD from life not 100 percent aligning with our dreams, wants, and desires than it does about the fragility of youth. Look, I'm not asking for anything super in-depth or cruel. A simple, "Much like a raggedy Chase Bank in downtown Manhattan that's covered in scaffolding, you are a work in progress. *Forever*. Get used to it and do the best you can." Not the most inspiring message, but at least it's honest. Anyway, I write all of this to say that when it comes to my somewhat fraught relationship with my hair, I assumed that I had, at last, by the writing of my first book, resolved my issues.

While that assumption was wrong, it doesn't mean I hadn't made progress along the way. To, at eighteen years old, 1) realize and admit to myself that I was getting relaxers not because I was experimenting with my hair, but because I was trying to fit within Eurocentric beauty standards, and 2) decide to go against the grain when the majority of Black women in the public eye and in professional settings were sporting chemically altered, bone-straight hair and/or weaves in the nineties / early aughts was a BIG deal and a much-needed step in my journey of self-acceptance. So I don't want to trivialize that; however, as I now look back on that evening with Miche, I can see old insecurities were bubbling to the surface once again.

Even though I had the privilege of interviewing Michelle on the final episode of the *2 Dope Queens* podcast, that conversation took place in the intimacy of her D.C. office. It felt slightly lower stakes because my cohost, Jessica Williams, and I divvied up the questions, and we had a limited amount of time with Michelle. Less time with her meant less chance of me screwing up. But her book tour? There was no way around it. It was going to be a big night: ninety minutes of one-on-one conversation with Michelle in front of twenty thousand people with a film crew filming everything for her soon-to-be-released Netflix documentary about her tour. And since I expected my appearance in the doc to be the equivalent of that rogue elbow we've all seen in a person's cropped profile picture on a dating app, I was gonna make sure my elbow was the most glistening and moisturized elbow that has ever been captured on 4K Ultra HD. Hence why my trusted glam team of Delina Medhin (makeup) and Sabrina Rowe (hair), as well as my number two, Mai, joined me in Philly. I can best describe Delina as Alicia Keys's Eritrean doppelgänger whose specialty is #RelatableGlam aka if you're trying to bag yourself an indie filmmaker auteur or want to serve an "I deserve this promotion" beat during an employee review. As for Sabs, she's a ball of lovable, positive energy who can execute almost any hairstyle and wears the cutest, most fashionable platform clogs. I stan a woman who values arch support! So there the four of us were, a multi-culti bundle of nerves and excitement.

A little over halfway through glam, I was told Michelle wanted me to swing by her greenroom so we could hang before the show. I panicked. My makeup was half done and I was wearing a jumpsuit that was less Elvis in Vegas and more Pep Boys "I'm about to upcharge you for a brand-new carburetor and there's nothing you can do about it" auto mechanic. But both my unfinished makeup and underdressed outfit took a back seat to my biggest concern: my hair. Sabs hadn't finished my cornrows or doing final tweaks to my wig. Aaah! There was no way I could chill with Michelle Obama until my hair was perfect. A completely normal thought, right? Except what most people mean by "perfect"—effortlessly fabulous, camera ready—isn't what I had in mind.

By "perfect," I was concerned with my hair not living up to the standard that Black women are held to. Anything less than magazine cover ready is generally unacceptable and opens BW up to ridicule. "Untamed" curls, edges not laid, and lacking a flawless sheen oft seen on a silk press are all crimes to be avoided, especially in public. Sure, in this instance, public wasn't really "public." I was backstage and would simply be walking from my greenroom past Wells Fargo Center employees, who most likely weren't paying attention to me, to Michelle's greenroom. Still, since none of those employees nor Michelle are confidantes, it felt too risky to reveal myself to them.

So there I was: a thirty-four-year-old accomplished woman with hopes and dreams and magical love in my life, both romantic and platonic, who was awash in shame and embarrassment that my natural Black hair wasn't "good enough." Sadly, those feelings are nothing new to the average Black woman and girl in America. We've been trained to despise our beauty and our hair, to make it look like anything except for how it does naturally, and to, at all costs, make sure our hair never betrays us. And the most fail-proof way of doing that is usually by manipulating our beautiful kinks and coils into something more in line with what's societally acceptable. If we can successfully do that, we can somehow hide our Otherness in plain sight.

As a Black woman, I'm deeply aware of how precarious my reputation and humanity are in the eyes of non-Black people. All it takes is one misstep for everything about me to be discredited, disregarded, and denied if my hair screams "I'm the culmination of America's wildest fears about Black people." So, even though I was no longer consumed by the myopic intention of fitting in with Eurocentric standards the way I was in my twenties, I was still keenly aware that the stakes are high, which is why I behave like an always-on-duty public DA, ready at the jump to defend my existence with my hair serving as number one character witness. Hence me not wanting those Wells Fargo employees to take one look at my hair and decide I'm not worth respecting and being treated like a human being. And double hence[3] me not wanting to let Michelle Obama down by my hair looking imperfect.

But this Miche, you say. She's from Chicago. She ain't siddity. She's down-to-earth. And most important, she's a Black woman. You are correct. She is all those things, so if I had popped by her room with my hair less than impeccable, I doubt she'd have even batted an eyelash, let alone looked down on me. But, y'all, let's be real, sometimes when it comes to Black on

---

3. Wait, can you do that? Someone get Ta-Nehisi Coates and Roxane Gay on the phone and see if their educated selves are out here multiplying hences.

Black judgment, we can be nothing but a bunch of Simon
Cowells minus the bad taste in jeans and ankie b's aka ankle
boots. We hold each other to extremely high standards because we know that each of us individually is expected by
society to represent our whole entire race. Therefore, we're
deeply invested in each other's lives because we know just
how much is on the line. That's why when Serena Williams
won the gold medal at the 2012 Olympics, we felt like we all
won and Crip walked alongside her. Or when a crime is reported on the news, we're collectively clenching our butt
cheeks until we find out it wasn't committed by a Black person
and then we do a small fist pump to ourselves, respectfully of
course, relieved that we're living another day without having
to pay for the sins of another. And, sadly, we're often first in
line to tear down or uplift each other, especially when it comes
to Black women and their hair.

Black women get dragged for poorly executed baby hairs,
teased for their ends looking dry, chastised for dyeing their
hair blond, made to feel inferior if their hair doesn't naturally
grow down to their butts. My favorite loudmouths, however,
are the boo-boo-ass, wannabe woke Black dudes who think
it's their job to "save" Black women by turning on India.Arie's
"Brown Skin" and reminding BW that they could love themselves if only they stopped relaxing their hair. Listen, heauxes:
1) Quit acting like you're doing the Lord's work when you're
actually just being condescending because you think you
know what's best for Black women, 2) Don't willy-nilly start
playing songs on Spotify because it fucks up the algorithm,
and 3) Finally, no one was asking for your opinion on how

Black women should wear their hair. Just because some of them rock chemically straightened or flat-ironed styles doesn't mean they're an army of Samuel L. Jacksons from *Django Un chained.* Maybe they want to switch up their hair or it's easier for them to handle when it's permed, or they just simply like the way their hair looks in an altered state. Whatever the case may be, it's really no one's business how a Black woman wears her hair unless she acts as though wearing it a certain way makes her better than other Black people.

Clearly, I'm #TeamMindYourDamnBusinessWhenItComesToBlackWomensHair for every BW, it seems, except for me. Try as I might, I'm not impervious to negative feedback about my hair, which is why I worried that the former First Lady would take one look at my less-than-flawless hair and think, *How could you walk around looking like that in front of people who aren't kinfolk?* I was afraid of letting her down in some way. Of course, I didn't have this level of clarity that night in Philadelphia as I do now. When I got the invitation to see Michelle, I practically Bruce Banner'ed and blacked the hell out from excitement, so I was purely acting on emotional muscle memory, which explains the immediate panic about my hair. I had Sabrina finish the last bit of my cornrows and plop on that wig so that Michelle wouldn't see my natural Black lady hair, which now, I'm aware of how absurd that is. Like, *hello?!?!* She's Black! She has Black woman hair! If I had to conjecture, she probably has 4C hair just like me, so she probably knew very well what my real hair looked like! And yet, I put on the "perfect" hair, so I could have the perfect greenroom experience with her.

311

Once the evening was over, I filed it away until two years later, when that night randomly popped into my mind. What jumped out at me was not how much fun I had with MO or the fact that the event was a major career and personal achievement, but my anxiety and belief that my natural hair was a liability. And as I sat on my living room couch, remembering that evening in Philadelphia, I wasn't saddened because I was still insecure about my hair, although I had every right to be. It would've been so easy to feel like a failure because I found out I wasn't "cured." Instead, I couldn't help but marvel at the genuine progress I had made since the *Becoming* tour. How I had felt about me and my hair two years ago was in stark contrast to the newfound feelings, the surprising ones of happiness and joy related to my hair, that I was experiencing during Covid.

It was a Saturday during the summer of 2020. British Baekoff and I were watching *Living Single* while I was styling my hair into mini two-strand twists. When the theme song kicked in, signaling a new episode, I was rapping alongside Queen Latifah. My eyes were closed and my fingers were on autopilot, patiently working the moisturizing cream into my freshly washed and deeply conditioned coils before twisting two small strands together. Even though my arms and hands were a little achy, I was beaming with joy because this painstaking routine transported me back to my childhood, when I would sit on a stack of telephone books between my mom's legs as she did my hair while we watched *Living Single*. Mentally going back in time allowed me to transcend beyond my usual playlist of negative self-talk and connect with the love my mom put into my hair each and every Sunday night in preparation for the following school week in a way I never had before. I wondered why I had spent all these decades undervaluing and discounting that meaningful love while readily accepting all the lies society sold me. And as I was recalling this special time with my mom and who little Phoebe was before she had internalized any destructive thoughts about her hair, I must have been grinning like a fool because I opened my eyes and Baekoff was filming me with his iPhone. He captured the happiness I'd spent most of my life hoping and wishing I would feel about my hair, but was convinced would forever be elusive because I have 4C hair.

4C hair. Where to begin . . . ooh! I know! If I see one more trifling bitch who clearly has a looser curl pattern using the hashtags #4CHair or #4CHairstyles or demonstrating an "easy wash and go" style, twist outs, a flexi-rod set, etc., I will commit identity fraud on all these women, open a bunch of credit cards in their names, max out the cards with purchases of hair products from Sally's Beauty Supply, Carol's Daughter, and Jane Carter Solution, and ruin their FICO scores. Yes, that is an elaborate scheme that will most likely backfire and end with me in pris—#Callback—but I. Don't. Care. I've had enough of these phonies selling pipe dreams. They know doggone well that for the average 4C woman, re-creating many of these looks requires a team of scientists including Dr. Fauci, Neil deGrasse Tyson, the ghost of George Washington Carver, a marathon of Whoopi Goldberg movies queued up, their therapist on speed-dial for when the style goes disastrously wrong, and a long weekend where Monday is a federal holiday, because trust, she will need the extra day off from work to get this mess together. Jokes aside, all many of these non-4Cers are doing is reinforcing the mindset that because our hair is not mirroring back what we just watched in the tutorial, our hair must be "bad." Now, before I continue discussing the ways in which the natural hair community, while well-intentioned and often a place of refuge, continues to perpetuate harmful attitudes when it comes to Black women's hair (especially those who fall under the 4C category), I must confess to something.

Full disclosh: I have 4A/B hair in the front third of my head while the rest is 4C, and those mofos ain't trying to work together. They're two mismatched classmates paired together for a science project. One student struggles to build the volcano alone while the other student shows up the day of the presentaysh and goes, "Lemme know when you need me to pour the baking soda in!" And they didn't even bring Arm & Hammer baking soda; it's the generic kind that just reads "baking soda" on the box in plain cursive lettering. Despite the friction between the two, they take first place at the science fair. That's kind of what it's like with my hair. Having combination curl patterns can sometimes be tumultuous, but in the end, they all come together to create something beautiful. There's just one problem: 4C is not seen as beautiful and aspirational like the looser curls of lighter-skinned or mixed Black women; therefore 4C hair is typically underrepresented inside and outside the natural hair community, which is irritating considering the fact that 4C hair is supposed to be one of if not the most important cruxes of the natural hair movement. Instead, 4C is seen as an unfortunate starting place that, with hard work and determination, can be transformed temporarily into something better, more palatable, and ultimately, good.

In the Bustle.com article entitled "How Black People Came to Believe 4C Was a 'Bad Hair' Texture," Kayla Greaves writes about how 4C hair went from being held in high esteem and considered attractive to being viewed as "difficult" and in need of taming. One of the people she interviewed was Dr. Afiya Mbilishaka, who is an assistant professor of psychology at the University of the District of Columbia and an expert in African cultural rituals and natural hair. Part of Mbilishaka's explanation echoes what I referenced earlier in this essay in terms of the opinion and understanding of Black hair changing with colonization. Greaves writes:

> Before the forced migration of African people began during the 15th century, the idea that 4C hair was somehow difficult to manage was non-existent. In traditional African societies, communities with 4C hair were equipped with the proper tools and methods to take care of their coils. "We had a lot of rituals connected to hair, that could actually prevent that type of hair texture from breaking," Mbilishaka explains. These societies would sometimes use ingredients like ochre clay and butter fats to preserve the hair and retain length—much like the methods the Himba people of Namibia still practice today.... Ironically enough,

Afro-textured strands were also believed to be linked to the heavens, Mbilishaka explains. "4C hair was actually used as more of an art form," she shares. "Our hair is the highest point on our entire body, and therefore considered most connected to the divine. In some degree our hair was supposed to grow up . . . as a way to connect to the spiritual world."

Wow. I wish I had known this when I was growing up in the nineties. Hell, I wish I knew this that night in Philadelphia. It would have saved me a lot of mental anguish knowing hair like mine wasn't always treated like the runt of the litter. Far from it. It was exalted and had meaning. It was art. That's why it's so exasperating when I click on the #4CHair or #4CHairstyles tag on social media and I'm bombarded with everything *but* 4C hair. Because when people from my own community, especially when those people are *other Black women*, erase you (intentionally or not), the message is: No 4Cs allowed.

That feels personal as fuck. And it hurts like hell. Lemme back up for a second.

While many reading this are more than familiar with hair typing, some may not be, and I don't want the uninformed to be lost the way I was when I watched *Tenet* and my clueless behind was searching for context clues like Inspector Clouseau so I could understand what the hell was going on. 4C is a term from Andre Walker's eponymous hair typing system, which was created in the nineties. After establishing himself as a celebrity hairstylist, Walker branched out with the AWHTS, which is broken down into four categories: straight, wavy, curly, and kinky. For instance, supermodel Kate Moss would probably be deemed 1A aka straight and fine hair whereas actress/playwright Danai Gurira is likely 4C aka kinky with tight coils. This system was then used to market his line of hair-care products. While he has subsequently admitted that this system was designed to push his products, the effects have lingered and in fact expanded over the years. So have his comments about those whose hair falls under the kinky category.

In an interview with *Elle*, Walker stated that women have to love and care for their hair, then proceeded to say, "Kinky hair can have limited styling options; that's the only hair type that I suggest altering with professional relaxing." Ululululu, limited according to whom, boo? Black women and girls have a plethora of options for their coily textures—Afro, cornrows, dreadlocks, frohawk, Bantu knots, flat twists, high puff with a head wrap, etc.—so for him to dismiss hairstyles because they're time-consuming to create or because some don't have the range to execute them is what's limiting. And whether he intended it to or not, this messaging reinforces the belief that kinky hair shouldn't be celebrated for what it is, but dinged for what it isn't: adhering to Eurocentric ideals. Toni Morrison once stated in an interview about white people and racism, "If you can only be tall because somebody's on their knees, then you have a serious problem. And my feeling is, white people have a very, very serious problem, and they should start thinking about what *they* can do about it. Take me out of it."

Similarly, leave Black hair out of the definition of what Eurocentric beauty is. If "white hair" is good only because of a false narrative that renders Black hair in all its uniqueness, malleability, and glory as bad, then what *is* white hair? If Black hair didn't exist, how would white hair define itself? Furthermore, how would white *people* define themselves if we didn't live in a world in which their self-esteem was built, in part, on denigrating Blackness? Many in the natural hair community, myself included, have wondered this, so when someone as revered, talented, and accomplished as Walker (who was Oprah's hairstylist for over twenty-five years *and* created Halle Berry's signature pixie cut, which many of us attempted to imitate only to have our hair end up looking like Julia Roberts's Tinker Bell wig in *Hook*) doesn't outwardly encourage us 4-type queens, it's disheartening and mind-boggling. I mean, ya had one job, dude! To remind Black women of their dopeness. And when he failed to do that and received backlash, he responded on his blog, but it just made things worse. He said, in short, that it was really a woman's "personal preference" and that chemical relaxers could actually lead to healthier hair.

To which my response was: Wut? When I used to get my hair chemically straightened, it ended up looking like the remnants of a forest fire in Yellowstone National Park. Just dry and brittle as hell with the ends breaking off. So, hair damaged and stripped of its nutrients is deemed "healthy" because it's . . . straight and "easier" to style, but arming my baby 'fro with the LCO method (aka liquid or leave-in conditioner, cream, and oil) so as to retain moisture and lock in all the nutrients—which, by the way, is *key* to achieving strong, healthy hair—isn't because of my tighter curl pattern? Bruh, come *on*! 4C-type hair can't be disrespected like this! I mean, yes, though relaxers have improved since the nineties, I'm sure this man knows that for many Black women, their hair is at its healthiest when it's not altered from its natural state. At least, that's certainly the case for me.

I always believed my hair was extremely fragile because when it was permed and I held a section of it in the air, the roots were thin yet somewhat sturdy. However, by the time I got to the ends, they were as see-through as the Chinese lanterns Lara Jean and Peter Kavinsky put their written-down wishes inside of before they sent those lanterns into the sky in *To All the Boys: P.S. I Still Love You*. Except in my case, my wish wasn't for teenage love to stand the test of time, but for something along the lines of "Can my hair thicken up like it's some roux in a plate of biscuits and gravy?" Seriously, it was demoralizing that society told me a perm is what's best for my hair when all it did was make it limp and lifeless. Fast-forward to now. My hair has more than rehabilitated itself in its natural state. My curl pattern can be tight or springy depending on the style, my hair now has the same level of thickness from root to tip, and there's no more breakage. And, of course, this transition from relaxed to natch hair was seamless. No hiccups. I looked like a *Jet* magazine "Beauty of the Week" model from the seventies every single day since I turned eighteen. Lies!

Without my mom doing my hair or getting a relaxer from a professional, ya girl STRUGGLED. I'm talking like if Helena Bonham Carter and her messy bird's nest of hair saw me, she'd be like, "Girl, I'm white as fuck. Hell, I'm practically *translucent*, and even I know you shouldn't be going out looking like that. Want me to call one of the three Black Brits I know to come fix this?" Point is, because for the first eighteen years of my life someone else did my hair, I never learned how to do it. And you can imagine how it went when I gave it the ol' college try.

Y'all, in my late teens and twenties, sometimes if I couldn't replicate a hairstyle, I cried like *Good Will Hunting*'s Matt Damon after Robin Williams told him it's not his fault. Other times, I gave up and had a barber cut my hair into a baby 'fro or shave it all off, so I wouldn't have to deal with my hair at all. And at my lowest, I'd look at pictures of biracial celebrities and models and think, *If only my hair looked like that, then my life would be easier.* Eventually, I sought help, and over the next several years, I bounced around various salons, getting all sorts of braided styles, faux locks, and Erykah Badu–esque massive Afro lewks done. I hoped that getting a knockoff version of these celebrities' hairstyles would magically cause me to feel positive about my hair, but usually, I just felt like an impostor—that is, when I wasn't distracted by a much bigger problem: I was broke as hell, and as a result, the quality of these hairdos depended on the kind of hair and services I could afford. Sometimes, getting my hair done on the cheap worked out in my favor, and other times . . .

You know how Martin Luther King, Jr.'s final book, *Where Do We Go from Here*, was an essay collection about the status of the Civil Rights Movement and how it could move forward? That title can also apply to those moments when, halfway through getting my hair done, I realize the hairstylist is going to have me out here looking like a gahtdamn fool and all I can think is, *Do I have sex for the next month with the lights off? Do I skip town and go live in a doomsday bunker? Do I become a performance artist and pretend this bullshit was intentional? Truly, where the fuck do we go from here?* Lol, Bernice and the rest of the King children are like, "Please do not mention my dad's work when writing about the ignorant moments in your life." Copy!

Anyway, the point is you can find pictures of my hair looking like a hot-ass mess. No one ever said anything, not even my friends and family, which I'm kind of annoyed about, but also appreciative of because their silence saved me the embarrassment of having to admit I was living paycheck to paycheck even though the evidence was there in plain sight. That's why I believe you can tell a lot about a Black woman's financial status by how her hair looks. Meaning if my locks are hella moisturized and shiny, you best believe I'm so flush with cash that I'm putting avocado on everything: toast, salads, face masks, whatever! Conversely, if it looks like David Attenborough is about to narrate a gaggle of squirrels playing slapbox on top of my head, then you already know I was chilling with Dante in the eighth circle of Hell: overdraft fees. Thankfully, as my career advanced, I got out of debt and was on camera more frequently, and I needed to elevate my hair game. Enter: Sabrina.

Having her around to help me get camera ready and indulge me and my chameleon ways when it comes to hairstyle and color was a lot of fun since she's a true artist. But, if I'm being honest, I mostly felt relief when we started working together. Deep down, I loved having Sabs do my hair because that meant I didn't have to "deal" with it. Ooof. After all that time to get in a better space mentally with my hair, I still treated it the way Seinfeld did his neighbor, with a contemptible "Hello, *Newman*." My hair was a nuisance that I begrudgingly had to address. And when I didn't want to, I'd have Sabs put it in a protective style or underneath a wig so I could ignore it. While I didn't hate my hair like I used to, I merely coexisted with it. That was progress, for sure, but it also made me sad. So, as per usual, I turned to the one thing that would lift me out of the doldrums: the natural hair community. But results were mixed.

Before I go any further, you must know how much I love the natural hair community. It was there for me when I grew dreadlocks for the first time, when I buzzed my head and was bald for a year, when I needed guidance on what products to avoid or incorporate into my routine, and when I needed hair inspo for season two of my HBO series, *2 Dope Queens*. But above all, the natural hair community is a place of refuge from a world that steals, ignores, or looks down on Black hair, and I don't know where I would be without it. However, I would be lying if I didn't admit that this same group has, at times, exacerbated my insecurity about my hair and made me question some of the things going on in the community. I'm not the only one.

Popular author, TV personality, and licensed psychotherapist Nikki Walton aka Curly Nikki expressed similar concerns on her eponymous blog in a post entitled "Has the Natural Hair Community Created a Hierarchy for Curl Types? #TheNewGoodHair":

There are fewer successful bloggers with 4C type hair. There are few products marketed toward [B]lack women with natural hair that has a kinkily coiled hair texture. Instagram accounts that celebrate 4C type hair have significantly fewer followers compared to the accounts that highlight "all" curl patterns and sparsely feature women with kinky hair, unless it is a celebrity or a high fashion photo.

I noticed this when I first dipped my toe in the community during the early aughts, which is why it is slightly distressing that many of these same problems (lack of 4C representation) still exist but in new formats (used to be websites and now it's social media). So despite the fact we're in a new iteration of the natural hair movement, products and techniques have advanced, and there is, undoubtedly, a wider acceptance of hair types than there was in the early aughts, the truth is the natural hair community is not inclusive enough. There's still far too much low- and high-key anti-4C behavior happening.

In addition to what Curly Nikki mentioned, it is still acceptable to mock 4C hair, to view Black women with 4C hair as less attractive or less capable in the workplace, and to appreciate kinkier textures only if they are on a light-skinned woman and/or if the hair is blown out so as to display its length. Many blogs, YouTube vids, and social media platforms place so much emphasis on getting kinkier texture to grow and visibly look longer that it's hard not to get suckered in to the point that you end up thinking this obsession with length came from within. Sometimes this avalanche of messaging makes me wonder if this is how men must feel when they see ads for penis pumps and other things that can cause self-doubt. Please note this will be the only time I empathize with #Peen-Probs because men and their penises are usually the root of many #CoochieConundrums.[4]

Anyway, back to anti-4C behavior within the natural hair community. In that same blog post from Curly Nikki, she explains that Black women with hair-care lines are "some of the fastest growing and successful entrepreneurs in the business sector" to the point that conventional (read: white) hair and beauty brands are witnessing a double-digit dip in profit for the first time in decades. Sound like a happy story? Well, it isn't, because it turns out that texture discrimination is part of what's driving sales. As Ebony.com's Trudy Susan writes in her article "The Sad Truth About Natural Hair Discrimination":

Curly and wavy girls dominate the branding in products mass marketed to natural hair. So while the recent rebirth and modern day celebration of natural hair has provided some balance for Black women looking to escape the media induced pressure to yearn for European imitated straight, long hair, now there is a new pressure for natural women to yearn for a specific type of natural hair. . . .

---

4. I spent more time on this than I care to admit trying to come up with the alliteraysh. #MuffMishaps was a contender, but it's a bit too playful for discussing the patriarchy, and #PussyPickles sounds like the cousin of the yoni egg, and is also ignorant AF. Anyway, the takeaway here is, why haven't I been nominated for a National Book Award yet?

Tight, coily and kinky hair naturals are underrepresented and by far under-celebrated, given their hair does not conform to the hair images being glamorized and glorified by many popular natural hair brands.

What about Lupita Nyong'o or Teyonah Parris, some might ask? Yes, they are in the limelight, but for every dark-skinned 4Cer, there is a litany of natural hair girls who have bigger, looser, softer curls being pushed to the forefront. They are the ones who get the most likes on social media, get the sponsorship deals, get booked for modeling gigs, become the face of brands.

It's no wonder why, at times, it can feel as though mixed women have hijacked the natural hair movement. Actually, "hijacked" isn't the correct word because it's not their fault that their hair type is the preferred visual representation of Black hair that we see in the media. While they should absolutely be represented and have space and commune, what about us 4C girls and women? Where do we go? Who is going to cheerlead us? Nurture our self-esteem? Be in the trenches with us? *That's* why I get irritated by non-4Cers encroaching on #4CHair and #4CHairstyles. Maybe it's a point of pride and ego in that I've earned my stripes, so to speak, by living with coily locks. Or maybe they want to be associated with the struggle without having to experience the struggle, because to be associated with the struggle also means being associated with its beauty.

Deeply textured, tightly coiled hair is staggeringly, stop-you-in-your-tracks beautiful. Only a fool wouldn't want to be synonymous with gobsmacking gorgeousness. But perhaps it's as simple as the fact that non-4C queens have had their own battles with how they are perceived because of their hair, and they feel a sense of kinship with us kinky folks. I accept that, but they also need to accept that our experiences and how we move through the world *are* different because our hair is different, and it's not divisive to call that out, but necessary. I've been made to feel that I am not enough, not worthy, not viable and valuable because of my hair. I've had it drilled in me that not being mixed or ambiguously Black and lacking the "aspirational" proximity to whiteness is a defect that can never be fixed. And I have been doing the painstaking work *every single day* to unlearn everything that I've been taught is wrong about me and my hair. So I can't pretend that every Black woman is in the same trenches when it comes to hair. We aren't, and that's okay because, frankly, none of us should be in there at all. We should be carefree and joyful about our Blackness and our kinky coils. At least, that is what I realized that afternoon on the couch, watching *Living Single*, when I was happy, proud, and grateful to have the privilege of working my fingers through my 4C hair.

Now, truth be told, the year and change since that joyful breakthrough hasn't been smooth sailing. There are moments when I'm discouraged by how long it takes for me to do my hair. My wash and gos are still a mixed bag, but I've noticed marked improvement. And, from time to time, I'll pine after soft, fluffy non-4C curls.

Despite all this, for the first time in my entire life, I truly, madly, deeply (only I can take this very Black pride moment and white it up with a Savage Garden reference) love my hair. I love its pliability, that it represents the resiliency of my people. I love that when I look at it in the mirror, I can hear the voices of those from the fourteenth and fifteenth centuries telling me that my tightly coiled hair is art and that my hair growing up, not down, is a sign of me connecting with the divine. These voices are starting to become as loud as the voices that told me my hair is something to be ashamed of. I'm not even religious, but the notion that my hair is in communion with the vibrations of the Universe brings me peace. Makes me feel full and special. That neither me nor my hair have to do anything other than just be.

And on days when I forget all of this and revert back to old habits of being furious at my hair and calling it every name in the book, I accept that, too, because it's all about the journey. So, nope, it's no happy ending. In fact, it's no ending at all, and thank God! I'm honored that every day I get to work through my shit and choose to recommit to loving my 4C hair in all its kinky, coily glory. I wouldn't have it any other way.

ACKNOWLEDGMENTS

Guys, why are we still here? The book is over. We laughed. We cried. We've come out of this more certain than ever that we are absolutely on the right side of history when it comes to outside clothes in our homes. Okay, *maybe* wisely not sitting on a Brooklinen duvet in outside clothes isn't worthy of being recorded in the annals of history, but perhaps it should be! Anyway, I digress. The point is, haven't I written more than enough words to meet my contractual obligaysh with this book? Why is there still more work to be done with this whole acknowledgments section? I mean, the people I love know that I love them, so do I actually need to do this? Can't we all go home? Wait. One sec. Am being told by my publisher that it's ignorant as fuck—their words, not mine; J/K, definitely my words—to end a book without doling out some thanks and gratitude. And now that I think about it, if British Baekoff has this same attitude when it comes to marriage vows and tries

329

to pull this stunt at our wedding one day (we're not engaged!) and stands at the altar in front of our loved ones and says, "You know I love you. Why do I need to say any of it in front of everyone? Isn't putting on this tux and giving you a ring enough?" I will absolutely curb stomp his ankles in my Sophia Webster stilettos—I'm avail for a sponsorship deal!—and cuss him out. So, okay. Fine. It's time to acknowledge some folks.

As per usual, I'm starting with my parents, Phil and Octavia. Thank you for being amazing, funny, and terrible at Face-Time. It's always sweet to watch the #TechnologyStruggle happen in real time. Hope I'm doing a better job of calling home more often. Breaking the workaholic habit is hard, but I'm trying. Love you!

My brother and sister-in-law, PJ and Liz. You are phenomenal human beings. So smart, with incredible moral centers. Plus, you're great parents to two of the most precocious and wonderful kids, Olivia and Trey. Can't think of a better advertisement of your awesomeness than how they're turning out to be. Love you!

British Baekoff, you are the tea to my crumpets, the bangers to my mash, the toad in my hole. #BritishFoodBeWeirdSometimes. Anyway, thank you for all your support, love, grace, sense of humor, patience, and willingness to watch U2 concert DVDs with me when I need my spirits lifted. Dating an author while they're writing a book is no easy feat, but you handled it with such aplomb. You are a steady and calm man and I've evolved exponentially as a person from being with you. Love you.

Mai, you've been building this empire with me brick by

brick from the beginning. I'm lucky to have you as my work wife. You challenge and support me in equal measure. Most of all, I love you more than you love me (lol), which is very on brand for our partnership. Your lack of effusiveness keeps me on my toes and makes me come back for more. Thank you for everything.

Sam, you are the best publicist that anyone could ask for and your friendship is one of my favorite things in the world. Thank you for your unfiltered honesty and sense of humor. We lift each other up always and I wouldn't have it any other way.

Team Tiny Rep Productions—Jose and Camille, thank you for going on this journey with me. Working with you reminds me of why I got into Hollywood: to make dope shit, have fun, and create a show that has something to say that'll resonate with others and make them feel seen. Thanks for lovingly dragging me when I make trash mom jokes.

I can't continue without shouting out my agent, Robert Guinsler. You believed in me when I was a little baby writer, just cranking out blog posts and freelance writing content. You saw what I was trying to do, fully believed in it, and have been on this journey with me for each of my three books. Thank you for your faith and for being my friend.

Team Plume! I love all of you, clearly, because we keep doing books together. Thanks for backing me and Tiny Reparations Books. Special mention to Christine. Building this imprint with you has been enlightening, exciting, and another "e" I'm fresh out of energy to find because I'm weary as per usual. ☺ Anyway, we have something special going and I can't wait to see what we do.

Acknowledgments

My editor, Jill. Hey, boo! I missed every deadline LIKE WE KNEW I WOULD but I got it done. Thanks for joining me not only for this book, but also for the entire Tiny Rep Books journey. Your passion for what you do is infectious. I promise I'll be on time with my next book. At Tiny Rep Books, I'd also like to thank Jamie Knapp in publicity, Alice Dalrymple in production editorial, and the marketing team of Stephanie Cooper, Natalie Church, Caroline Payne, and Tiffani Ren.

I would be remiss if I didn't thank my social media team aka Swim Social for everything you are doing to help build my career. Elena and Emily, you are so smart, funny, and talented. Thank you for saying Yes to the Dress and working with me.

Glam Squad—Delina, Sabrina, Ryan. You keep me looking cute, youthful, and on trend. Thank you for making my dream of being a low-budget Zendaya a reality. Love you and the vibes you exude. I wish I could live in your energy forever.

Next, I want to thank myself. Yep! I'm not going to fake humility and pretend that this book *happened* to me when I had to work my behind off in order to bring it into existence. Writing is too difficult a task to complete without self-belief and dogged determination. So I'm grateful for all the times I wanted to quit, but didn't; all the times I found my groove and allowed myself to enjoy the process of writing; and all the times I decided to not compare myself to other authors and just put myself on the page. That's hard to do.

My friends—Karen, Nore, Michelle Buteau, Bono (he called me his friend once, so it would be rude not to mention him here. #IAmThirsty), Jamie Lee, Amy Aniobi, Jordan Carlos, Baron Vaughn, Vanessa Bayer, Neil Punsalan, Whitney Cummings,

Acknowledgments

Jameela Jamil, Josh and Katya Sussman, Abby Sasser, Austin Channing Brown, Wanyi Zee, Hari Kondabolu, Milena Brown, Alex Richenbach, Beth McGregor, Alison Stauver, Kathy Iandoli, Emma Gray, Ilana Glazer, Abbi Jacobson, Caroline Modarressy-Tehrani, Jonathan Groff, and others I'll kick myself for forgetting to mention. I'm grateful for all of you. You make my life full, and as we're all getting older and we have to juggle the hecticness of our lives, I feel your presence daily and it helps me to keep going.

Spotify and Apple Music—thank you for being the soundtrack I wrote to. Many a day when I felt like I couldn't finish this book, you got me though with '80s and '90s R&B and pop playlists. Good looking out.

About the Author

Phoebe Robinson is a stand-up comedian, writer, producer, and actress. She is best known as the cocreator and costar of the hit WNYC Studios podcast *2 Dope Queens*, which was turned into eight one-hour critically acclaimed HBO specials. She's also the *New York Times* bestselling author of *Everything's Trash, But It's Okay* and *You Can't Touch My Hair: And Other Things I Still Have to Explain*. Additionally, Phoebe was a staff writer on the final season of *Portlandia*, hosted the critically acclaimed podcast *Sooo Many White Guys*, and starred in the movies *Ibiza* and *What Men Want*. Most recently, she founded Tiny Reparations, a production company under ABC Studios. Tiny Rep's first project, a talk show entitled *Doing the Most with Phoebe Robinson*, premiered in 2021 on Comedy Central.